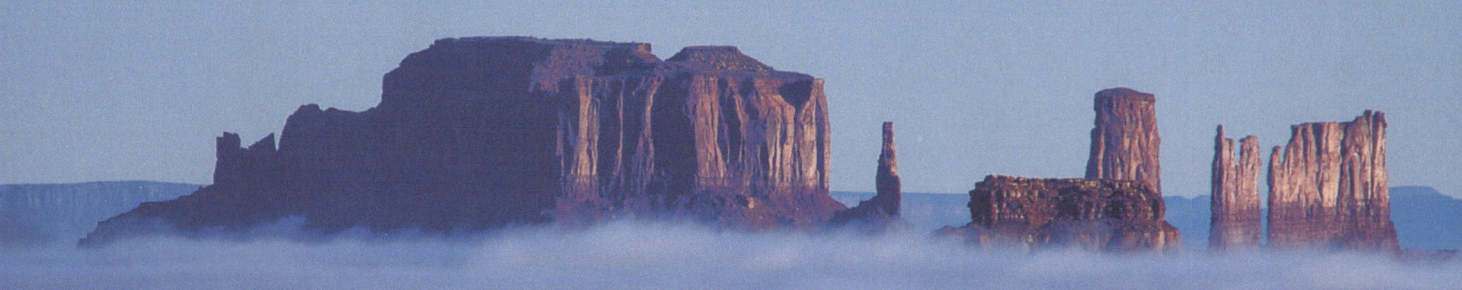

Unbounded Chronicles

Wild West, wildlife, the tranquil coasts, and more, like you've never seen them before

Text and Photography by David Schneider

Cover: *Yellowstone Cloudscape*

Title Page: *Butte's Fog*

Right: *Ready, Waiting*

Contents Page: *White Tracks*

Preface Page: *Evening Elk*

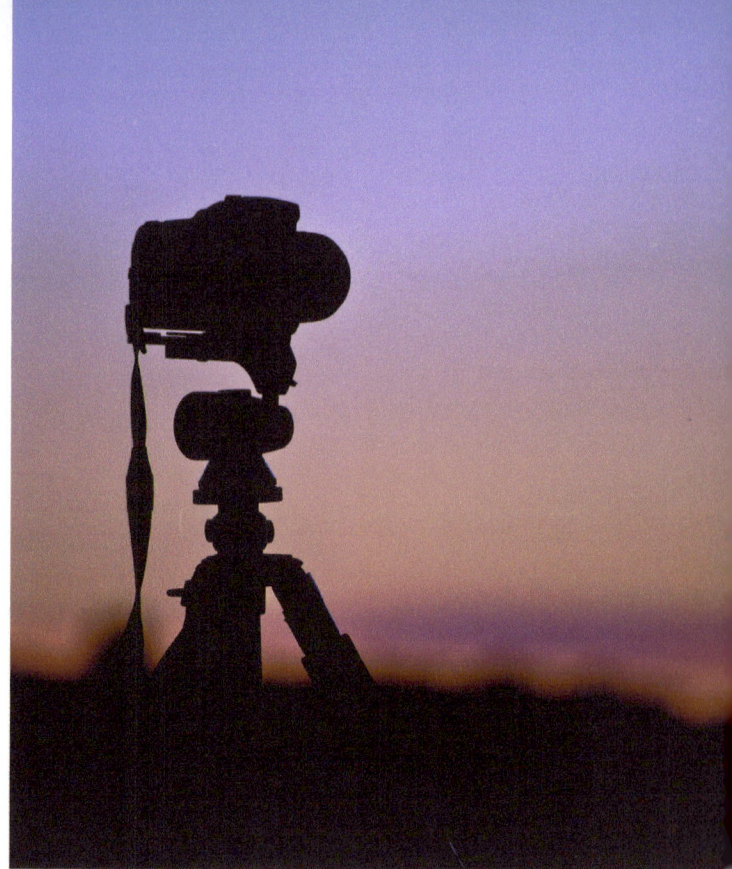

ISBN: 978-0-9838967-4-6

Unbounded Chronicles: Wild West, wildlife, the tranquil coasts, and more, like you've never seen them before © 2015 by David Schneider. All rights reserved.

Text and Photography by David Schneider

Edited by Bobbie Christmas

Created, produced, designed, and printed in the United States

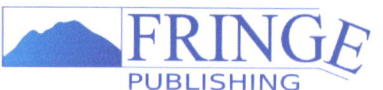

FRINGE PUBLISHING

An imprint of Fringe Innovations

For more information about our books, write Fringe Publishing, PO Box 555, Tijeras, NM 87059, call (505) 750-4PIX, or visit www.fringepublishing.com

Contents

Preface

It's hard to believe that here we are in my second book; it seems like just yesterday, or maybe earlier this morning, I was working on *Sojournic Tales*. Time really does fly when you are having fun. Since *Sojournic Tales*, I've been out on the road photographing, documenting, practicing patience, and doing my best to stay warm.

In *Unbounded Chronicles*, I delve deeper in the stories behind the photographs and some of the adventures that went into them. Often, when making the photograph, the story accompanying it is written in my mind at the same instant; those powerful connections are always my favorites. I'm delighted that I can share a few of those with you. I have been privileged to witness some miracles of nature and life. I am honored to share those with you, as well.

I hope that you see the world as I see it: full of light, beauty, mystery, magic, and hope.

david

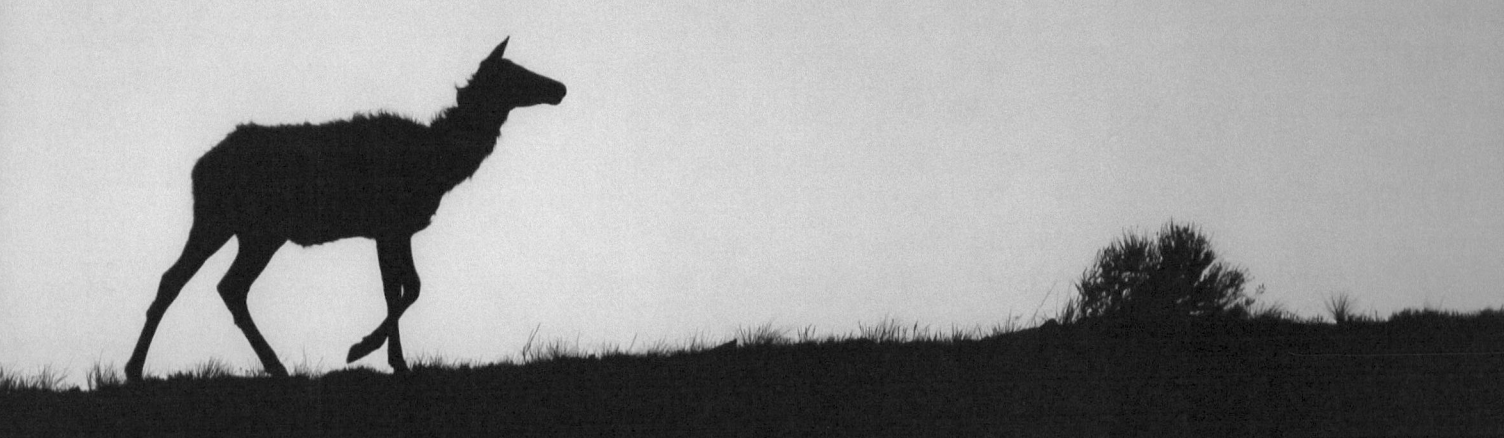

For Joseph, Kris, Iris, and Jeff, who set me in motion along this adventure. Thank you for showing me the path.

Desert Southwest

When we think of the Desert Southwest, we tend to think of a dry and dusty place; a land where tumbleweeds roam free and a lone cactus graces the empty, distant horizon. In actuality, the Desert Southwest is full of wondrous places and amazing sights which take your breath away and hold you captive among its beauty.

Mitten's Sun

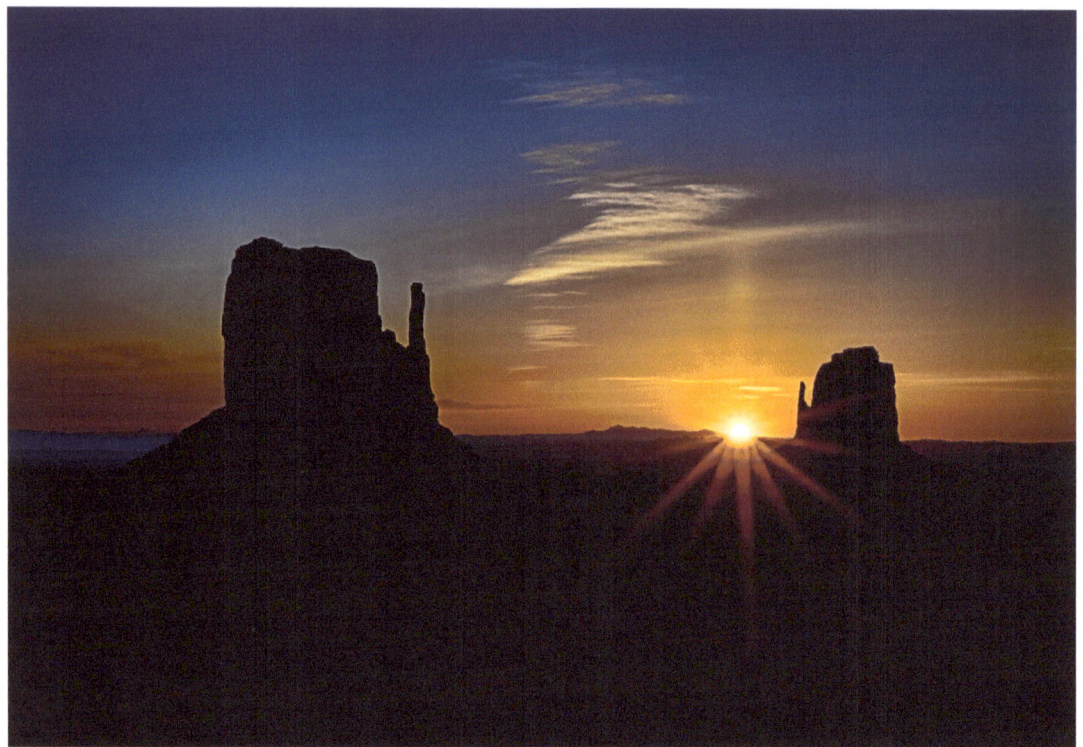

Every time, and I mean every single time I see a sunrise, I silently give thanks for being able to witness another incredible spectacle, for every single time it is a truly amazing sight. Granted, some sunrises are more colorful than others, but they are all wonderful in their own right, and each begins a new day. It is fitting, then, that we begin with a sunrise.

This particular sunrise was extraordinary in every regard. I was in Monument Valley in the Navajo Nation, standing between the monuments known as The Mittens. It's easy to see why they have this name, since they resemble a pair of mittens. At first I thought this sunrise would be typical: pretty and wonderful, and a delight to watch. I had no idea, though, what the morning had in store for me nor the treat that I would be given. As the night's colors shifted away from dark indigos into the shades of dawn, I was surprised that the usual pink was nowhere to be found. Gradually, yet steadily, the sky lightened as the grip of night was vanquished. Slowly at first, then rapidly as the sun found its stride and began to rise, the colors rose on the horizon with it, seemingly pulling the sun up with them.

All at once the sun breached the horizon, sending its rays out far over the land, heralding the start of a wonderful new day. The Mittens stood draped in shadows, adding a stark counterpoint to the sun's reach. The mountains and hills in the background were bathed in violets that added another dimension of color to the already incredible scene.

Mitten's Sun is my tribute to that moment in time and an excellent beginning to our adventure.

Mystery Saucers

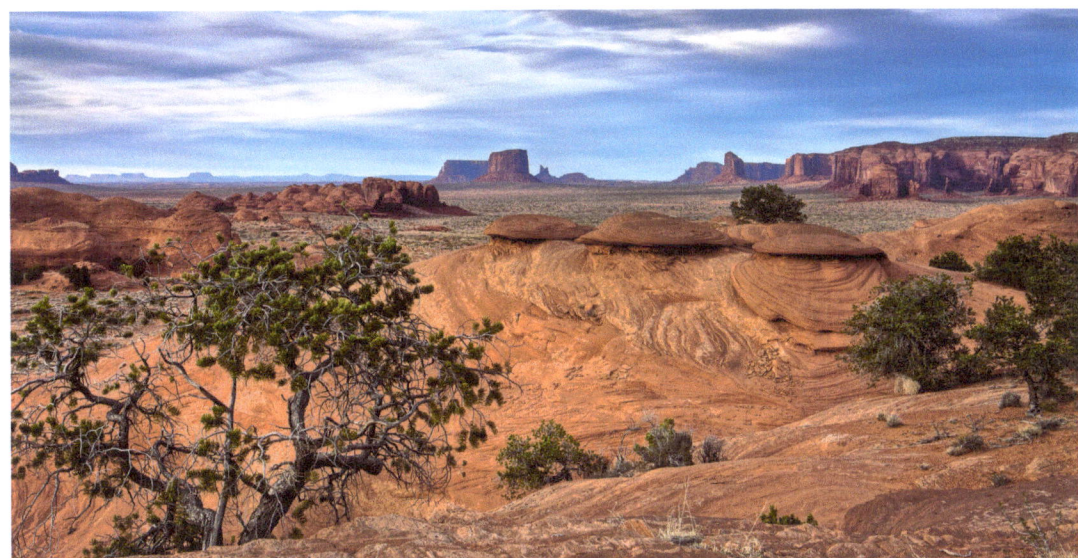

The Southwest is full of contrasts. One of the contrasts I find fascinating lies between the well-known, big-name places and the equally pristine and beautiful areas that few seem to know about. Perhaps that reason is part of my fascination with Monument Valley and the far lesser-known Mystery Valley.

Mystery Valley is, as its name suggests, a place of mystery. It is right next to the far more famous Monument Valley, which receives most of the area's attention. Still, Mystery Valley has wonders all of its own, and it rewards handsomely those who visit. In fact, you can see the monuments of Monument Valley from Mystery Valley. In this photograph, we are looking north into Monument Valley.

Although it lacks the tall monuments of its neighbor, it does have a rich and deep culture. Throughout the valley, often where you least expect it, are the remains of ancient dwellings. Some are tucked into alcoves, and all are strategically located. The ruins are no longer occupied, but they are certainly not forgotten, either. They are sacred places, and their very presence can be felt throughout the valley. They are a poignant reminder of those who came before us.

Mystery Valley also sports some impressive rock formations, such as these saucers. Wind and erosional forces have sculpted the sandstone into swirled discs reminiscent of flying saucers poised for liftoff to places beyond. Combined with moody skies and the distant buttes, saucers make for an incredible, surreal landscape, one that completely lives up to the moniker of Mystery Valley.

Mystery Valley is a location that sings to me. While some folks see only the starkness of the land, I see the beauty and richness of the desert.

HooDoo Sunrise

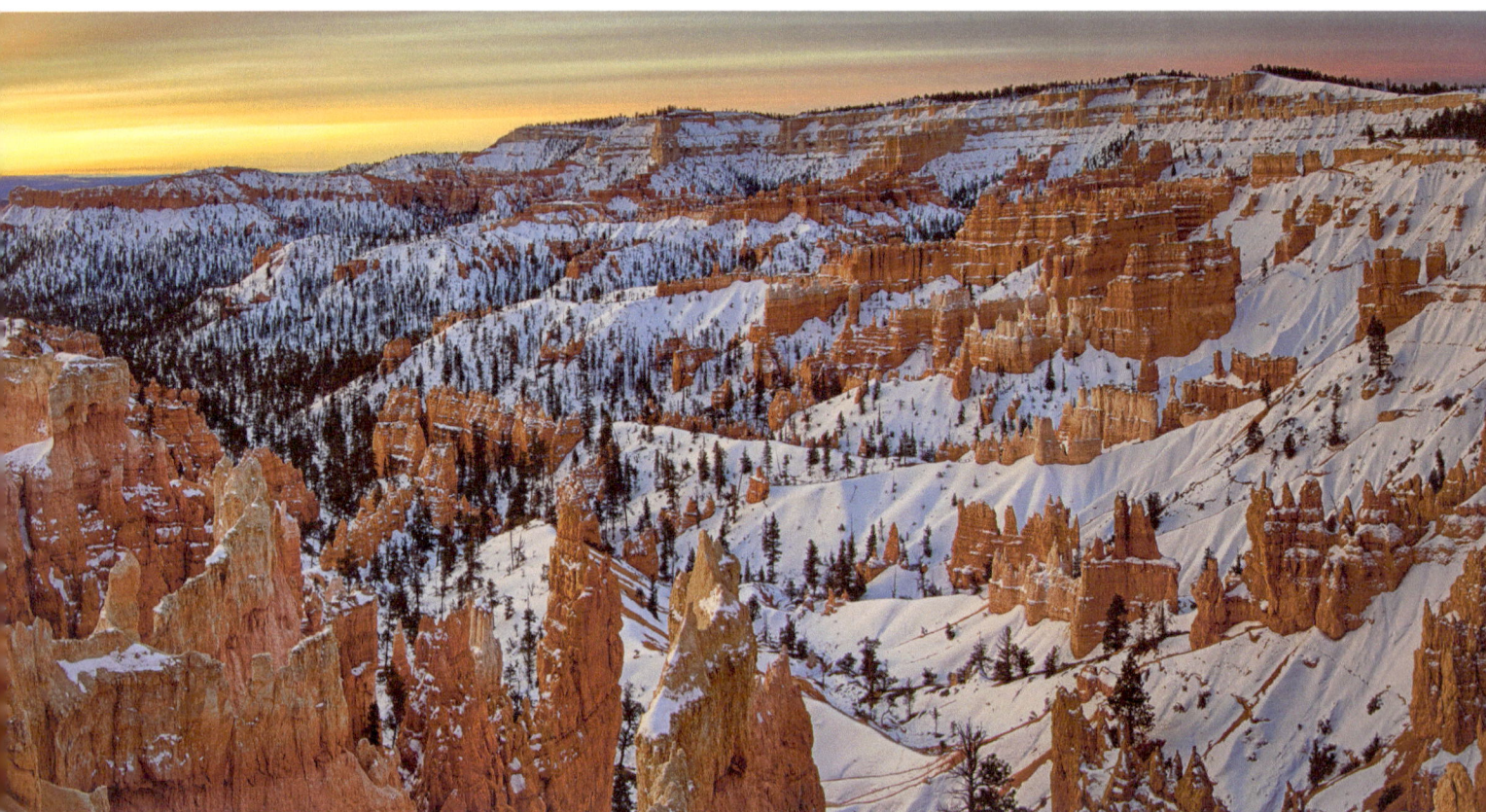

The Southwest is filled with locations that feature fantastic sunrises. When asked about where my favorite location is, I rarely answer, even when pressed, for the truth is that everywhere is. The Southwest is filled with so many amazing sights that whittling them down to a favorite is impossible, yet there are a few excellent stories to tell, like a certain winter sunrise in Bryce Canyon National Park.

The great thing about Bryce Canyon is that it takes on a different feel and flavor as the seasons change. During the summer months, it is hot and dry and sometimes quite stark, yet beautiful and awe-inspiring at the same time. During the winter months, the same scene takes on a softer, more serene feel. Naturally, all these changes make for compelling photographs.

I was up well before dawn this morning and curious how the morning would turn out. The previous day had clear skies, yet as the day turned to evening, the skies began to fill with a solid layer of clouds. This change didn't bode overly well for the morning, but one never knows, for there is only one way to find out what the morning holds. The temperature of this morning was well below zero, which, all things considered, wasn't a huge problem. The bigger issue was the wind. It wasn't enough to be actually "windy," but "breezy" would be a decent description. The pre-dawn cold of below zero and the steady breeze combined to make an exceptionally cold morning. With the breeze finding its way through every layer of clothing I had on, the February morning turned absolutely brutal.

I waited, none to patiently, for dawn to do its thing.

Soon enough, which is to say just after an eternity in the cold, there was enough light to see. Crud. The sky looked to be filled with the solid layer of clouds from the night before and didn't look photogenic in the least. I was alone at the edge of the canyon, perched high above a set of hoodoos that I had located the night before, and I hunkered down to wait it out. I figured someone would find my frozen body in late spring, if nothing else.

The sun continued its slow rise.

At first I was sure the whole morning was going to be a bust. Surely nothing could happen. The sun continued to rise, my core body temperature continued to plummet, and still nothing was happening. I checked my watch: the sun had broken the horizon, but I couldn't tell it from the clouds. Ah well. At least, I thought, I had watched another sunrise, and I gave thanks for it, as I always do. I turned my back on the canyon to begin to pack up my gear. After a few moments of getting my gear ready and wondering if I had once again frostbitten my fingers, I looked up. The day seemed brighter, by far, and eventually it occurred to me that I really should turn around. Imagine my surprise.

There, before me, was *HooDoo Sunrise*.

Against all odds, the sun had found a way to sneak some color past the watchful eye of the clouds. The soft warm pinks and yellows glowed in the sky, a beautiful counterpoint to the whites and oranges of the snow-covered hoodoos. The carpet of snow didn't feel like it was smothering the hoodoos, but rather wrapping them up, hiding their base, and saving the bottom of the canyon for spring to unwrap. Still, I adored the contrast of the bright orange hoodoos as they poked out of their cocoons. The orange was especially prevalent that morning since the sunrise was full of pinks and reds. To make everything perfect, the wind died down for just a moment, just long enough for me to make this photograph.

Shortly afterward, the sun ducked behind a cloud bank, the last I saw of it for the next couple of days, it was perfectly okay with me.

I can't wait to see what the hoodoos hold for me in the next season. Whatever it is, it is sure to be amazing and beyond beautiful. Maybe I will even thaw out by then.

Mesa Sun

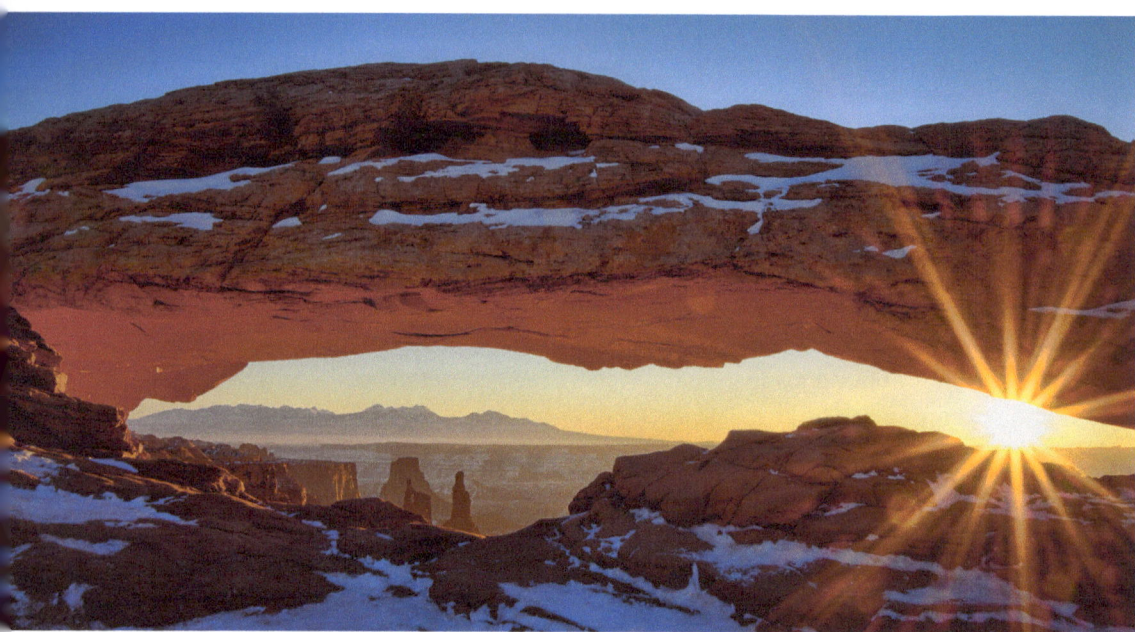

While we're on the topic of Utah sunrises in the winter, let's go to the other side of the state to Canyonlands National Park, home of the famous Mesa Arch. Mesa Arch is a popular sunrise location, but it is not nearly as popular in the winter, probably because the weather is, surprise, so darn cold. Naturally there I am again, in that cold. You would think that at some point I would begin to catch on that winters are cold, but the connection somehow continues to elude me.

On this January morning the world held its breath and was utterly quiet. The instant before the sun breaks the horizon is always a magical, yet tense, moment, and breaths are usually held. There is a certain stillness before that moment, a sense of anticipation, a sense of wonder and awe, and the dual senses of solemnness and joy, all rolled into one.

The first ray of light peeked out, at first tentatively, but quickly followed by conviction. The world was even quieter than before, if that was at all possible. Without any further prelude, the sun roared over the horizon, and its jubilant rays spread everywhere, bringing light and life to the day. The world let out its collective breath and the day had now well and true begun.

Mesa Arch glowed brightly as it too celebrated the sun's arrival, liberating it from the dark of the night. The valley far below basked in the dawn's early light and began to soak in what warmth it could from the cold winter day, for the temperature was well below zero when this photograph was made. As the sun rose higher and began to clear the arch, the warm dawn glow faded, but the memory of that amazing sunrise will live on forever.

I think we're finished being cold for now. Let's warm up a bit, shall we, although later we'll return again to the cold. We'll put it out of our minds for now, however, and step into some wonderful, bright, warm sunshine.

Valley Monuments

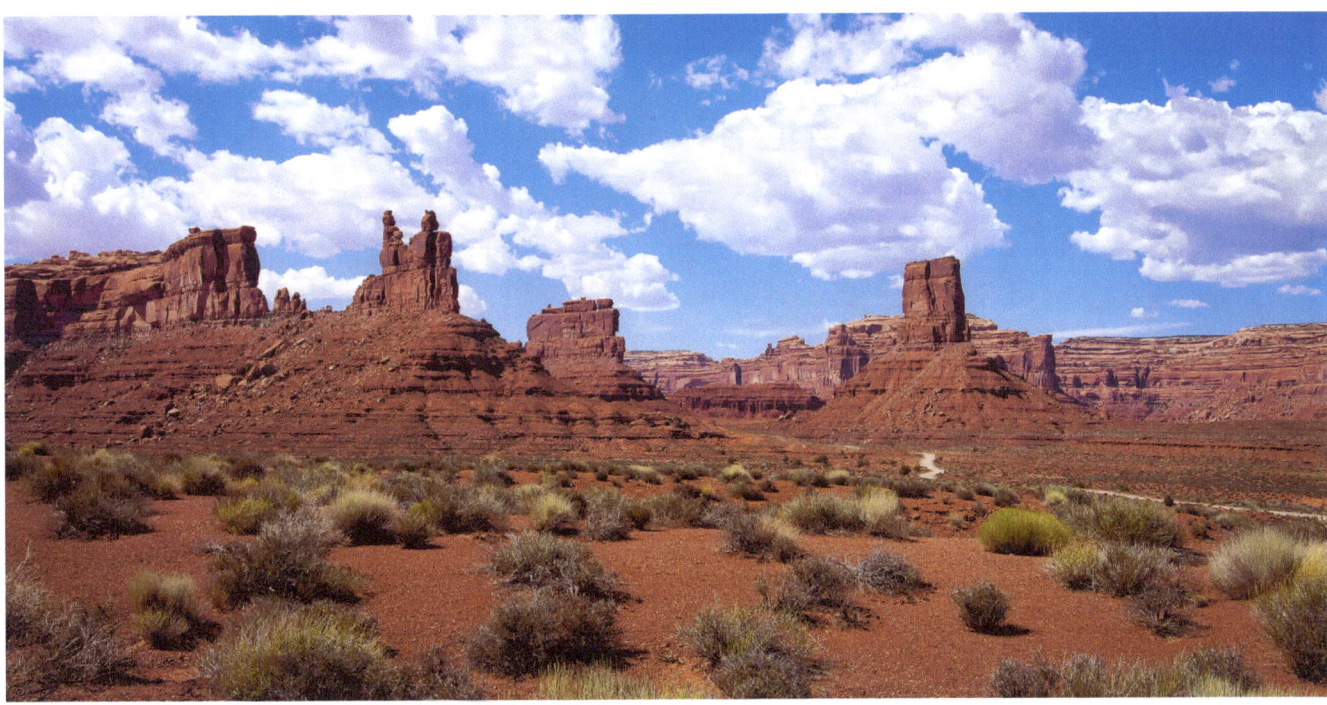

For our sunshine fix, we'll stay in Utah for one more story, and because I am still chilly, we'll warm up in the deep desert in the middle of summer. Yes, it is an extreme jump, but at least we won't be cold anymore.

The desert Southwest calls me, its alluring song whispering to all that I am. No matter how hard I try to stay away, time and again I am drawn into the depths of the Southwest, where I always find the peace and solace that I hold dear. There is something about the shifting sands, tall red rock spires, and azure skies that resonates deeply within me. Needless to say, I spend quite a lot of time looking for exactly these places.

Just north of Monument Valley lies another extraordinary area: Valley of the Gods. This valley is where Road Canyon exits Cedar Mesa and opens back up into the desert, and it is missed by many of the few people who travel through this area. As the canyon falls away, monuments—the tall, red rock buttes and spires that dominate the landscape—take over, standing tall and proud, piecing the very sky. These buttes are impressive from far away; up close their size overwhelms your senses.

Still, there is something pristine about this known, but little traveled, area. The landscape remains pure, just as it has been forever. Traces of humans remain here, but very few. Overlooked by most people, this area is exactly the kind of place that I seek and exactly the kind of place that settles my soul. Valley of the Gods describes it perfectly.

TearDrop's Valley

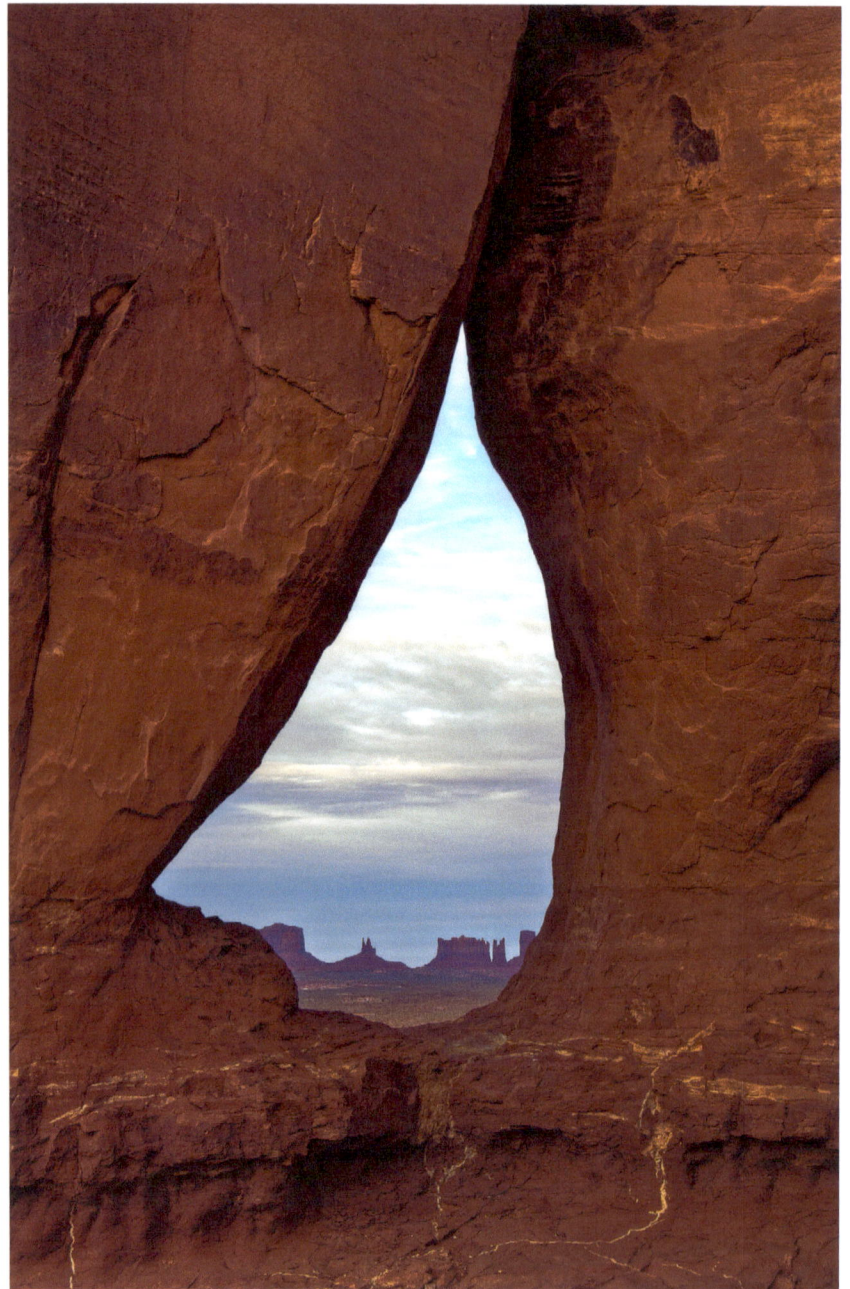

"Curiouser and curiouser!" cried Alice, so surprised at the view through the arch that she completely forgot how to speak proper English. "Now my own tears of joy shall match Tear Drop Arch perfectly."

Truer sentiments could not possibly be said, for the sheer beauty of this small hidden arch just outside Monument Valley often causes tears in one's eye. If the grace of the arch isn't enough, then the view through the arch certainly shall be, for there, off a short way away lie some of the buttes of Monument Valley itself. A view within a view, and both equal to each other.

The Monument Valley area has numerous small treasures such as this arch. One just needs to know where, and often, when to look. This particular view is just at sunset, moments before the colors of the day faded. Still, the reds of the rock were strong, highlighting the arch perfectly. The sky and clouds beyond, still blue at the top and shading into deeper tones below, provided the perfect backdrop for the valley itself, resplendent in the mauves for which it is so famous. Alice and the rest of us watched in silence, all of us with a tear in our eye for the beauty of the arch.

For now, however, it is time to leave the Monument Valley area. We'll be back to it, though, soon enough.

Antelope's Window

Our adventure continues in the Navajo Nation. As much as the vast landscapes represent the classic beauty of the desert Southwest, there are other features, too. Slot canyons cut through the landscape, and within their tight and narrow confines exist patterns that defy the imagination. Antelope Canyon is one of these places.

Antelope Canyon, or more precisely, Antelope Wash, is a series of slot canyons known for extraordinary walls of sandstone. Over the eons, water has carved through the wash, creating slot canyons from the soft rock. Water, being water, doesn't move in a straight line and takes the easiest path; as a result, the canyon walls are wider in some places than others, and the floor is often far from level. Along the way, fine lines meander and swirl throughout the canyon walls. Lower Antelope Canyon has a secret that few know about: light beams.

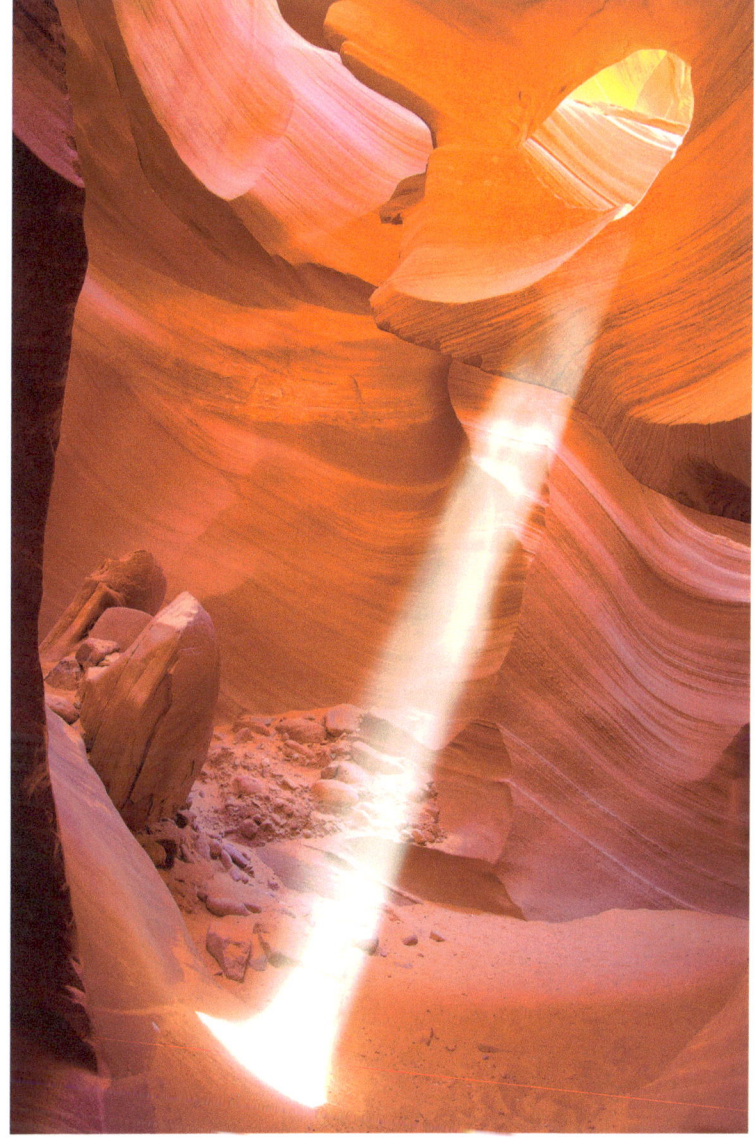

Like the well-known Upper Antelope Canyon, Lower Antelope Canyon does indeed have light beams, and one in particular shines directly through a "window" in the canyon walls, providing an dazzling effect. The light beams happen only at a certain time of the day at certain times of the year and happen only on bright sunny days, which, for this area, is most days. Still, it is a matter of timing to capture any one particular beam.

This particular photograph is my absolute favorite of all of my ones from these canyons, and it is easy to see why. Amazingly, I have seen people walk right by this phenomenon without ever turning around to see it. Beauty is everywhere around us, and nature's light shows are unparalleled, but you have to know where and when to look. You have to keep your eyes open to what is around you. This photograph reminds me always to keep looking around me and always keep an open heart and mind.

Alstrom Panorama

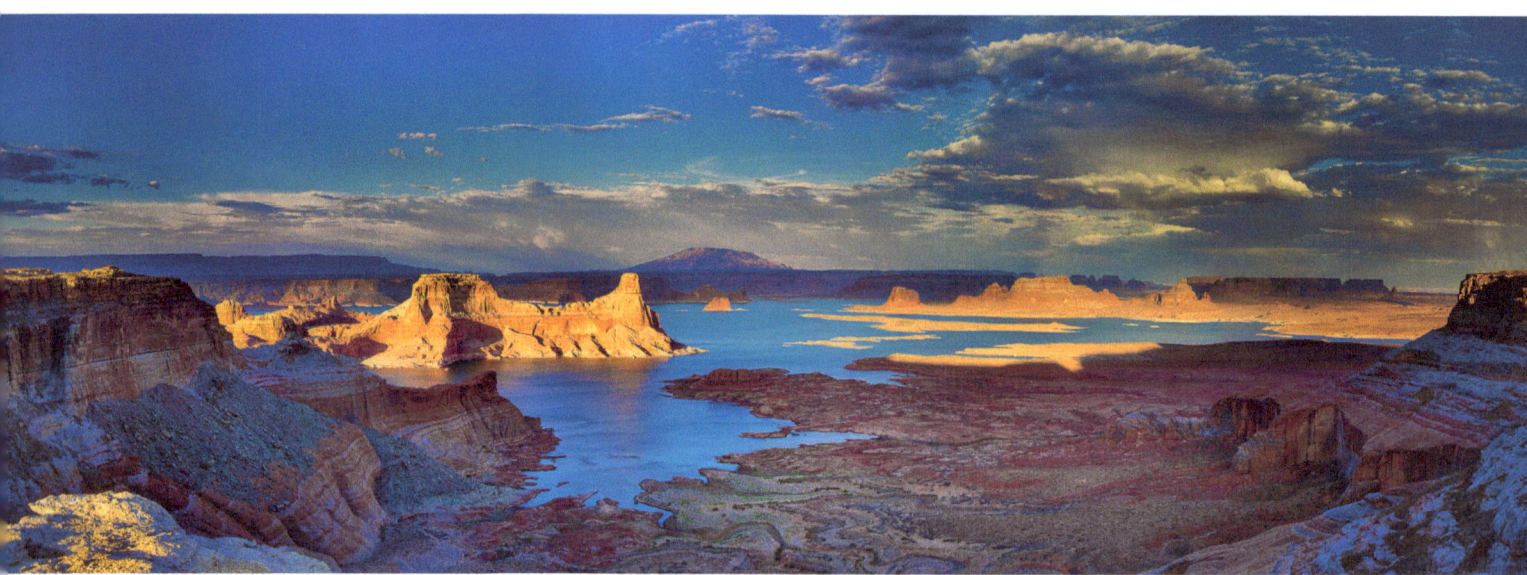

Often, when we think of the Southwest, we think of trackless reaches of sand, perhaps broken by the occasional tumbleweed. To be fair, such places exist; however, rivers run through the Southwest. Some of those, such as the Colorado River, are significant. If you happen to build a dam on such a river, you completely change the landscape. That's exactly what happened when the Glen Canyon Dam on the Arizona and Utah state line was built, forming Lake Powell and forever inundating and changing the surrounding landscape.

Long ago, at least before the 1950s, this particular view simply did not exist; now, however, this point is one of my favorite places in all the Southwest. Although not the hardest place to get to, it is not without its challenges. It is literally a case of being "so close yet so far," since you can see the destination across the desert, but getting there is harder than it initially appears. It is an eighteen-mile trek through some difficult roads, and calling them roads is being charitable, through deep sand and over slickrock to reach Alstrom Point. Clearly, though, the journey is worth it.

The prominent butte in the left center is Gunsight Butte. I love how the clouds seem to be reaching for it, yet it eludes them and stands mighty in the last, golden waning rays of the sun. The mauves of the desert night are beginning to creep through the land, and the lake itself lies quietly, preparing for a gentle evening. The more you look, the more you will find, and this panorama captures it all.

When water meets the desert, the results can be awe-inspiring. We'll visit water with a chapter all its own later on.

There is an interesting prelude and postscript to this photograph. That morning, Mary Beth and I left Page, Arizona, somewhere around four in the morning. The plan for the day was straightforward: we would visit a couple of places around Page and then head out to Alstrom Point for the sunset. We did the right thing before we left and checked with the Glen Canyon rangers and the Bureau of Land Management office about the roads and weather. All the rangers said everything was fine and we would have no problems. With a full tank of gas, luckily, we headed off to Alstrom Point.

On the way out to the point, off in the far distance, Mary Beth noticed some rain clouds. I brushed those off because they were so far away. As you can surmise, they were not nearly as far away as I thought they were. We made it to Alstrom Point with plenty of time to spare, and we enjoyed the sweeping panoramic view and dramatic sunset. I was delighted because I knew in my heart the panorama I wanted would turn out, so we headed back to Page in the dark over the rugged jeep trail.

For a long while, everything was fine. We were making excellent time, and I was already thinking about a good, long hot shower. The far distant rain that wasn't very far away had different ideas for our evening, though. As we came down a slight slope to head over a wash, Mary Beth noticed that the headlights seemed to be shining on something very bright and wet looking. Luckily she convinced me that it was a wise idea to perhaps get out and take a look around. Good thing we did, because the road that we had followed on the way in was completely gone. Not a trace of the road was there, or if it was, it was a few feet beneath the swift moving wash. It turns out the rains were quite close, and a small thunderstorm sprang up behind us while we were out at the point. The desert, being a desert, doesn't take well to a sudden influx of water, and the situation can become, quickly, very dangerous. We were in just such a situation.

Going forward would not be an option and possibly not an option for days, while the wash dried out enough to be passable again. We were still ten miles or so from pavement, and thus, help, so walking out was not a viable option. We did the only thing that made sense, which was to turn around and head out of the Grand Staircase-Escalante National Monument the back way, over more jeep roads. We made good time to a very steep road that headed up and out of the area called the Kelly Grade. Up, up, up we went into the darkness of the night, which was probably a good thing, because the Kelly Grade is a dirt jeep road, very narrow, very steep, and with many hundreds of feet of dropoff with no guardrails. Truly a case of what you can't see won't hurt you. We took the back jeep roads through the National Monument, passing some of the most beautiful areas you can imagine, in the dark.

We picked up the pavement again in Escalante, Utah, about one in the morning. We were not far from Page as the crow flies, but we were not crows. Sighing, we drove the long way around, passing Bryce Canyon National Park in the dark, whizzing by Zion National Park in the dark, and passing through the Paria area in the dark. I quietly whimpered as we passed each place and quietly made a promise to come back to visit each one in the daylight as soon as I could. We finally arrived back at the hotel at four in the morning completely exhausted. We passed by the same bemused hotel clerk who watched us leave the day before, and our day finally came to a close.

This photograph holds a lot of memories for us.

Malpais Palisade

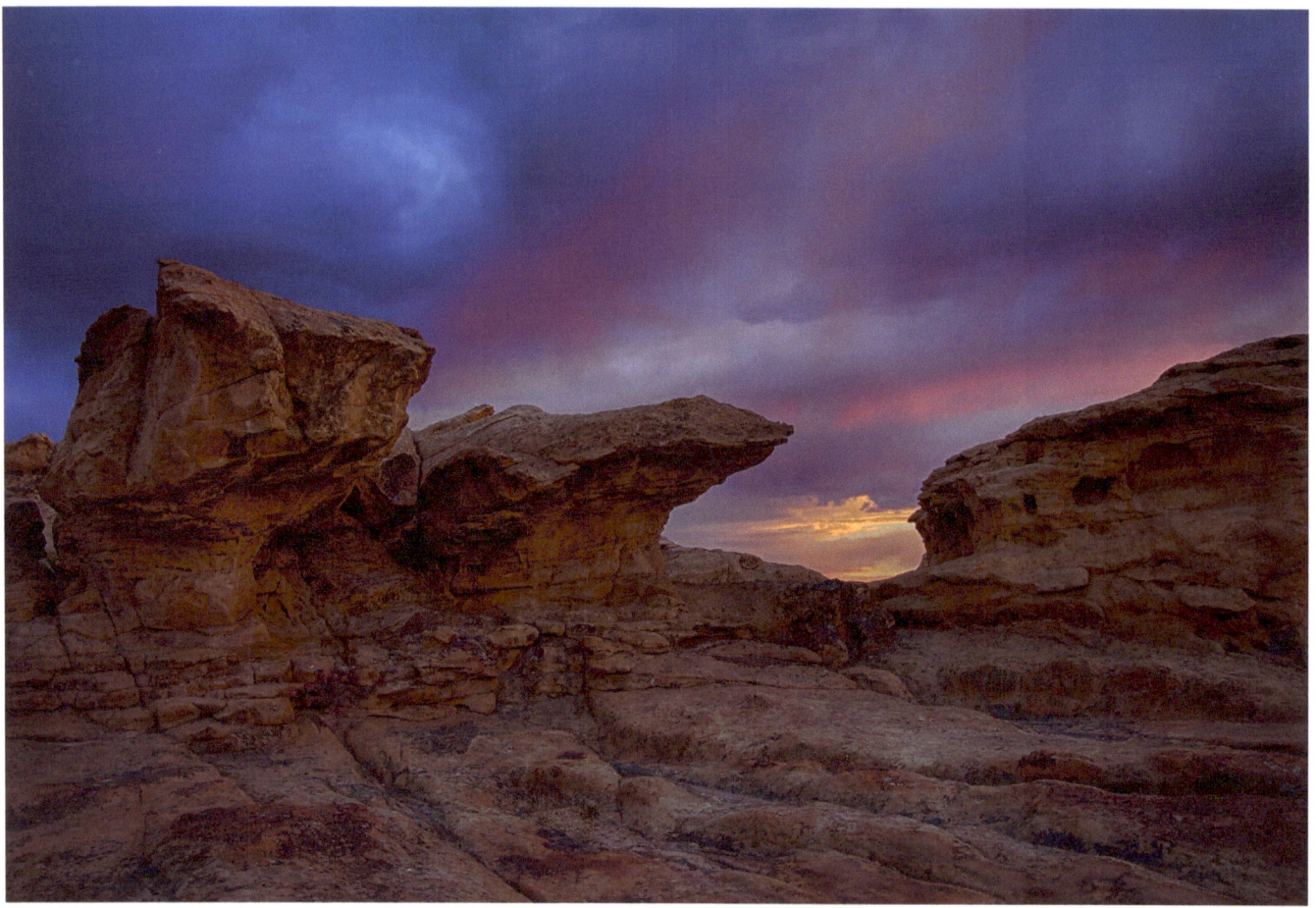

Utah and Arizona are not the only places that have the classic desert feel; New Mexico has some hidden gems of its own.

The sky was calm that summer evening, perfectly flat and gray from horizon to horizon, as far as the eye could see. Since I was standing far above the valley floor on top of the sandstone bluffs at El Malpais National Monument, I could see quite a way. The sun made its afternoon journey unseen, above the featureless sky.

The clouds, I knew, had a mind of their own. They were drifting to the east, probably because they wanted to be nowhere close when the sun decided to set. Wisely they scurried away, beginning to break apart in their haste to get away.

The sun was indeed perturbed when it began its final descent and let everyone in sight know it. It sent out tendrils of fiery pink and purple, with a heart of oranges and yellows immediately around the sun itself. The clouds reflected all the colors, mirroring the sun's displeasure far and wide, glowing with a light all their own. The red rock of the bluffs stood fast, a palisade from the clash of clouds and sun, protecting me, and in the process, providing this glimpse into a fiery Southwest sunset.

At least that's the story I tell, but it isn't quite the entire story of that night. Mary Beth and I were sitting at the bluffs watching the day draw to a close. Unfortunately for us, the day was going to go longer than this portion of the National Monument was open, meaning we would miss the end of it. I spent about half my time watching the sky and its show and the other half watching the road into the bluffs for signs that a ranger would come by and chase us out. Sure enough, my worse fears were realized, and before the day ran its course, a ranger drove up.

She was a very nice ranger and spoke to us for a bit. It didn't take her very long to figure out what I was doing and how disappointed I was that it was time to go. Right as it was time for us to all leave, however, she decided that it was time for her to take a break. She sat down on the bluffs with us, not saying a word after that, and we all watched the most colorful show nature could provide in complete and companionable silence. After a while I stood up, stretched, and went over to my camera to make *Malpais Palisade*. I made just one image during this sequence, just one, and didn't say a word. We all sat together again until the light faded away and then bade each other a good night and headed off.

To that ranger: Thank you. Thank you very, very much. That kindness means the world to me.

Tree Magic

Trees are all around us and often completely overlooked, yet trees have their own magic that is shared with us when we quest for it. These stories reveal a small part of the magic that happens with trees are involved.

Aspen Sun

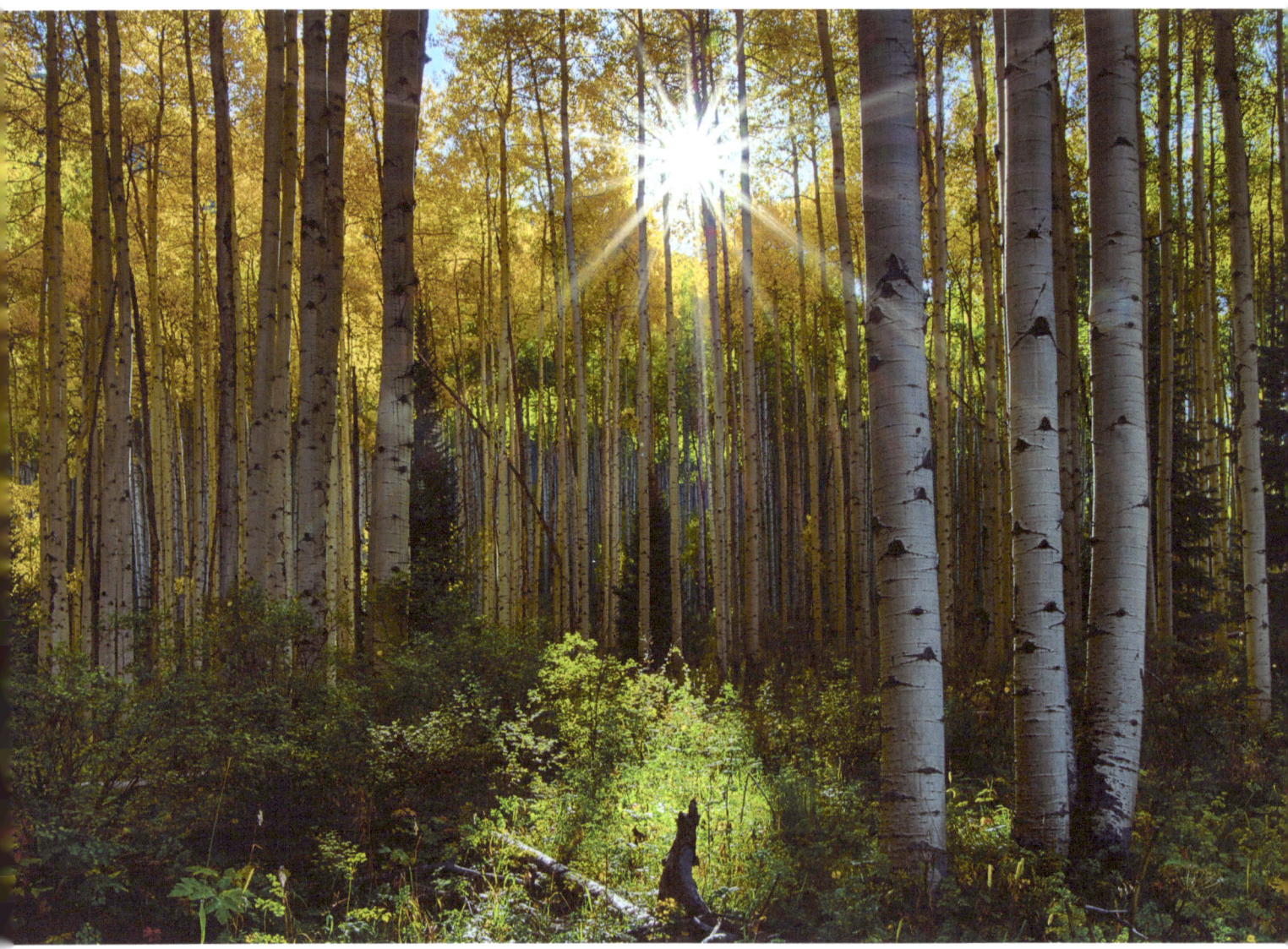

There is something special about an aspen colony that goes above and beyond what you might expect. Sure, there are the obvious explanations of the white bark and the quaking, whispering leaves, but it goes well beyond that. To stand among the aspens sensing the life enveloping you is a powerful experience; you can feel the connection to the aspens and through them, the world around you.

Aspens are colonial, meaning all the trees are part of one single organism, arguably making them the largest organism on the planet. As you walk through the trees, you are walking through the colony itself. As you touch one tree, you feel not only the tree itself, but the entire grove of aspens. Because the roots and offshoots are below ground, a stand of aspens is highly resistant to the ravages of time and is able to withstand almost anything. These thoughts and more were going through my mind as I stood there, attempting to absorb the entirety of the colony. The cool Colorado fall morning had been overcast, as mornings near Aspen, Colorado, can sometimes be.

I had scouted the entire area looking for the exact right location for this photograph. I knew what I wanted to accomplish and knew it could be special. All I needed was the right spot at the right time, and it might work out. After a day or so of scouting, this exact spot was the one that sang to me. There was something about how the trees parted "just so" that spoke volumes to me, and thick, dense, yet jumbled forest floor made me welcome for reasons I cannot quite explain. I knew this was the spot, but alas, the weather was not going to cooperate.

I busied myself in the area, for that is an easy thing to do when you are surrounded by aspens. There is always one more tree to view and admire, each one telling you its story, and each one telling its neighbors your story. By the time I had visited a few trees, I felt as if I was among a group of old friends, and my mood brightened considerably. As it turned out, the day had brightened considerably, too. The sun broke free of the clouds and its light spread quickly throughout the forest, bringing warmth to everything it touched. In that special moment *Aspen Sun* was made, which is a celebration of the aspens and friendship with the trees.

Ironton's Story

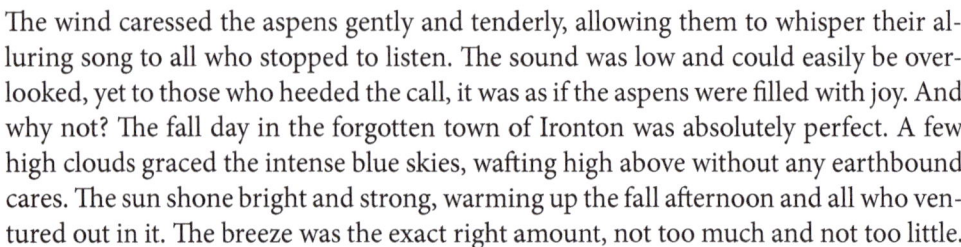

We'll continue with the aspens in one of my favorite locations: Ironton, Colorado.

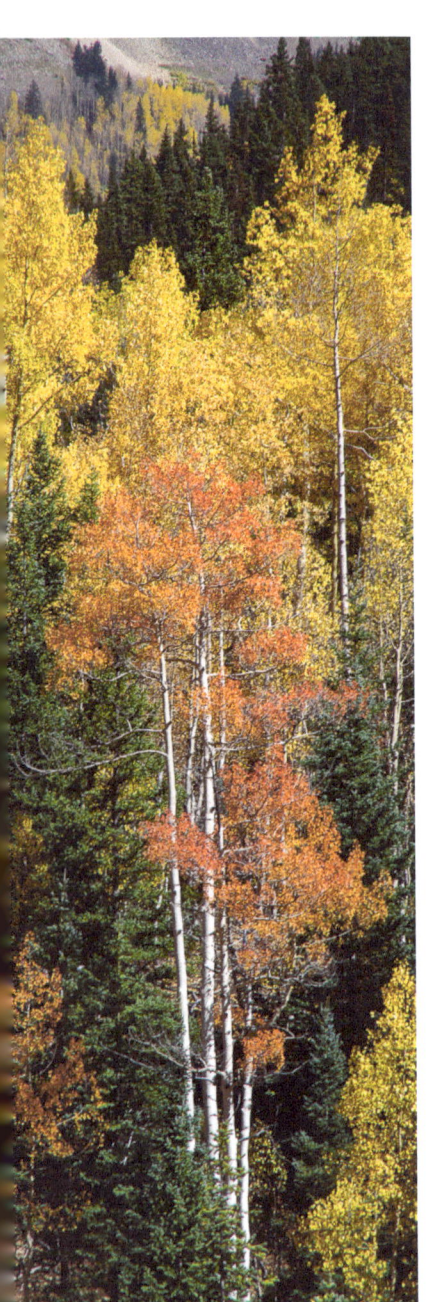

The wind caressed the aspens gently and tenderly, allowing them to whisper their alluring song to all who stopped to listen. The sound was low and could easily be overlooked, yet to those who heeded the call, it was as if the aspens were filled with joy. And why not? The fall day in the forgotten town of Ironton was absolutely perfect. A few high clouds graced the intense blue skies, wafting high above without any earthbound cares. The sun shone bright and strong, warming up the fall afternoon and all who ventured out in it. The breeze was the exact right amount, not too much and not too little.

Ironton in days gone by certainly wasn't quiet. It was a bustling mining town, and its miners tirelessly worked the Red Mountain area looking for silver and other precious minerals. The town itself was fairly large, and it easily supported the miners and their families. With more than one thousand residents, or so those who remember say, it served the area well and was a major transportation hub. You wouldn't know it, of course, from the remains, but if you stop and listen, you can feel the town, and you can feel the fire it must have had. These days, however, the town lies empty of humans and is slowly fading back into time. Most of the buildings are long gone, although a few still stand. Aspens grow tall and mighty now; back in Ironton's heyday, they must have been small trees clinging precariously to life.

Now that the miners are gone and the town has faded away, the aspens have grown tall and strong, reaching toward the sky, their canopy closing the town in from above. Ironton may be all but gone, but the aspens help keep it alive.

The fire hasn't truly gone out, either. Today it lives on in a single red aspen just at the edge of the town. To me, the fiery red aspen reminds me that Ironton still has much to offer and is still alive. For some reason, Ironton and I get along well, and I make it a point to stop in and visit when I am in the area. My visits are, naturally, quiet, but that's okay. The memory of the days gone by live on, the stories carried to me by the aspens, and we remember fondly the days of yesterday.

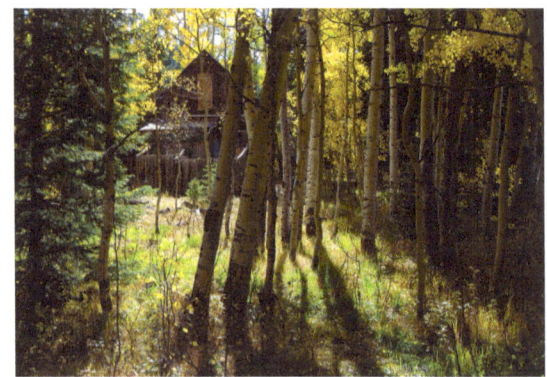

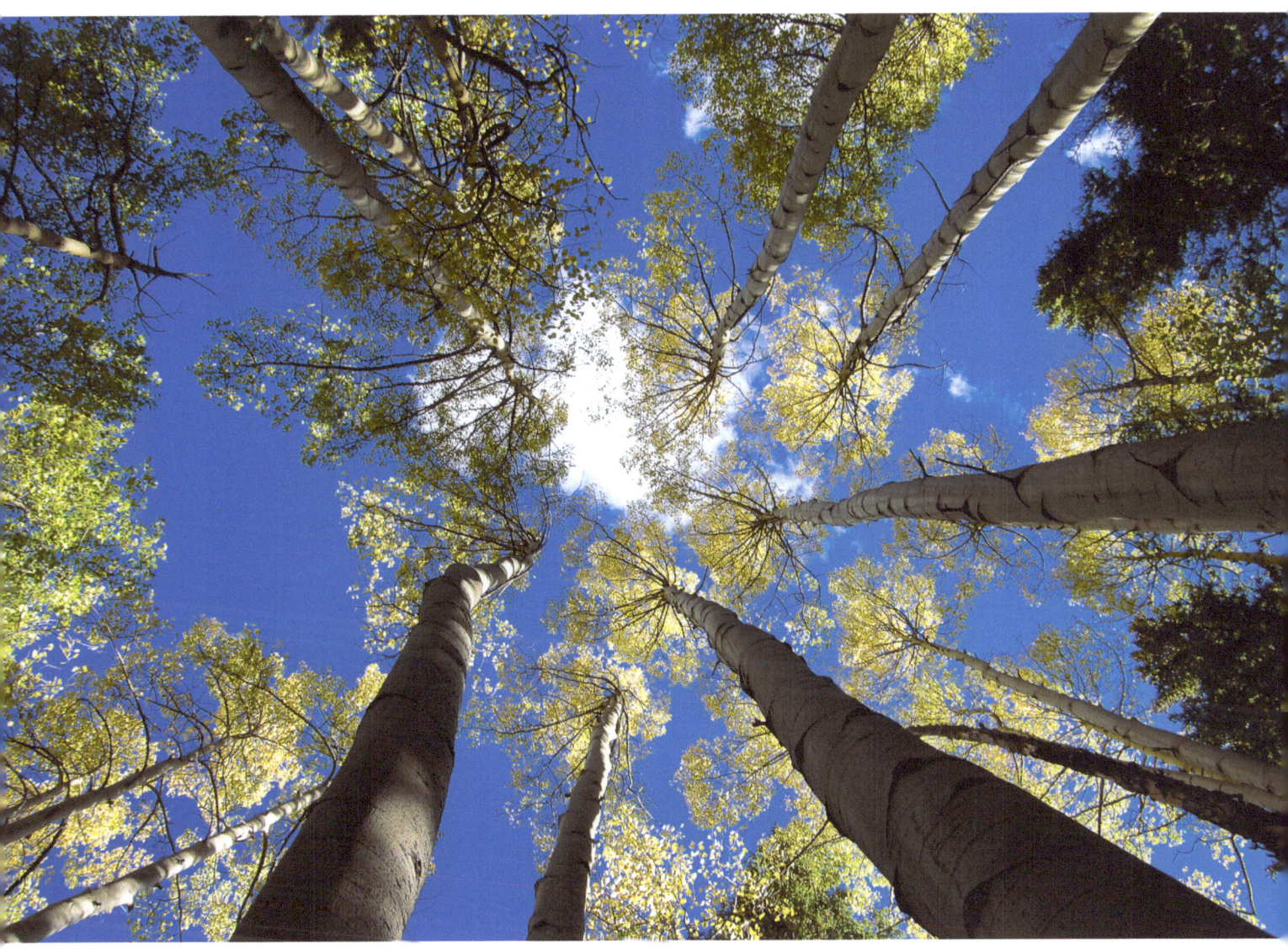

Kebler Tales

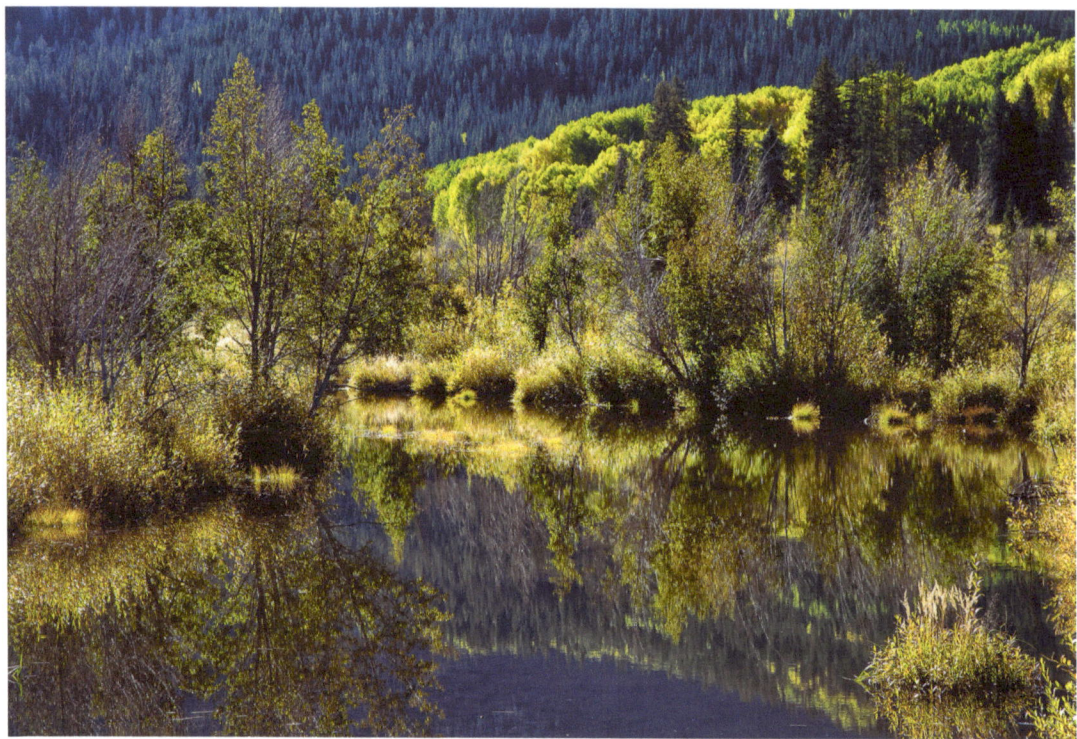

There are a few other places that I particularly enjoy for aspens and tress, besides Ironton. Kebler Pass in Colorado is one of those places, and I adore making detours, sometimes lasting several days or even longer, over the pass just to see. Although often noted for its soaring aspens, Kebler Pass has many smaller hidden treasures for those who know where to look.

This vignette struck my eye one fall day. The pond, really quite a small pond, was dead still, and the slight breeze that had sprung up earlier seemed to forget to visit. The reflections were outstanding, and the color beyond vibrant. How could I not make a photograph of the scene? The warm glow coupled with the symmetry of the reflections completed everything. After I made this photograph, I remained here for a while, enjoying the view and reflecting on how magnificent our world truly is.

Eventually, however, the afternoon glow began to fade away and it was time to leave. That's okay, though, because Kebler Pass holds more treasures.

The next morning I went farther along the pass, looking all around me, but also looking at the ground, for you never know what you might happen to see. I was fascinated with the leaves on the forest floor and the patterns they made. I wandered farther into the forest, deeper and deeper, looking for something, although I wasn't quite sure what I was looking for. I knew I would figure it out sooner or later. Out of the corner of my eye I spied the perfect leaf in the perfect fall color, waiting for me. I went over and looked, marveling in the beauty of that single, solitary leaf. Bright against the fallen aspen leaves around it, it splashed its red everywhere, standing alone, but also standing proud and tall. It seemed not to care that it was close to the ground instead of high up in a tree. Sunlight splashed through an opening in the canopy high above, lighting the area. I would like to think that the trees were letting the sun through for this one leaf. Perhaps that was indeed the case.

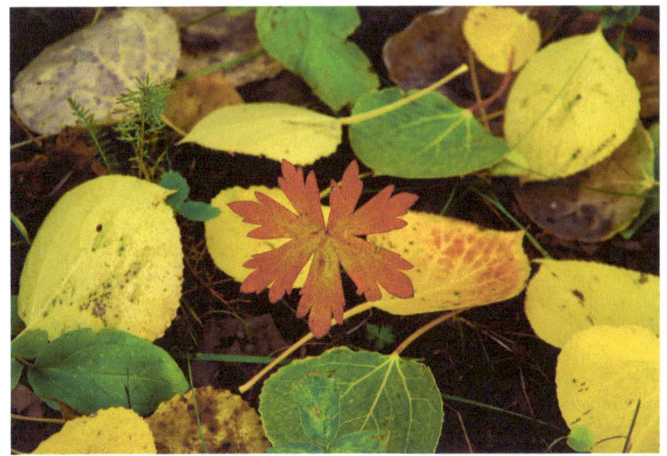

For the longest time I fussed with making the perfect photograph of the leaf. I looked at it from every angle. I looked at it from above, and I looked at from the side. I looked and looked and then looked some more. The more absorbed

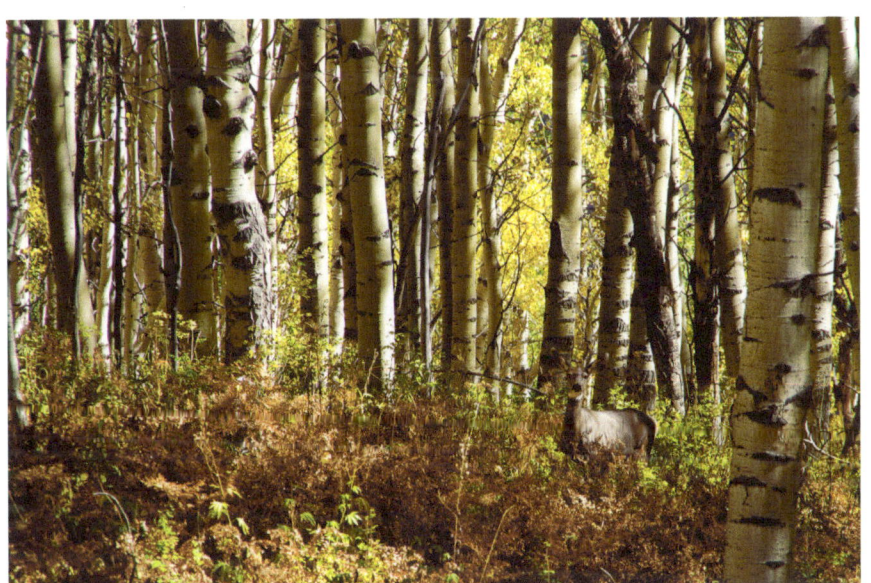

I became, the more I felt the forest around me, watching me, encouraging me, and paying keen attention to what I was up to. I didn't feel alone at all, and I felt the curiosity of the forest all around me. While I might have started out alone, the forest had joined in my quest for the one perfect photograph, and together we made this one.

I then finally looked up and realized that I was being watched by more than just the trees.

Kebler Pass, for good reason, is definitely one of my favorite places.

Maple Visions

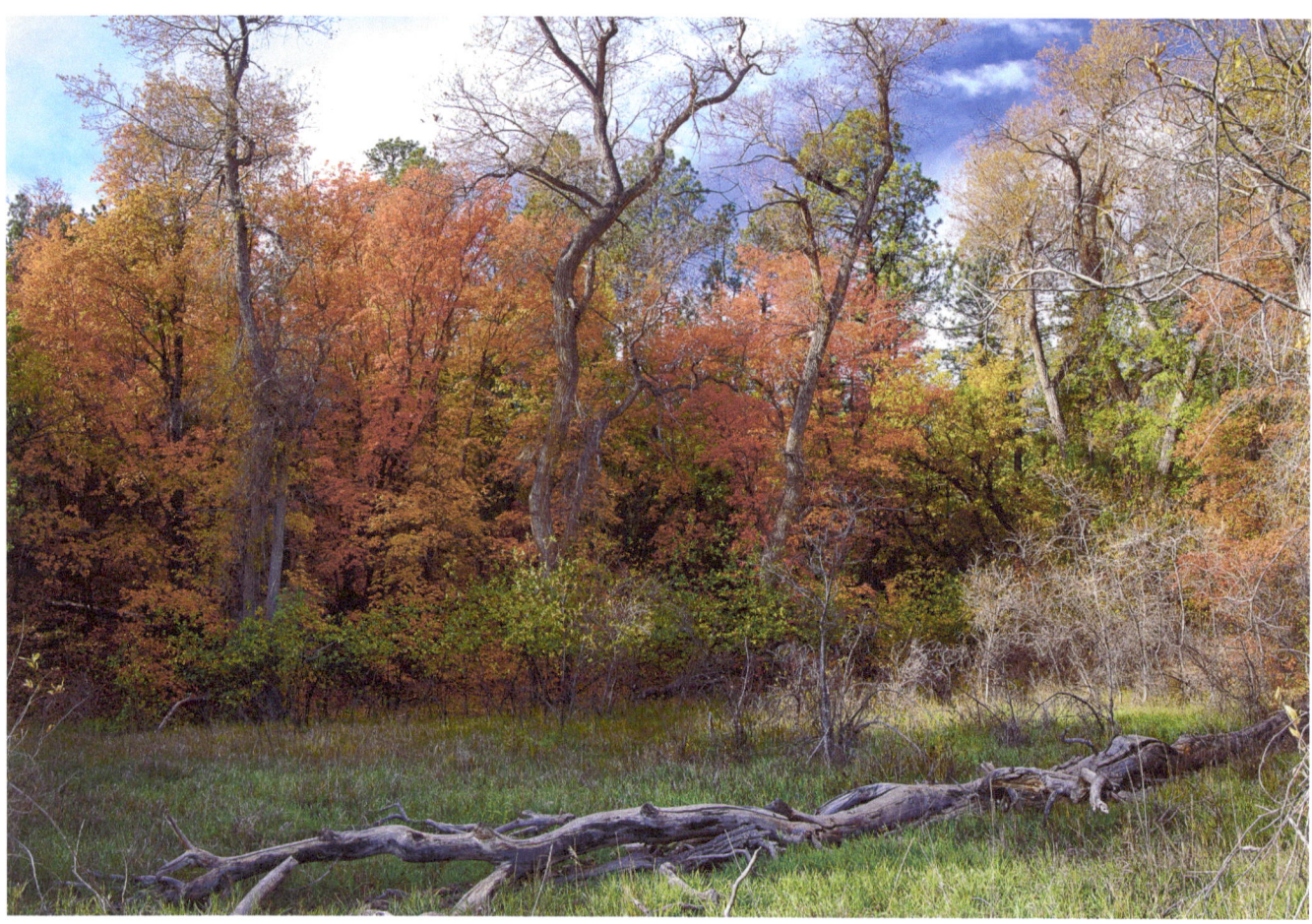

Often when we think of trees and the Southwest, we think of aspens. Deep in central New Mexico, however, there is a small pocket of the most unlikely of tree, the big tooth maple, that puts on a fall show that easily rivals the one aspens produce. The leaves of the big tooth maple do not turn gold, but rather red, and in the process make a stunning sight.

The Manzano Mountains, not far from Albuquerque, are home to this pocket of maples. Every year in the fall, they turn from their usual green and catch fire with shades of oranges and red. The reds, especially, are absolutely stunning and take my breath away. I don't live very far from this location, so I drop by it frequently to spend some time enjoying it. One beautiful fall day I was greeted with the most amazing site; the maple leaves were every shade one could possibly imagine, with a few new shades thrown in for good measure.

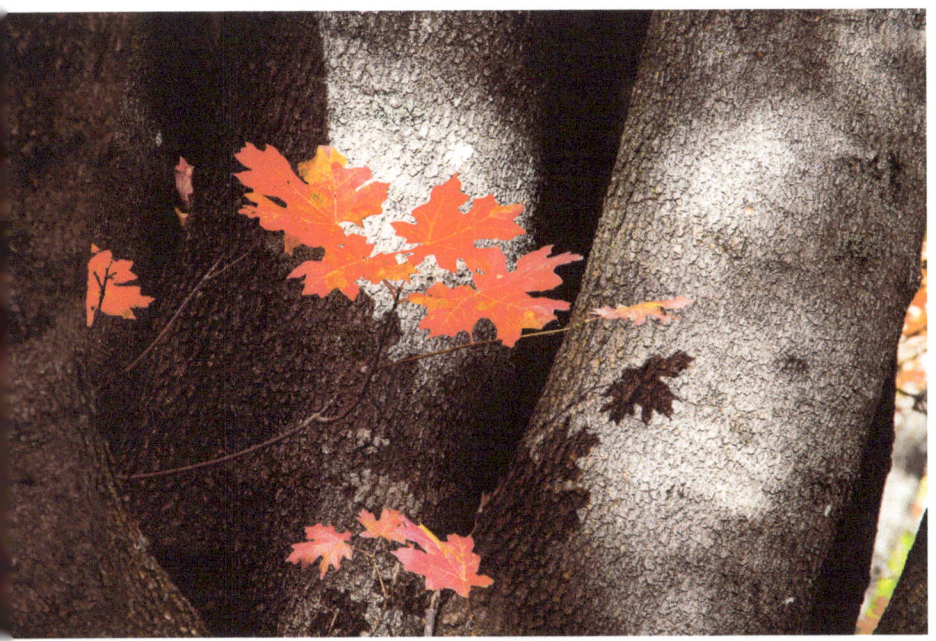

Not just the large stands of leaves are amazing, for even a few leaves can shine in their own right; *Maple's Shadow* is a perfect example. In the shadow of its far larger neighbor, the small maple branch casts its own shadow on the larger tree. I like that metaphor as much as I like this photograph, and I like this photograph very much. It reminds me that something doesn't have to be big, mighty, sweeping or soaring to be beautiful, and it reminds me to keep my eyes wide open, because you just never know.

The last scene from the Manzanos is another that struck me deeply. As fall arrives and the maples really come into their own, their vibrant red leaves stand out against the usual forest colors, complementing and enhancing the surrounding foliage. I love the way the verdant wild grasses cover the gentle slopes, and I adore how the maples lean over, creating a pathway that draws me into the forest. The dappled sunlight caresses the area, providing exactly enough light without being overpowering. The serenity of the forest is strong here, and every time I look at this photo I feel the peace and tranquility of the late afternoon in and among the big tooth maples.

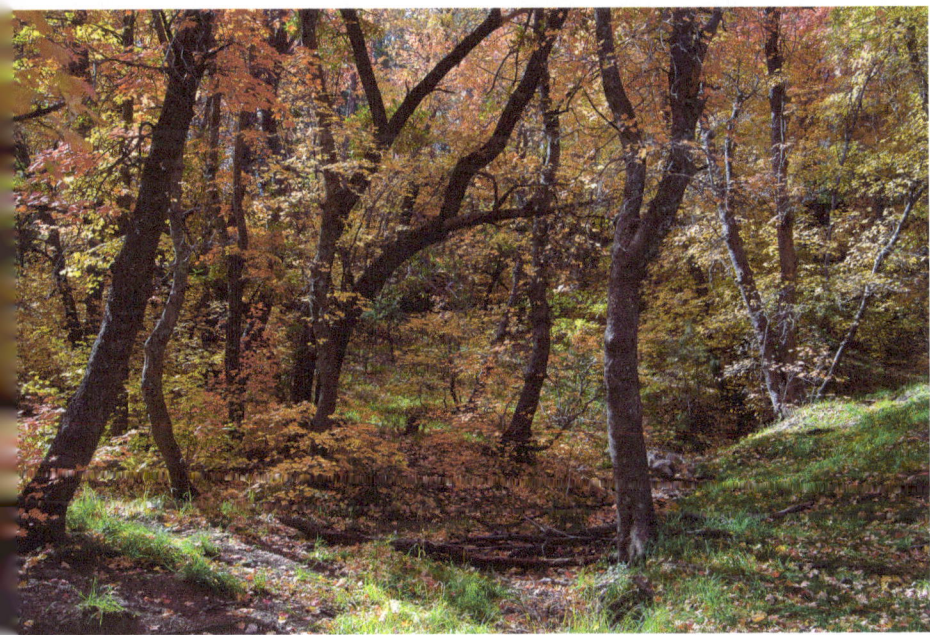

Sunset Maelstrom

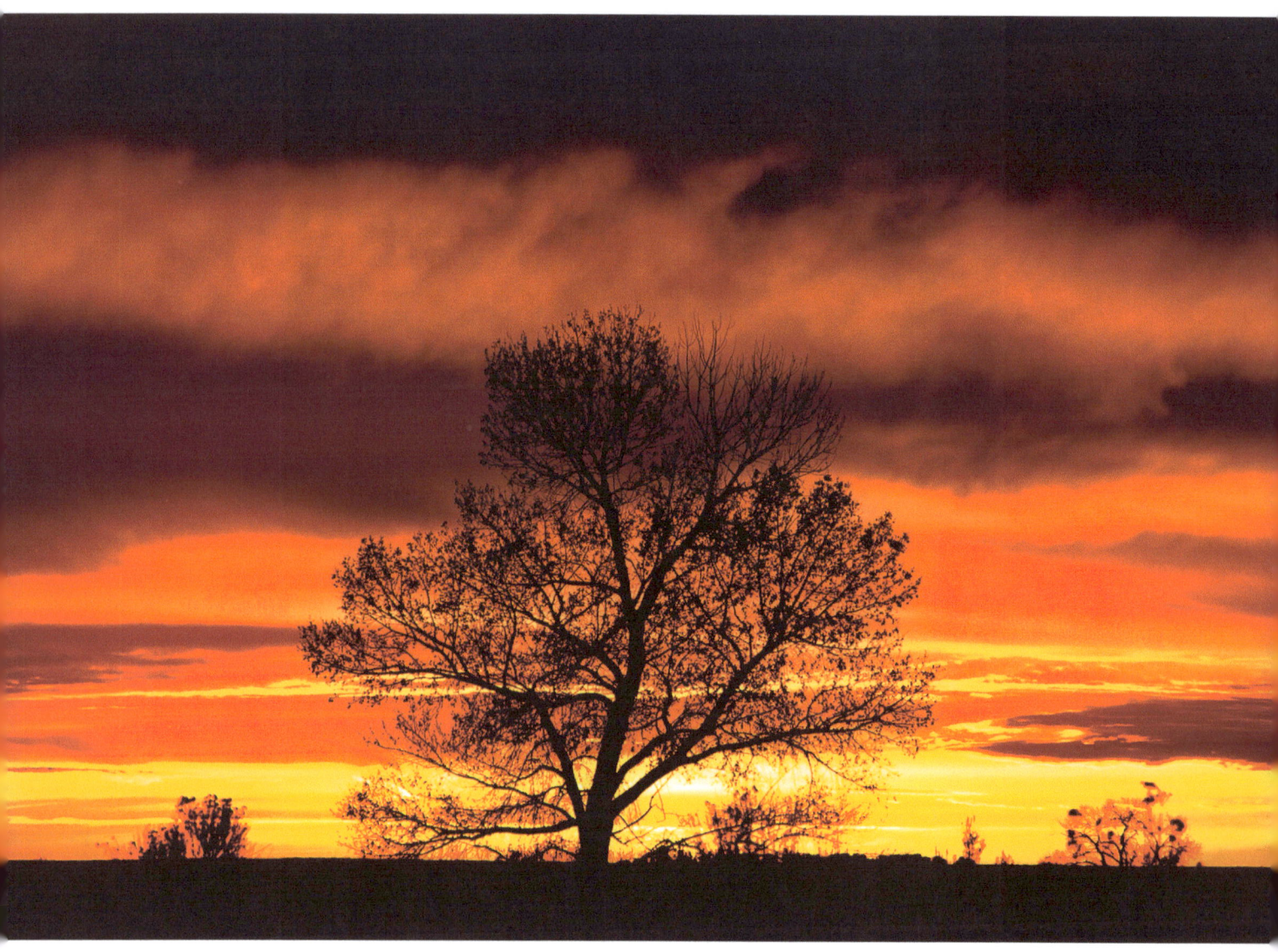

We'll leave this chapter with a dramatic sunset.

It had been a very long day for me. I had been up since well before dawn photographing Mesa Arch, and since it was winter, that meant being quite cold. Today the temperature was fourteen below zero, so cold meant cold, the sort of cold that seeps deep into your bones and takes up residence. The kind of cold you feel for hours and hours afterwards, and even as I write this, I am still shivering.

I had been chasing the light all day, and aside from the productive time in Canyonlands National Park, had very little to show for it. A thick, heavy cloud deck moved in over me, and was not going to budge. My time in Utah was up, so I pointed my vehicle southward toward home and began the long drive into the dreary day. Along the way it promised to get better, but didn't.

Somewhere around Lewis, Colorado, I realized everything was about to change. At last I drove to the edges of the cloud; finally there was promise for something that could make the photograph I was hoping for. I raced down the road, carefully watching the clouds and the moment. The sun finally dipped below the thick clouds and found a space to light up the maelstrom above. The sun was angry at having been hidden all day and determined to let everyone know how it felt.

Unfortunately, as dramatic as the sky was, I was completely lacking something compelling to make the photograph. The colors grew and intensified, and just when I thought it couldn't get any better, it did. Still, as stunning as the sky was, it was just that, a sky. I continued to race down the highway, looking for an opportunity. I had almost given up and decided that I would simply enjoy the fiery colors, when I saw the absolutely most perfect tree I could ask for, brilliantly silhouetted against that sky.

I stopped the car and jumped out. Alas, I was just not tall enough to make the photograph work, so I looked around for something, anything, higher. I saw a snowbank, and while not ideal, I decided it would have to do. I ran up the snowbank, and as I was slowly sinking into it, I had just enough time to make this photograph. I couldn't have been happier. Sure, I sank into the snowbank, and sure, I ended up more than wet, but I knew this photograph would turn out, and I never felt a thing.

Bosque's Birds

The Bosque del Apache National Wildlife Refuge is home to an extraordinary number of birds throughout all the seasons. These stories represent some of my favorite experiences there and some of my most memorable moments.

Bosque Surreal

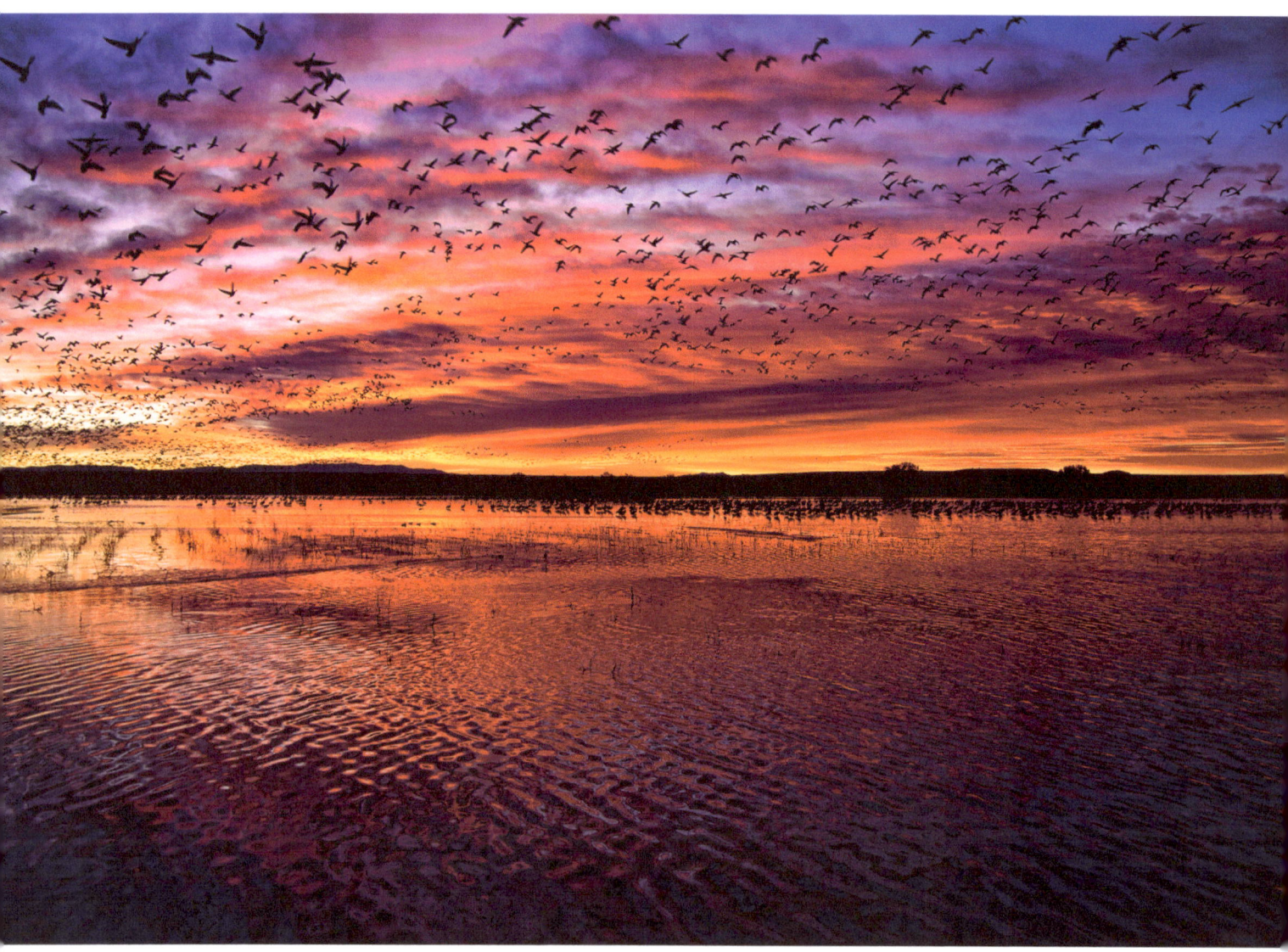

The Bosque del Apache National Wildlife Refuge in New Mexico is world renowned for the birds that flock to it. Any time of the year finds birds, at least temporarily, making their home there. As the seasons change, so do the birds, making each visit completely different. No matter what time of year, there is always the possibility that you will see something exceptionally interesting.

On November 19, 2011, at precisely 7:03 a.m., something exceptionally interesting did indeed happen: *Bosque Surreal*.

The morning was cold, as only a mid November morning can be, the kind of cold that deceives you, for although you have dressed in layers, donned as much insulated clothing as you possibly can, and have taken every possible precaution, the cold somehow slices right through all that and right into your bones. The longer you stand there, the more the cold seeps deep into you, even though the thermometer claims it is not, in fact, negative 500 or so. The thermometers in the Bosque del Apache must all be in collusion, or something, for it was at least that cold, if not more so.

As dawn began slowly to wake up, the skies lightened accordingly. From the first moment of the first light, it promised to be an extraordinary day. Color came before the light, it seemed, and in the far distance pinks, reds, purples, and oranges all teased their entrance. As the sun rose higher in the sky, the colors, instead of fading, intensified and grew more vibrant.

The birds out on the ponds remained seemingly oblivious to the show nature was putting on, or perhaps they knew the best was yet to come. If it was the latter, they were completely correct.

By 6:45 a.m. the colors seemed to be at their peak. As much as I had hoped the snow geese would fly up and into the color, my hopes were dashed. The disappointment of that moment was crushing. I was cold. I was tired. I grew colder still, and the color ran out of the skies before my very eyes.

Just before 7:00, however, it all changed, and it changed in an instant. Against all odds, the colors came back into the sky, and this time they came back with a vengeance. Where they had formally played and danced across the sky, now they seared across it, with the reds fighting for dominance with the purples and the oranges shoving aside the yellows. The purples, in turn, pushed right back against the reds and showed off their vibrancy, and the yellows were tired of the oranges and showed them how it was really done. The only question was if the snow geese would fly.

At 7:03, they did. Oh, how they did!

As one, all of the snow geese in the pond rose into the air to greet the morning. As one, the snow geese covered the sky from edge to edge. As one, they merged into the morning scene, and in the process, created *Bosque Surreal*.

By 7:04 the colors were fading. Shortly after that, the morning gave way to a far more traditional one, although by that time the snow geese were far away. I slowly let out my breath and realized I wasn't cold anymore, not even a little bit. I stood for the longest time, marveling at the spectacle that I had seen, and more than pleased at the result.

Solo Flight

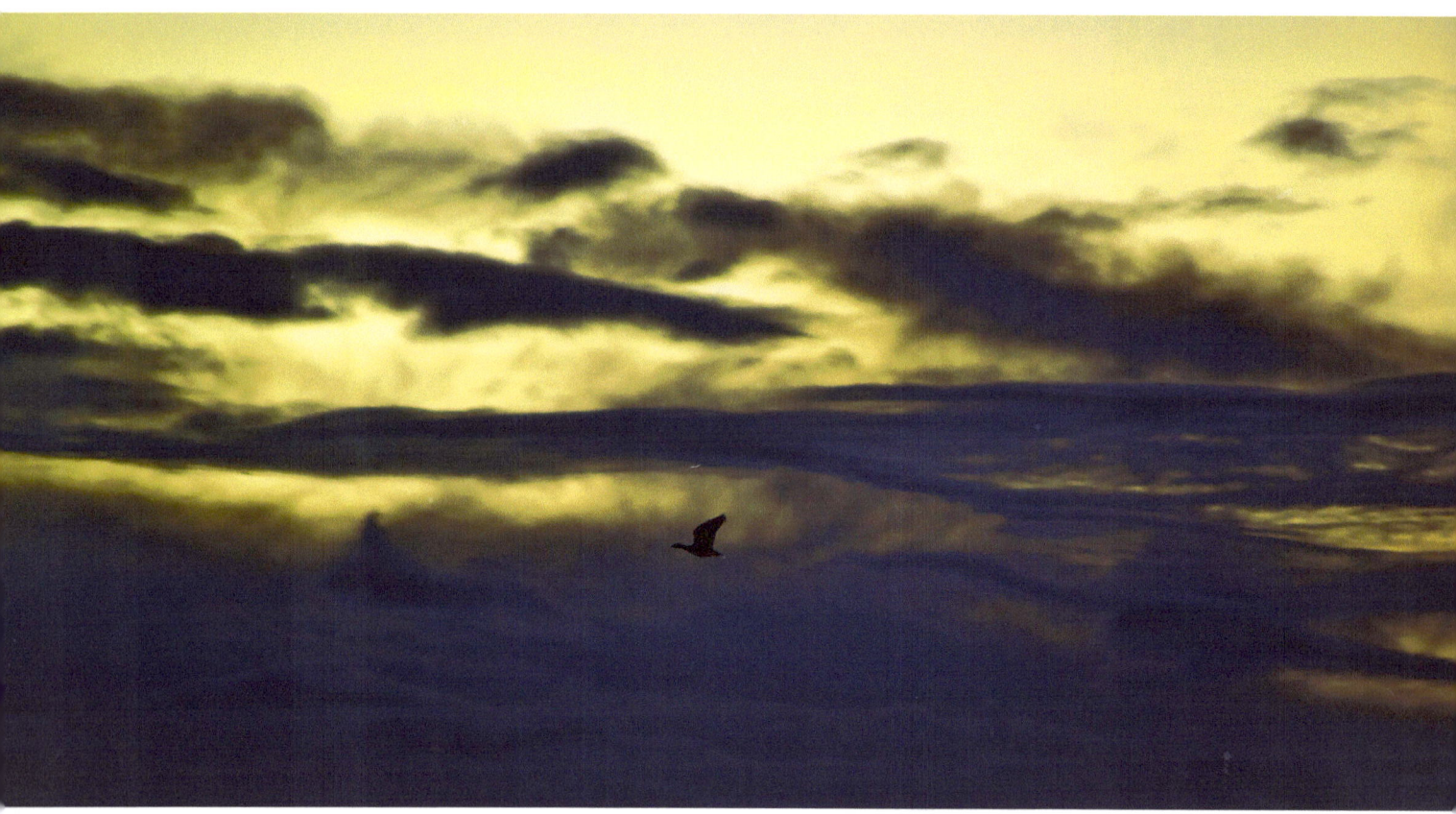

Despite the amazing gift that I had been given, the morning was not done with me.

After I made *Bosque Surreal* and the snow geese had departed, I lingered on by the pond's edge. I was in no hurry and wanted to simply enjoy the morning. Although the intense colors had drained from the sky, the yellows lingered on for a bit, apparently deciding if they should stay or fade away. A single, lone snow goose knew where it wanted to go and headed off to find its comrades. As it gained a little bit of altitude, it flew near the yellows and through the wisps of lingering clouds. In a the blink of an eye, *Solo Flight* came to be.

It was, and still is, one of the best mornings I have ever experienced in the Bosque del Apache.

Crane Intensity

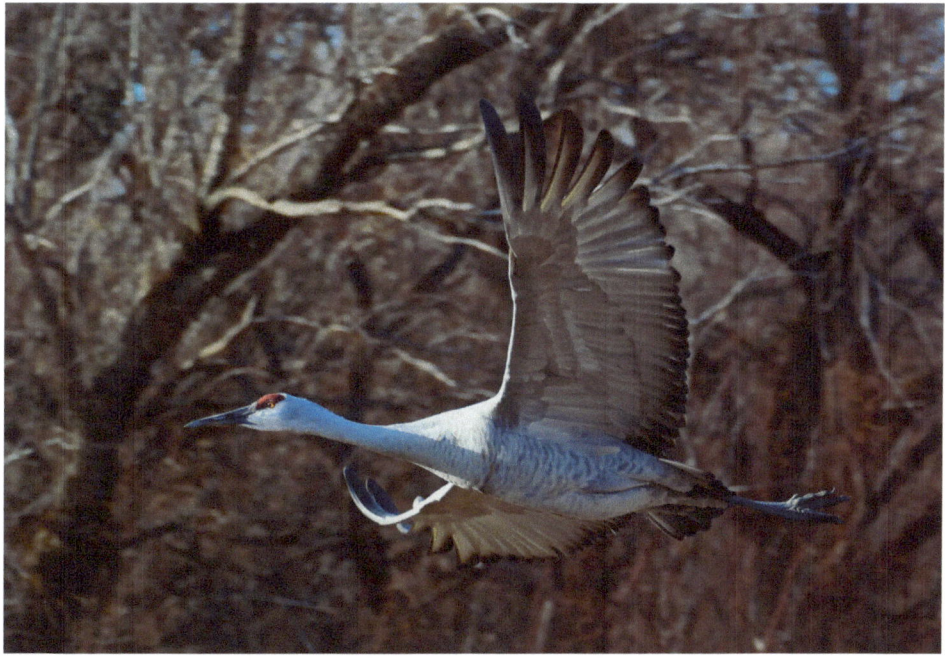

The fall day was calm and still. Late afternoon often offered a mixed bag of opportunity, and I never really knew what might happen, if anything. Perhaps the birds prefer to remain far afield and out of sight, although perhaps they will decide to come in early. It is hard to say what will happen on any given day.

On this day the Bosque was relatively quiet. The few cranes there all seemed to be far away and content; in any event, they weren't moving much. The snow geese were out and about and had not yet decided to come back in for the evening. There wasn't anything for it but to wait and see if anything happened.

The afternoon wore on and all remained quiet, which is always a difficult time, because you end up being lulled into afternoon's clutches. One lone sandhill crane, however, had a completely different view of the afternoon.

Out of the corner of my eye I sensed the movement and saw the crane flying low to the ground. Opportunity, it would appear, was headed right toward me. I prepared to make the photograph as quick as I could, and as the crane flew by me I was ready. The look in the crane's eye shows the intensity of the flight. The crane knows where it is going and what it wants. I am more than pleased with this photograph and how it came out. I never know what the afternoons will hold for me.

Hawk Takeoff

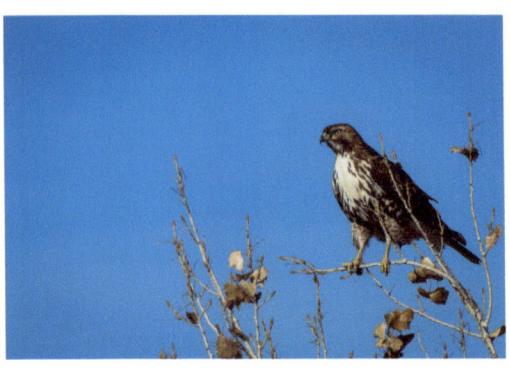

"Patience pays off. Patience pays off," I kept telling myself over and over, again and again. "Patience pays off. Patience pays off." Over and over. It had become my mantra.

The hawk, apparently, also believed my mantra.

I had spotted the red-tailed hawk earlier, perhaps a half hour before, and stopped to wait for it. While it sat alert and restless in the top of a tree, it was only a matter of time before it spied a potential meal and took off for it. I thought this would be a fine opportunity to make a photograph and didn't think it would take very long. I had not yet settled into my mantra.

A couple of moments passed, and the hawk continued to look around. Twice it ruffled its feathers as if to take off; I was completely ready. Twice it settled back down. I remained ready. A few more moments passed, and again the hawk looked as if it was going to take off. I wasn't expecting any warning regarding imminent takeoff, so I remained braced and ready. It wasn't long before I said to myself, "Patience pays off." I would say it quite a few times to myself before I made the photograph.

I have no idea how long we sat, the hawk and I, although we had completely different agendas. It would twitch and rustle and I would be ready for the split second I knew I would have. It would settle back down, but I dared not let down my guard. I considered abandoning the attempt, but I was too invested in it not to see it through until the end. Surely the hawk would take off right now, right?

"Patience pays off."

We continued to wait, the hawk and I. After a while, above the faint rustle of the leaves, I was certain that I heard the hawk say, "Patience pays off," but it was probably just my imagination. The wait continued.

Between heartbeats the hawk's wings unfolded and it was no longer sitting still. I had the blink of an eye to make my photograph, and I did. The hawk flew off for its dinner, and I headed off into the afternoon. We each knew in our hearts that indeed, patience pays off.

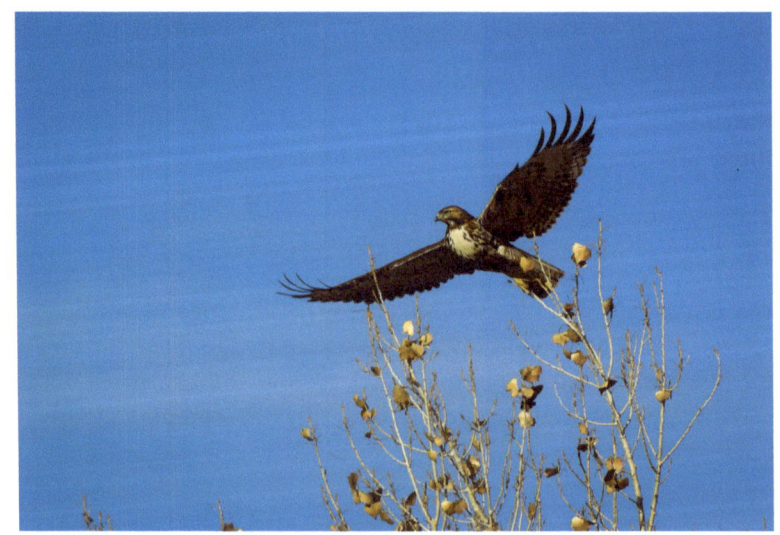

Egret Takeoff

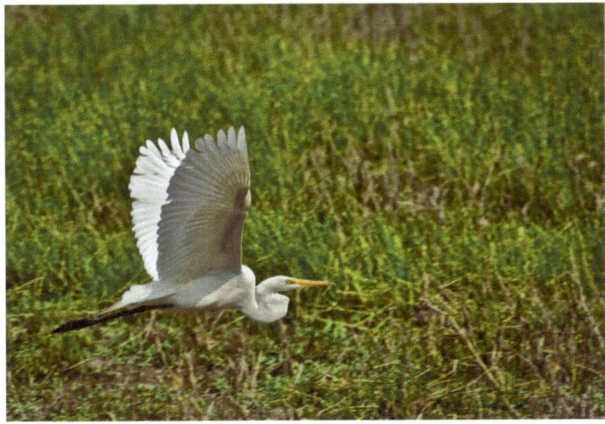

The snowy egret stood silently, watching the ground for what seemed like hours on end. Barely twitching, its feathers flowing in the gentle breeze, it was motionless, and its eyes never left the ground in front of it. This snowy egret was hunting dinner in the Bosque del Apache in the summer, and snowy egrets are very good hunters.

On land they look for small mammals, reptiles, or whatever happens by. With a lightning-quick strike, they spear their prey. In water, they become fishermen, and they are equally good at that sport.

In any event, this egret had decided that the hunt would not pay off. With what looked like a shrug, yet surely wasn't—was it?—it spread its wings wide and fell forward into the breeze. With two quick beats of the wings it was airborne and level, flying low over the field, perhaps looking for a more suitable dinner location.

After a short flight, it landed again and before you could draw another breath, once again turned into stone. The hunt was afoot again.

Geese Drop-In

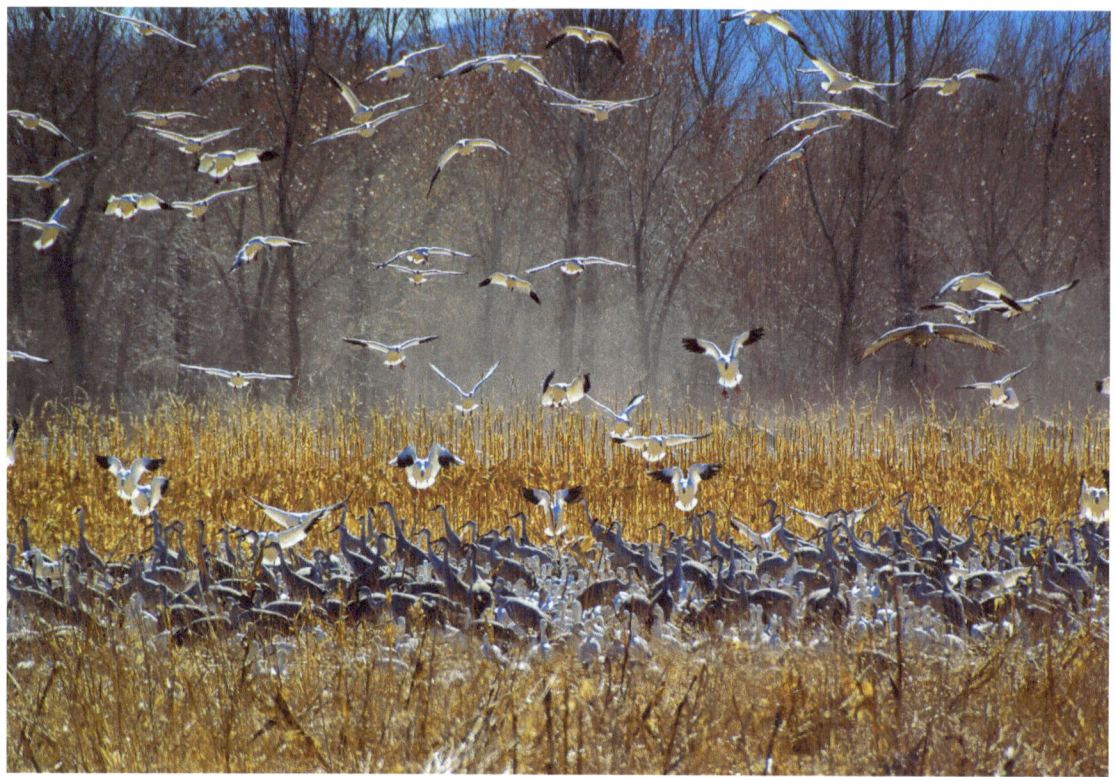

It was a quiet winter morning at the Bosque del Apache, and the sandhill cranes were enjoying it immensely. It was sunny, the temperature was quite reasonable for January, and most of all, the field had plenty to forage on. In short, it was an absolutely perfect day.

That is, until the geese decided to drop in for brunch. At first it was just one snow goose that decided it would join the cranes, but where there is one goose, there are thousands, and before the cranes realized what was about to happen, the geese began to land. What was a quiet morning turned, in a heartbeat, into an intense, noisy affair. What was a serene field with plenty of room to spread out turned into a crowded, cramped space, with geese underfoot everywhere. What was the perfect spot to feed turned into something considerably less so. Worse, geese are flighty, constantly taking off and landing, and in the process, stirring the dust up constantly.

The sandhill cranes, though, suffered their fate admirably. They, to the best of their ability, ignored their uninvited guests, choosing instead to focus on their brunch. And the geese? They were happy with their newfound bounty and stayed on for dinner.

Landing Sequence

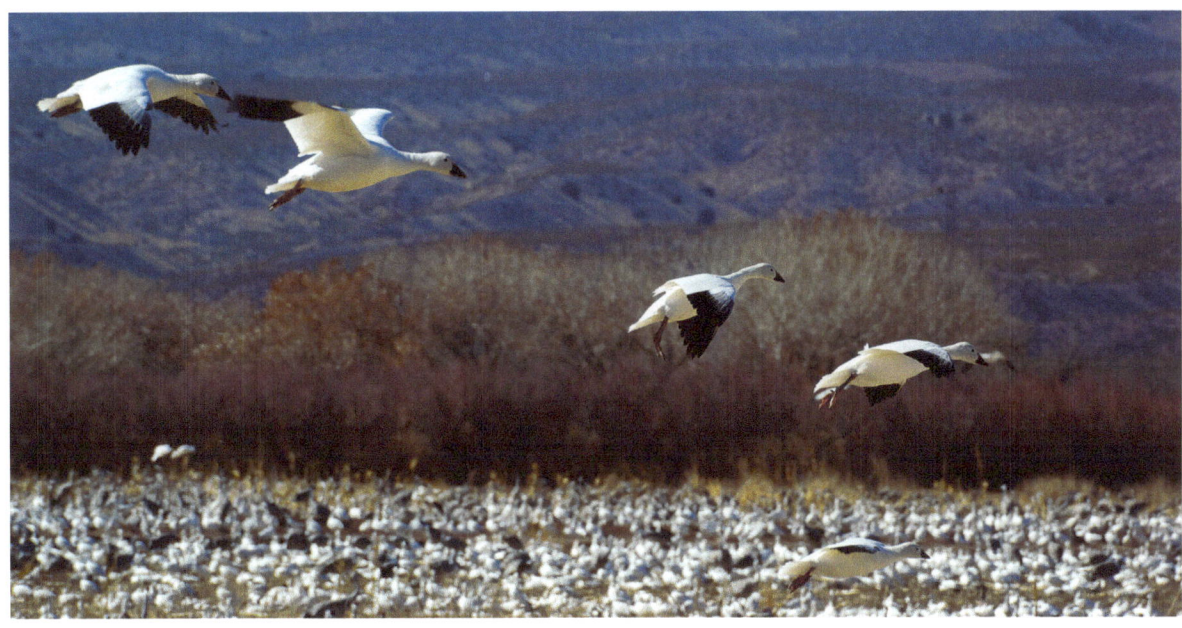

The Bosque del Apache is known for its birds, specifically the massive flocks of sandhill cranes and snow geese that winter there. Crowds of people gather in the predawn hour to watch the "fly out," in which thousands of birds take off at once. This sight is awe-inspiring to be sure.

But what happens when the birds land?

They do not, as a rule, all land together, instead landing either by themselves or in very small groups. One by one, two by two, they spread their wings wide to slow down, extend their feet, and drift ever so gracefully and gently to the ground as if gravity simply didn't apply to them.

This whimsical sequence shows four such snow geese drifting in for a landing. They each seemed to be on the exact same flight path, and they landed right next to one another in the end. But for the brief moment just before touchdown, they demonstrated for all to see an absolutely perfect landing sequence.

I am very pleased with how this photograph turned out, and I smile every time I look at it.

The Bosque del Apache is an interesting place, full of life and especially full of birds. Any time of the year is a perfect time to visit; you'll find small, intimate scenes of birds, whimsical scenes, and of course the grand spectacle of the winter fly out. It remains one of my all-time favorite places to visit, and I always come away with a newfound appreciation of the birds and other inhabitants who rely on the wetlands.

Flower Power

Flowers have the incredible ability to bring happiness to us no matter what troubles may be around us. Wildflowers have the strongest smile power of all, from carpeted fields of flowers to a small, solitary one growing on the forest floor. Flower Power explores some of these flowers.

Bluebell Skies

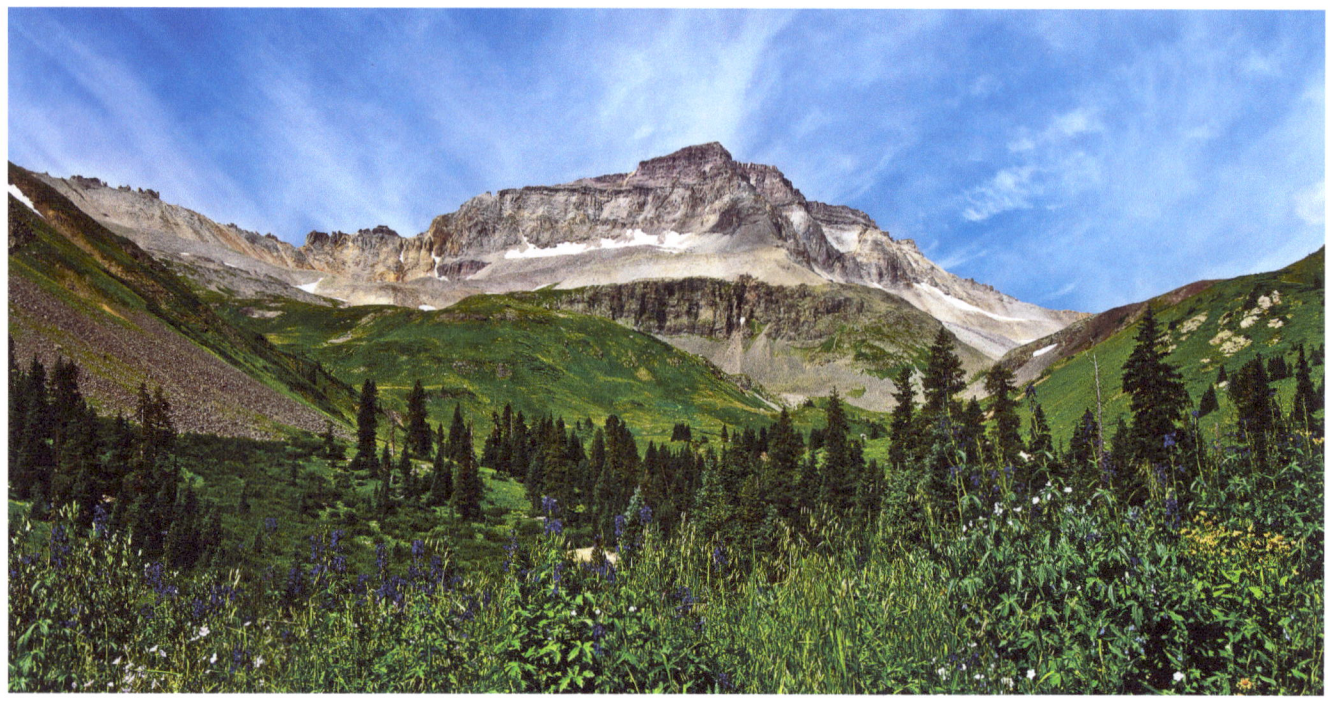

High above the small mountain town of Ouray, Colorado, lies the Yankee Boy Basin, so named for the famous Yankee Boy Mine that was located there. Back in the day, the narrow, winding and often treacherous road that leads up from Ouray to the Yankee Boy Mine saw a reasonable amount of traffic, since there were quite a few mines along it. The mines have played out, and the only people traveling up into the basin are Jeep enthusiasts and people like me. The road remains difficult, and there are a few blind corners with a 600 foot drop on one side and sheer mountain walls on the other. It is a popular road among adventurers for this reason, but not without peril.

Once you make it to the top, however, the beauty is beyond compare, especially on a summer day when the bluebells are out. The sight makes you forget all about the difficulties of the ascent. The mountains rise above you and surround you, holding you tight within their grasp. This scene, I think, evokes the feeling quite well. Tall, lush plants carpet the basin, broken by the summer wildflowers. Beyond the tall grasses, fourteen thousand foot peaks reach toward the sky and catch it, sometimes. The clouds break over the peaks, giving them a wide berth, lest they be caught as well.

Summer in the upper Colorado basins is a beautiful time of the year. The bluebells all around add a perfect crowning touch.

Yankee's Columbine

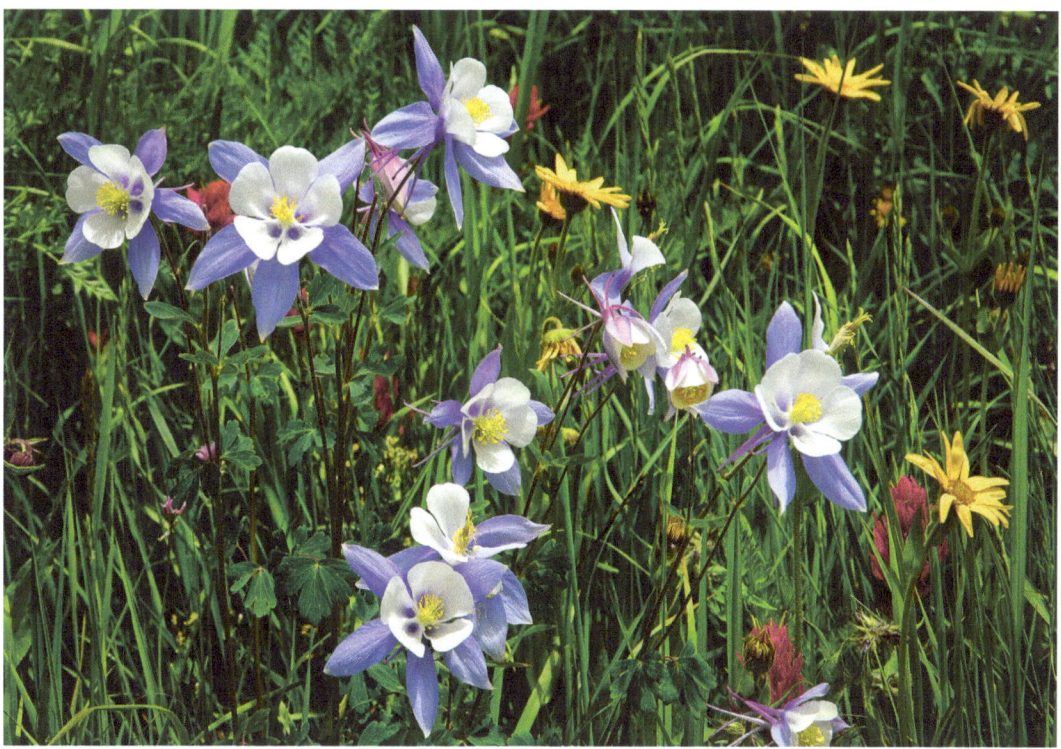

While admiring the soaring views of the fourteeners, mountain peaks that exceed fourteen thousand feet that surround me in the basin, it is easy to become lost in the vastness. This portion of the San Juan Mountains has soaring peaks and colorful basins, and when you turn 360 degrees the perspective hits you as you realize the sheer scale of what is surrounding you.

In the summer time, though, also in Yankee Boy Basin is found a small and delicate flower, the Rocky Mountain columbine, nestled within the tall summer grasses. As breathtaking as a fourteener is, the columbine has the same power and attraction, but on a scale that is far easier to grasp.

It is not hard to see why the columbine is Colorado's state flower. The choice is an obvious one. The state made that decision back in 1899, and it has been a sound decision ever since.

This small scene spoke to me as I made this photograph; the counterpoint of the sparse yellow and red set off the purple and white hues. *Yankee's Columbine* captures the beauty of it perfectly.

Arching Color

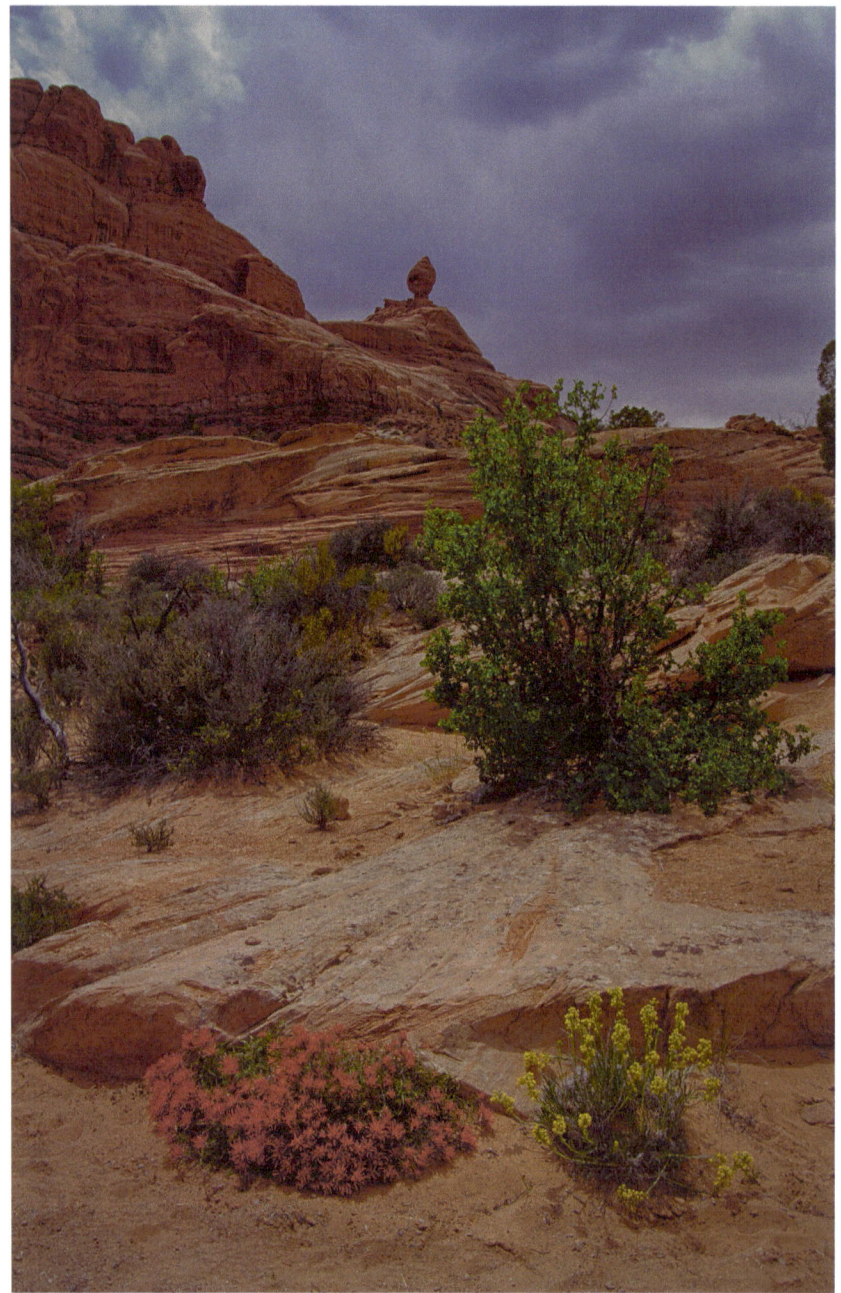

The high mountain basins of Colorado are not the only place one can find flowers and contrasts. The deep desert has a few surprises as well.

It had been a hot, dry day in Arches National Park, Utah. The wind, although gentle, was blowing and making a dry day even drier. There had been rain recently, but it was already a distant memory. As the hours went by, the heat was becoming relentless.

In the distant sky was the hint of relief, though. A thickening of the clouds low on the horizon perhaps promised that moisture would come. The day slowly turned into a race of heat versus the incoming summer storm, and eventually it was well apparent that the storm was going to win the race.

The flowers knew it, too. They appeared to become more vibrant than they had been earlier in the day, although perhaps it was merely that ominous backdrop that made them appear that way. They reached for the sky, wanting to catch and taste the sweet water as it tumbled to the ground. Best not to waste a single drop!

Shortly after I made this photograph, the storm delivered as promised. Skies opened up, spilling the much-needed water onto the flowers and the desert.

Perfect Day

We'll continue our close-up look at flowers, but this time, we'll head back to New Mexico on a warm summer day.

Every now and then everything in the world lines up perfectly. The sky is bright and sunny, with some fluffy clouds here and there. There is a gentle breeze, just gentle enough to move the air and keep you cool, yet not enough to actually blow anything out of place. The temperature is absolutely perfect too, and you are neither too hot nor too cold, and if you could adjust it to anything else, you wouldn't. The birds are chirping cheerfully in the distance, while the gentle "buzz buzz" of nearby bees provides a counterpoint. The flowers are in full bloom, reaching for the sky, their colors contrasting with everything else, yet also blending in perfectly.

Exactly that day happened to me in the El Malpais National Monument in New Mexico. All these factors lined up for me to experience a stellar moment in time, making this photograph a natural extension of that moment. The Indian blanket flowers were so colorful as they reached toward the sky that it was hard to believe they were real. The bees on them had no problem believing they were real. The sky behind provided the ideal photographic backdrop. Everything I could ask for lined up perfectly on this perfect day. The day was everything I could have asked for, and more.

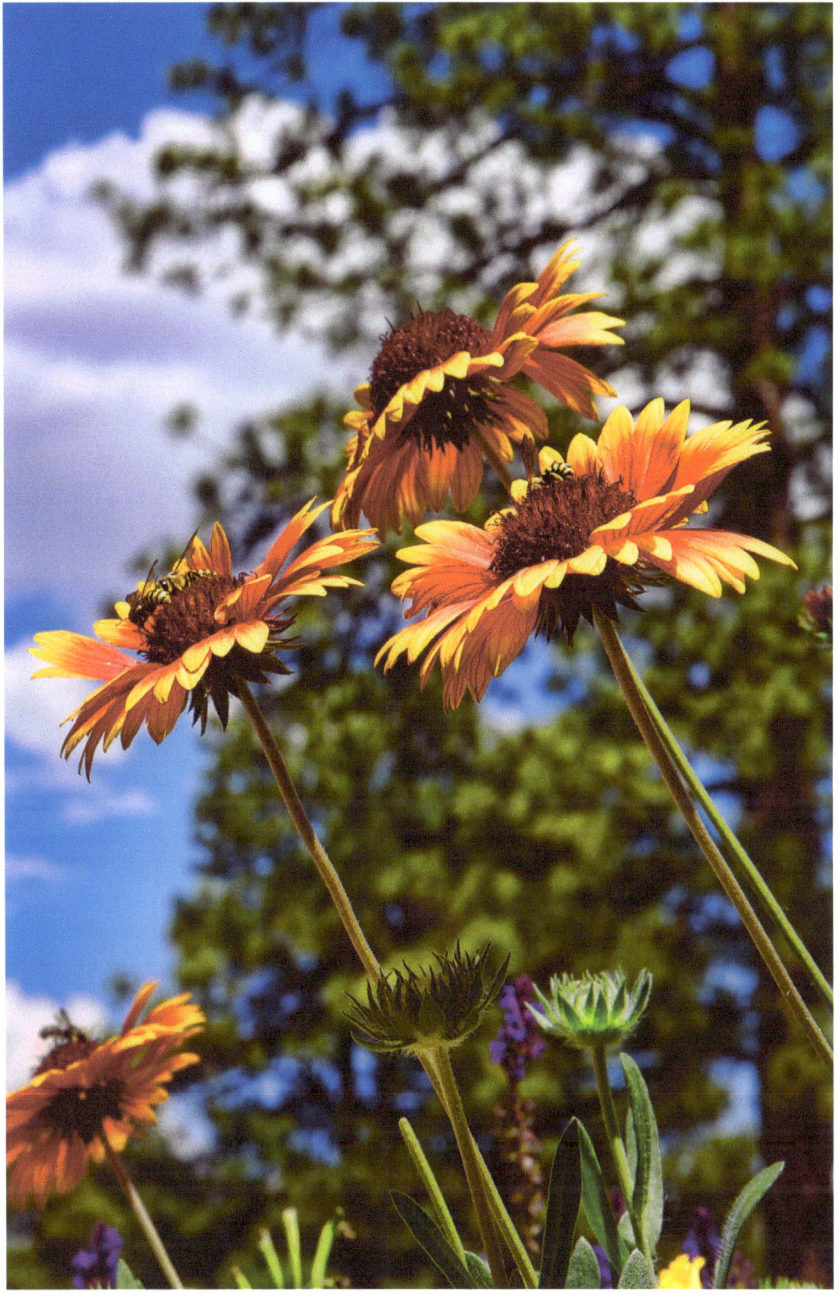

Calypso Orchid

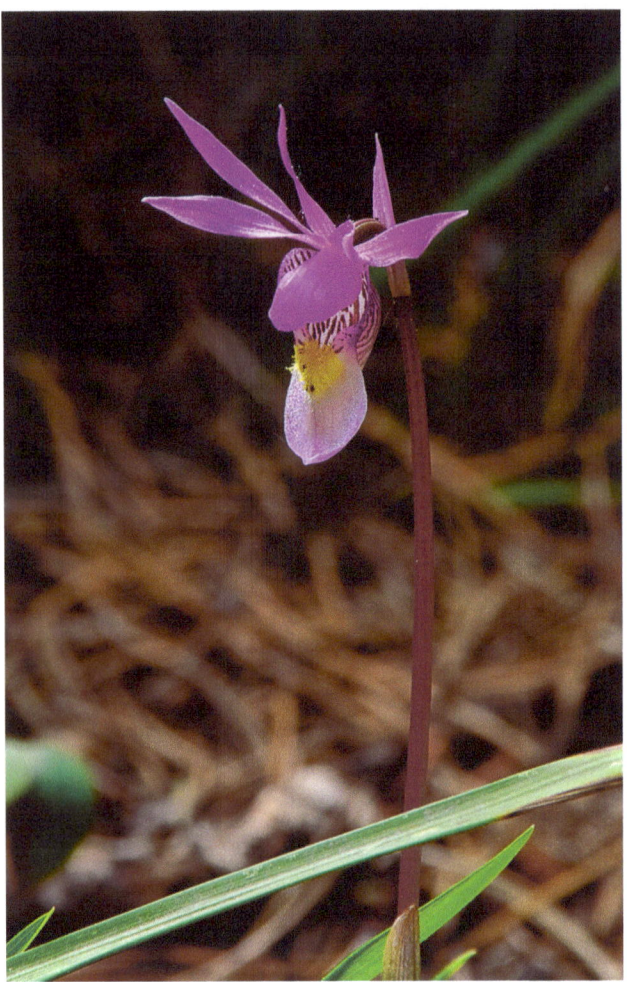

We've looked at vast, soaring mountain peaks surrounded by bluebells and columbine. We've seen flowers anchored in red rock, holding their own against a summer storm, and we've seen Indian blanket flowers make a perfect day. These common flowers all thrive in the Southwest and are admired by everyone. Let's go deep into the forest and look at a small, delicate orchid, an endangered species in North America, and take a look at a flower equally as beautiful, but hardly ever seen.

As you go off the beaten path and far along the outer reaches of some trails, in the eastern forests of Rocky Mountain National Park, Colorado, the trees become thicker, denser, and the colors become slightly more muted, since the sun has a hard time finding a pathway to the ground. Far fewer people visit this area, and fewer still hike very far. You have to keep your eyes peeled for what we are looking for: it is only a couple of inches tall, blends in perfectly with the forest floor, and prefers to grow in shadier areas, all of which combine to make spotting it difficult.

If you are lucky and time the season just right, you might find the small, delicate calypso orchid, which is the most magnificent color purple you can possibly imagine.

This orchid, while not uncommon, is endangered in the forests of Rocky Mountain National Park. It does not transplant at all, because its symbiotic relationship with the very soil it chooses to grow in, and if you are lucky enough to see one, it is best left alone. Perhaps one day it will be able to make a complete recovery, but for the time being, its beauty remains for only the luckiest to find. I was fortunate to locate a few and even more fortunate to be able to photograph one. I cherish this photograph and the journey I made to create it.

Beauty is all around us, all the time, if only one knows where to look. The calypso orchid reminds me always to keep looking.

Finch Attitude

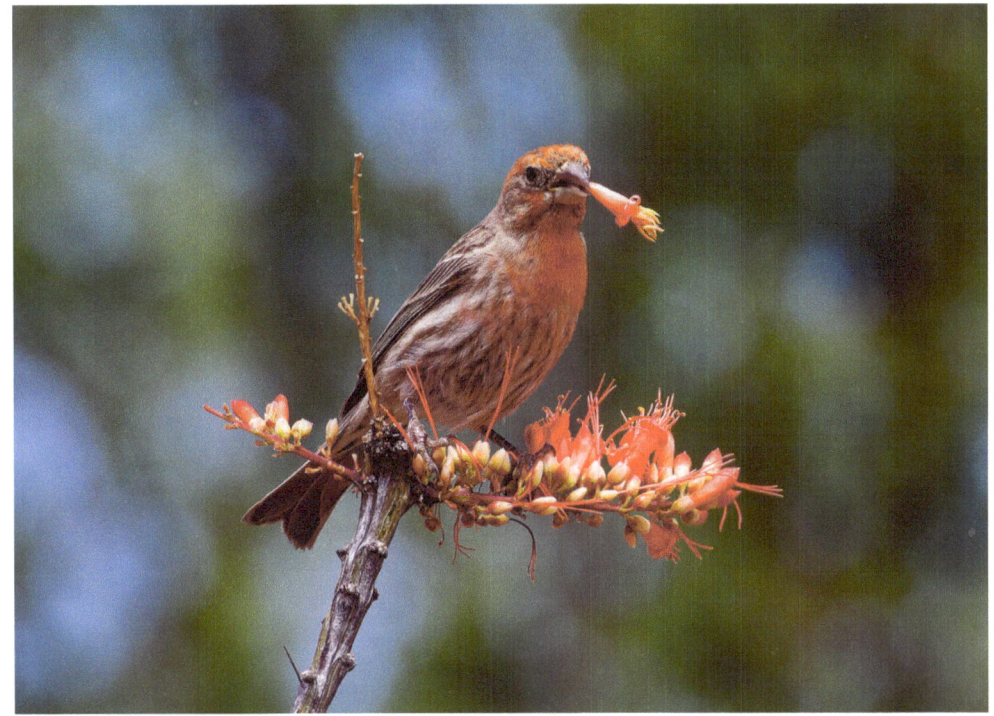

We'll finish up our short foray into flower power with a reminder that as much as we humans enjoy flowers, many other animals, including birds, do as well. When I was south of Tucson, Arizona, I encountered a finch who was holding court. He was, to put to it mildly, quite the character, and he certainly enjoyed his flower. I had stopped to ask him a simple question, but getting an answer was far from easy.

"Now then, as I was saying," the finch continued talking over me, despite my attempts to stop him and finally get my question in. Finches can be quite the talkers; that's for sure, and once they get going, it is exceptionally difficult, if not absolutely impossible, to say anything at all. "You have to find the best ocotillo flower to eat. Not just any old ocotillo will do, and you need to make sure that it is in full bloom. Now here, in southern Arizona, there are a lot of these, so you have a good selection. Best to fly around looking carefully at each one. Be choosy! You don't want to waste you time eating just any one. It's the red in the flowers that makes your breast red, so you need the brightest ones."

Whew! I was breathless just listening to him. I was pretty sure that the flowers didn't have much to do with making his breast red, though, and I had the temerity to try to question him. "Um, are you sure..." was about all that I managed to interject before he carried right on, while giving me a stern eye for my attempted interruption.

"Red makes red; any good bird knows that. If I ate blueberries, for instance, you would think that I was just an ordinary bluebird, wouldn't you? That's why I eat only red flowers, and that's why you should, too, if you know what's good for you." With that, he flew off with his flower, and I could finally breathe again.

I realized then my question was never properly asked, let alone answered, although in all of that, I also managed to forget why I was there in the first place. Finches!

Bird Prose

There is something profoundly powerful about a bird upon the wing. As they fly high in the sky, soaring where we can only dream, we often wonder what it would be like to be a bird. These birds stood still long enough for me to get to know them individually.

Finch Fellows

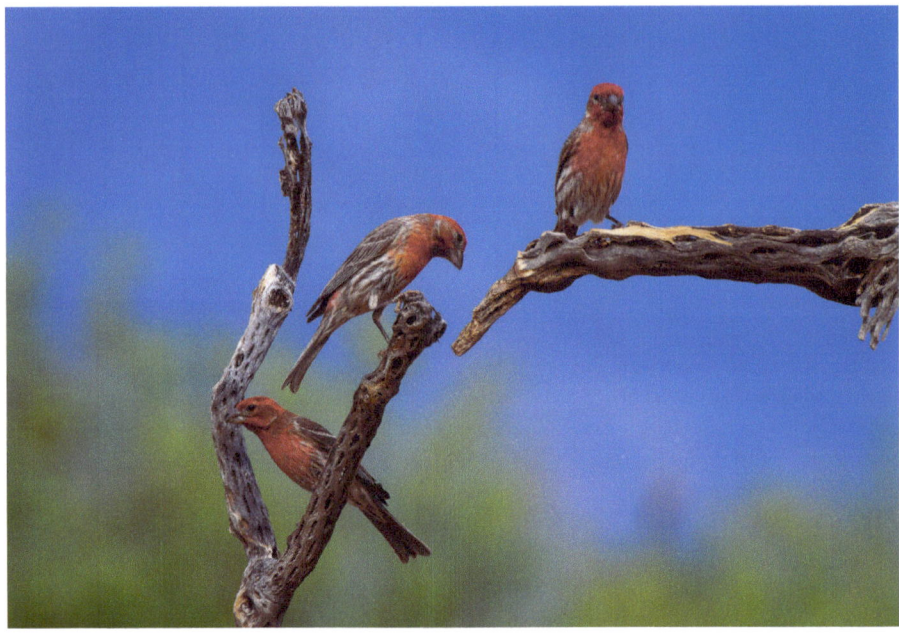

Since we just happen to be on the subject of finches, there is something whimsical about the house finch. A small bird, they seem to be quite active and even playful. They flitter about with an abundance of energy, and it seems that they never, ever sit still, at least not for long. The male's bright red chest provides a splash of color, and they are one of my favorite birds to watch and enjoy.

And to photograph.

These fine finch fellows gathered on a couple of pieces of cholla cactus in southern Arizona. It was a sunny spring day, warm, yet not too warm, the faintest whisper of all breezes to keep the air moving, and a blue sky above. Food was aplenty, so foraging was not a problem, which left a little extra time in the day for play.

Much to my delight, these three stayed in the branches and sang to whomever would listen. Since they are active, they were all doing their own separate thing, which made for this playful photograph. Here's to blue skies and warm days!

I was nestled in a small oasis in the desert, and I stayed there for several days. The location was ideal, and I had been there before. It had the most important ingredient, a small pond that attracted wildlife, especially birds, and it had plenty of forage to keep them there. I spent a couple of days hunched over in a blind, watching and waiting, waiting and watching, looking for certain combinations of wildlife to happen. The last time I had been there I had seen and photographed male cardinals, and I had seen and photographed female cardinals, but I had not seen, nor photographed, both a male and a female together, and that was something I wanted. I found myself back at this pond, back in a blind, waiting and watching.

For days.

This is not to say that the days were not fruitful, because they were. I was privileged to see many different birds, some of which I had never seen in person before, and that was a thrill.

Pyrrhuloxia Pose

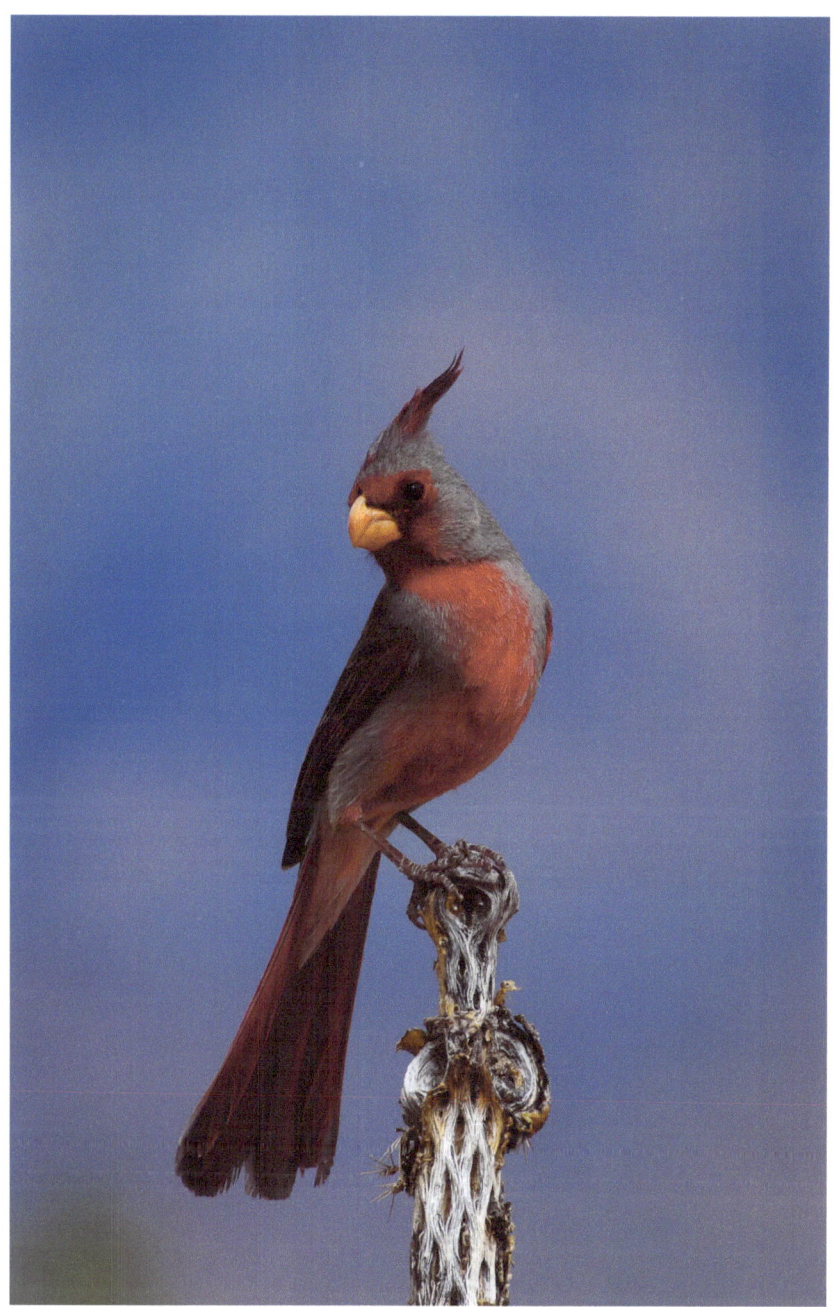

The pyrrhuloxia, or desert cardinal, is a regal bird. Unlike its cousin the northern cardinal, the male is not bright red all over, but it does retain much of the distinctive reds, and especially the crest. It's strange that this bird is nicknamed the desert cardinal, though, since both species readily live in the desert, leaving one to wonder why the northern cardinal didn't get the nickname.

It is, in any event, one of the oddest-named birds there is. Pyrrhuloxia is actually a combination of the genus names *pyrrhula* and *loxiz* and could be loosely interpreted as meaning flame-colored and crooked. It is as good a description as any, I suppose. Then again, desert cardinal seems so much easier.

It was spring and breeding season, and the males were looking their best. They have to, of course, to attract a female. It didn't take long before this beautiful bird came to rest not far away from me, and I was delighted the first time I saw it in person. What an incredible bird! He flew to a stump and perched there, looking at me. He cocked his head this way and then that way, perhaps to see me better. To me, he was trying to make sure I was able to photograph his good side, complete with the stunning backdrop behind him.

As beautiful as he was, though, he was not the cardinal I was seeking. I continued my wait in the blind.

Cholla Cardinal

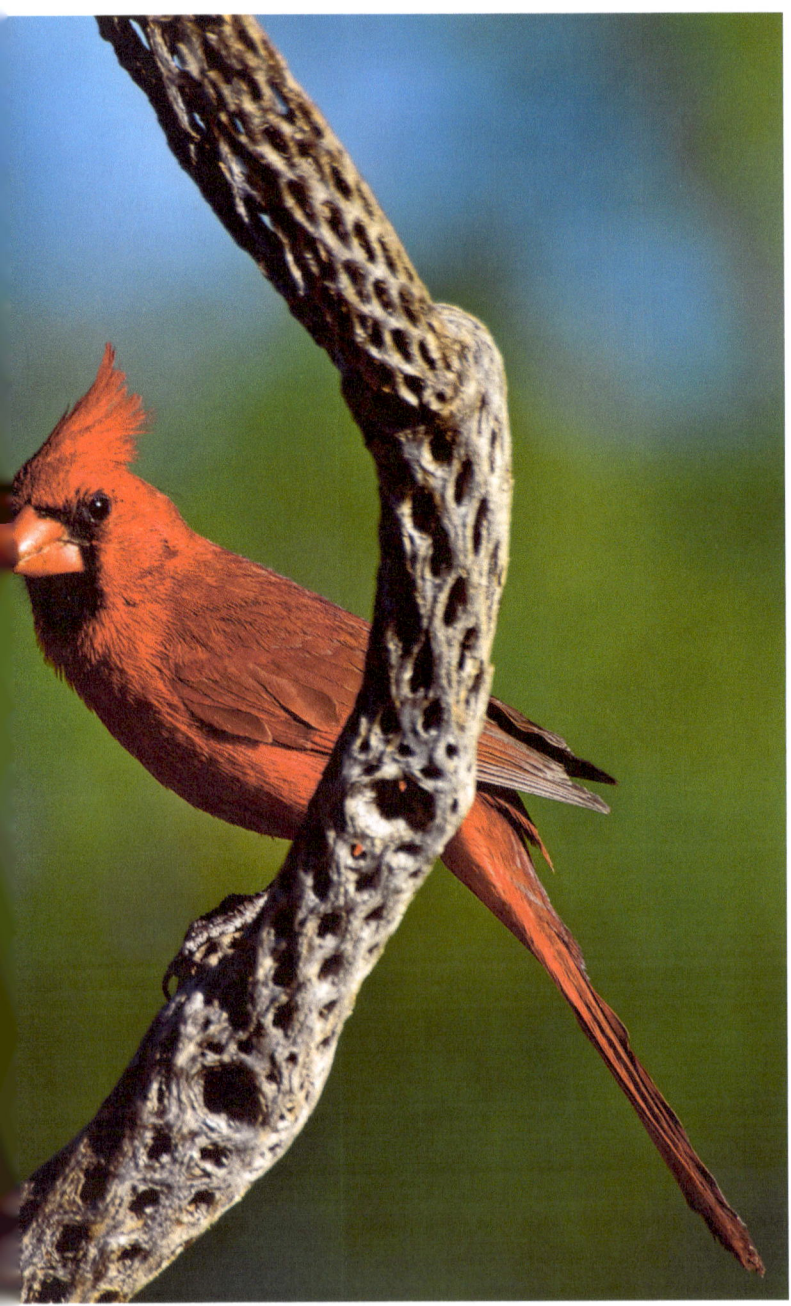

While I waited, I thought back to the previous year and the cardinal I had photographed then: *Cholla Cardinal*. It was this photograph that was the basis for my coming back again this year.

The exceptionally vibrant northern cardinal, with its signature bright red feathers and orange bill, holds a distinction that no other bird can claim: it is the state bird of seven states (Illinois, Ohio, Indiana, Kentucky, Virginia, West Virginia, and North Carolina).

Ranging throughout the Midwest and eastern states, it is also found in southern Arizona and northern Mexico, as well as most of Texas. This finch, for the northern cardinal is indeed a finch, is popular wherever it is found. I don't always find it perched on cactus, as is the case here. This fine fellow stopped for a while in the crook of a piece of cholla cactus, making this a uniquely southwestern piece.

This bird does not migrate, meaning you can hear its clear call of "cheer cheer cheer" or "purty purty purty" year round, lending cheering and prettiness throughout the year. Best of all, the northern cardinal population is on the rise, and there are no conservation issues with this fine bird.

The next time you see a flash of red pass by, it just might be the cardinal heading out to forage or perhaps returning to its nest, but in any event, adding joy and beauty to the day.

I continued my wait, which turned out to be longer than I expected.

Cardinal Love

Patience does pay off, as I continue to learn.

It took a long while, a couple of days, in fact, but finally my quest came to a conclusion. As I sat in the blind waiting for the exact moment I was looking for, I had several times when a male and female were close to each other, but not quite close enough. Once, I did photograph them together, but then I realized it wasn't quite what I wanted. After photographing the birds together, it dawned on me that what I really was looking for was a male and a female interacting.

That is exactly what I was able to accomplish.

I cannot say with absolute certainty that this is a mated pair of cardinals, but after watching them for a good bit, I believe they are, and they are certainly together and interacting. At long last I had managed to achieve my desired photograph, and I couldn't be more pleased with the result.

Cardinals usually pair with a single mate, and they select each other based on their physical appearances. Healthy-looking cardinals will produce healthy offspring, and that in turn increases their odds of survival. It should also come as no surprise that cardinals are at their best for singing during the mating season. The cardinal mating rituals, such as feeding each other seeds, is a true delight to observe, and the bond that these birds form will last upwards of a year and maybe even longer. I was able to witness this incredible bond of nature, and at long last my time in the blind was at an end.

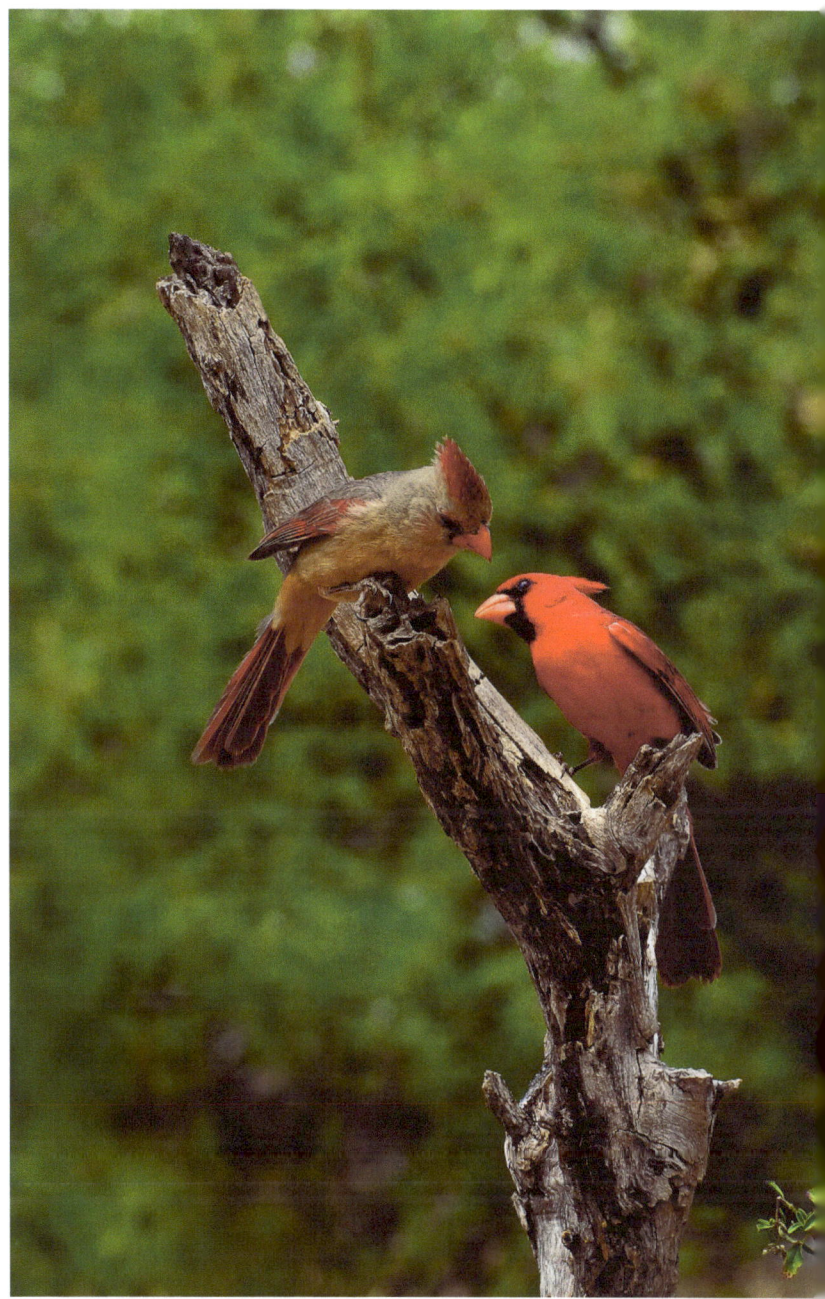

Bluebird Family

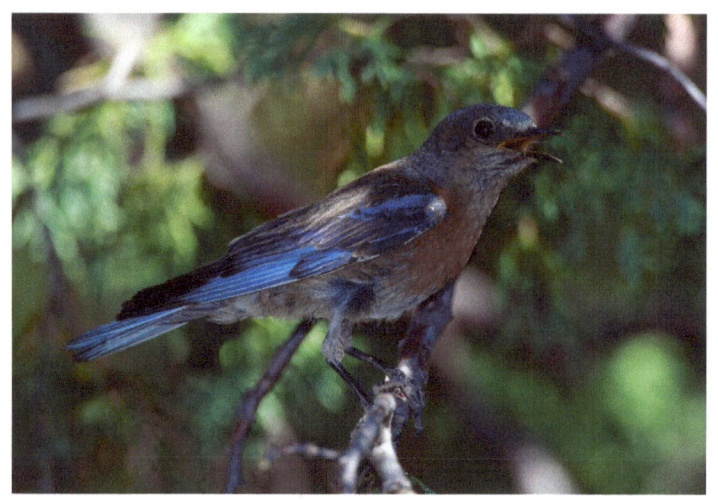 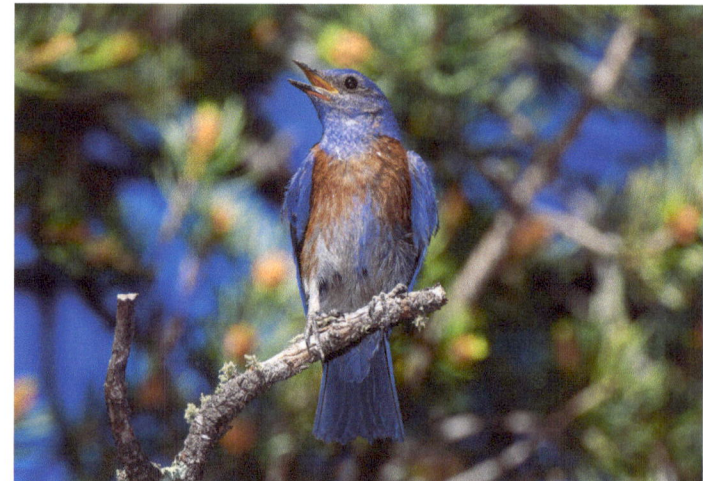

For whatever reason, I seem to have an affinity for birds. They fascinate me, and I enjoy watching them and watching how they interact with the world. As interesting as a single bird is, a mated pair is far and away more fascinating, and a family, well, that's about as good as it gets. To say that I was delighted that a pair of western bluebirds decided to raise their family right in front of my door is an understatement. I spent a tremendous number of hours with these birds, and I came to think I was part of their family. They thought so, too.

We routinely do our best to attract birds to our house. We put out numerous feeders, each with a different type of, we hope, delicious bird food. We keep bird baths and make sure they have water in them, and we put up birdhouses to see who might decide to take up residence. One fine spring, I noticed a bluebird or two nosing around a box not far from my front door. I didn't want to get my hopes up, but still, I couldn't help it. I thought it would be the most wonderful thing of all to have a bluebird nest there. Sure enough, a male and a female bluebird checked out the box and decided it was just right for them. Before long I had a pair of bluebirds coming and going, busy making the box their own.

I watched them closely. They were naturally wary of me, so I kept my distance. Over time, I would like to think, they grew to tolerate my being in the general vicinity. They were not, by any means, pleased to see me, but neither would they take flight the moment they saw me. We reached an understanding that I was there merely as a very interested observer, nothing more. The days wore on with our newfound arrangement, and I continued to check in on them many times throughout the day.

The male was a beautiful western bluebird. He looked in excellent condition, and he was clearly a very skilled hunter. He must have had all the right stuff, for his mate was also beautiful and matched his hunting skills. Together they made a fine couple.

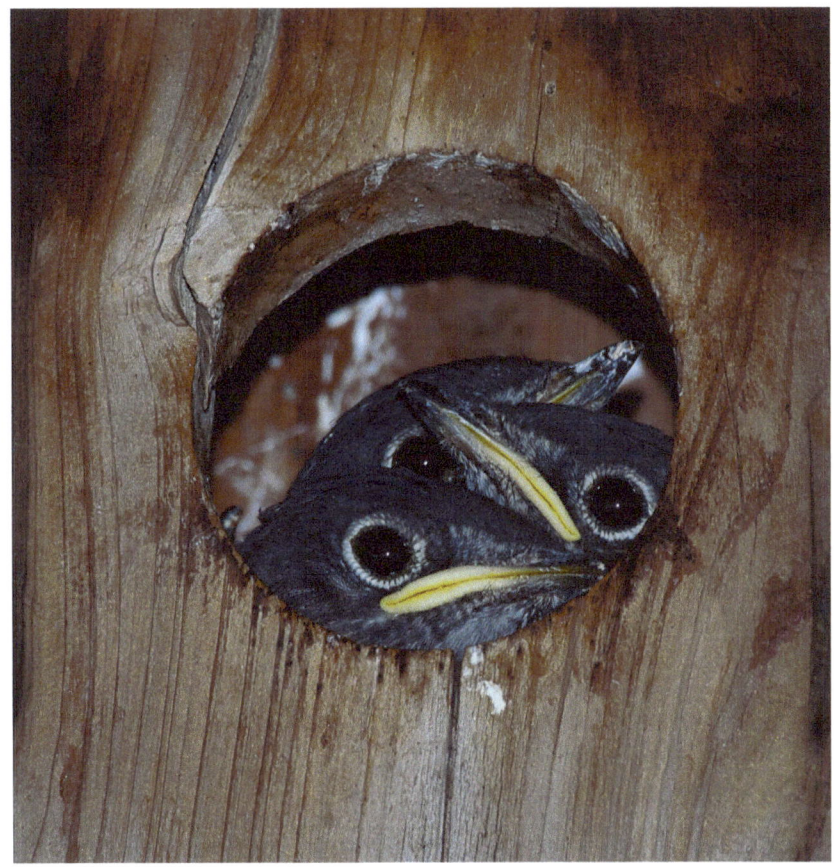

One day I heard the sound I had been hoping for the last few weeks, a small, ever-so-faint, barely audible "Cheep!" Success! When I walked into the house my grin wouldn't fit through the door, and Mary Beth didn't even have to ask why I was so happy.

From that point forward, you could find me sitting on the front porch watching my birds, for they had truly become my birds. My family. Over the next few weeks, I would learn an incredible amount about bluebirds.

The babies were growing. I couldn't see them yet, but I could sure hear them, and they were getting louder by the day. Mom and Dad would fly back and forth, hunting for small insects. They would perch on a branch looking out over the yard, and then in a quiet "swoosh," turn into a blue streak, snatching the bug from the ground, or as often as not, from midair. Back to the nest they would go, and carefully, gently, make sure a baby had its meal. The babies were quiet for a moment after each meal, but within a blink of an eye would start up their endless "Cheep! Cheep!" Day after day I watched this ritual. Flight after flight Mom and Dad would hunt for food for their babies.

Before long, although it felt like an eternity, I saw the first beak in the birdhouse. The babies were getting bigger! Once I saw the first beak, I saw it time and again, or more likely, I was seeing a different baby. I still didn't know how many were there, other than there had to be more than one. Eventually I saw the first eye looking at me. I can't imagine what the baby bird thought when it saw me, for it was cheeping as usual. As soon as it saw me, it went dead silent and slid away. Another eye looked at me, perhaps the same one, perhaps not, and was quiet. And then another, or the same. Who knew? It was impossible to say.

The days continued to slip by, and I continued to sit hour after hour in my usual spot. Mary Beth decided that my meals should be served there. At least I think she did. I had thoughts only for the baby birds. By this time, they too had come to tolerate me and would no longer stop cheeping when they saw me. They would, however, spend a very long time looking at me and I them, as we stared at each other across a few feet and a very broad evolutionary gap. I finally saw all three beaks at once, and I knew how big my family was.

Mom and Dad continued their hunting and feeding. Along the way I learned that a bluebird could hover, yes hover, in mid air for a moment before swooping in. I honestly had no idea they could do it, but they were masters at it. I also learned that Mom and Dad were getting very, very tired.

In the beginning, they appeared to find the perfect insect and make sure a baby had it. Later, however, they gathered up whatever bug they could find and almost threw it at the nest. When they went to hunt, they stopped on a branch, but gone were the earlier blue streaks. Now they rested, and for all intents and purposes, panted, before grudgingly taking off. Clearly, raising bird babies is a whole lot harder than I imagined. Still, the parents were troopers about it, day after day. By this time the babies and I were on very good terms. I never, ever went close to the nest, but we all spent a lot of time watching each other.

One morning I went out to take up my vigil, eager, as always, to see my babies. The moment the door opened again, Mary Beth instantly knew, for my face told the entire story. I'm not saying there wasn't a tear or two or more in my eye, but I'm not saying there was, either. I was despondent, yet elated, too, for my babies were out in the world, new birds on the wing, living their lives as they were meant to be. My sadness turned to joy, and I was able to walk out on the front porch and look to the sky, hoping to see three new blue streaks. Mom and Dad had left, too, headed off for a well-deserved rest, I suppose.

I don't know what it is about birds that fascinate me so much. Certainly moments like those reinforce my love of birds, and it is an incredible thing to be able to witness and experience nature at her finest.

Even to this day, every time I see a western bluebird, I wonder if it is one of mine. Sometimes they don't fly away as I walk by, and I know the answer.

Roadrunner Pause

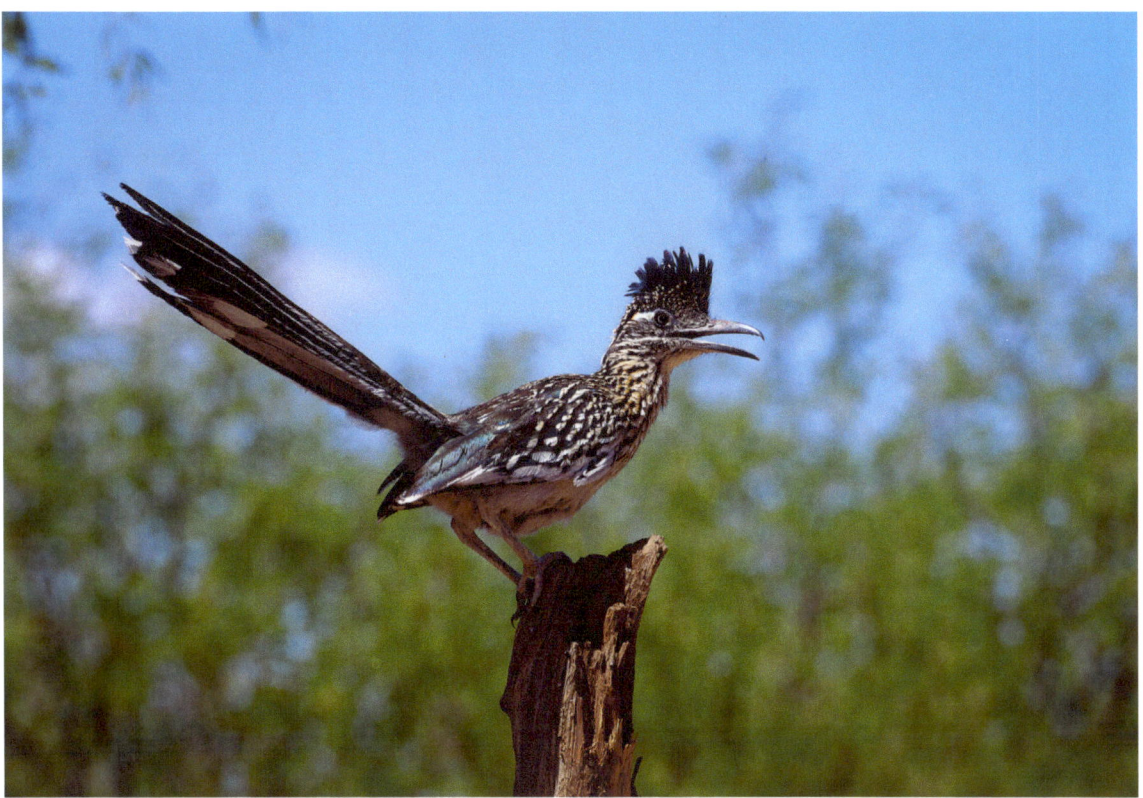

I didn't mind the waiting to make this photograph for it was a bright sunny day, and I was simply soaking the scenery all in. The day was warm, but not overly hot, so I was comfortable, although after a while, my mind and attention began to wander.

The next moment, and without me quite realizing it, a roadrunner materialized on a branch before me. One moment it was empty, and the next, not. That's the way of roadrunners, for they are as quick as their reputation makes them out to be. He paused, opened his beak to say something, and...

Just like that, was gone again. Not even a whisper of the wind marked his departure.

The roadrunner is a beautiful bird. Although it prefers to stay and run on the ground, it will walk or hop for short distances. It can fly perfectly fine; it simply would prefer to be on the ground. When they pause their tail will often pop up, giving that ever-so-classic roadrunner look. With the comb spread out it makes for a very interesting and photogenic bird.

Into Autumn

Autumn holds sway over almost everyone, for who among us can resist the allure of the golden leaves of the aspen tree, the flaming reds of the mighty oaks, and the myriad of fall colors? These stories explore the transition from summer to winter and the beauty that is revealed during fall.

Fall Bells

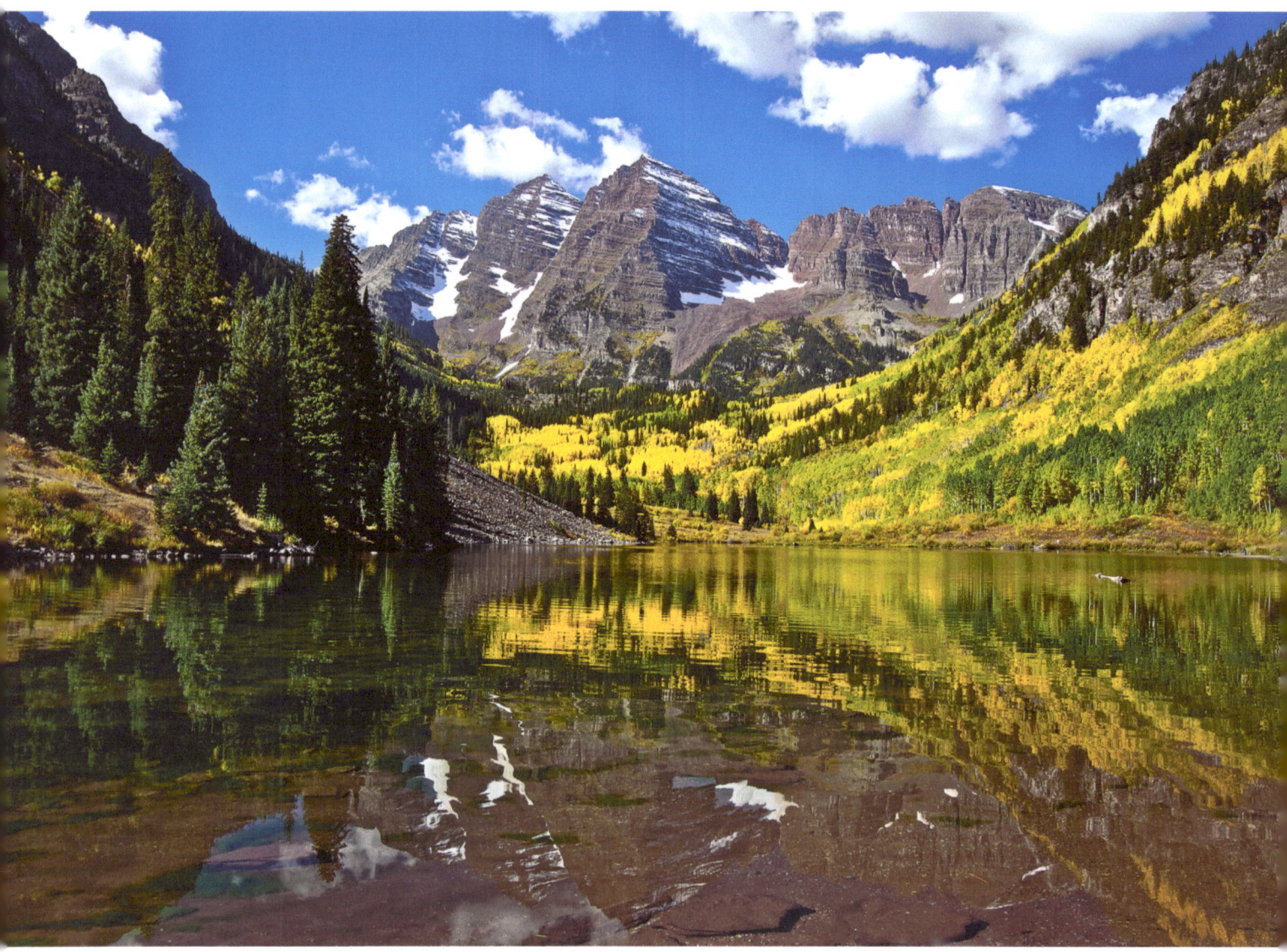

It is appropriate to fall into autumn with one of the most iconic autumn shots in the Southwest of all: Colorado's Maroon Bells in the Rocky Mountains.

It is in the fall, when the aspens are in their peak color, that the Maroon Bells really come into their own. These magnificent peaks, which are technically called "bells," tower over Maroon Lake, rising up out of the wilderness and into the sky itself. As the aspens turn into their fall colors, the sight intensifies until, right at their peak, the colors are almost indescribable. With aspens stretching down one side and evergreens the other, the contrast becomes picture perfect.

Maroon Bells is a well-known location for photographers and tourists alike. It has the reputation as best being photographed at dawn, just as the sun's rays break the horizon, causing the bells to glow a beautiful maroon color. Photographers line the edges of the small lake, so crowded that elbow room is hard to come by. Right on cue the maroon color creeps over the bells, fading quickly away right after sunrise. Just as quickly fading away are the photographers, believing that the show is over. They are on to the next location.

Later in the morning, however, when the sun is much higher in the sky, something else magical happens, although not nearly as many people are there to see it. The full colors of the hillsides come alive in the sun, lighting up in vivid golds, yellows, and greens of a glorious autumn day, bringing alive the majesty that is *Fall Bells*.

The Maroon Bells Wilderness has more beauty in it than just Maroon Lake and the bells themselves. Trails start out from the lake, going low and going high, allowing one to walk in the wilderness. Despite the crowds that come to see this panorama, the trails remain mostly uncrowded, providing solitude. For those who have the time to explore, the wilderness will reward you well; of course you're always in sight of the iconic mountains, which makes the trek all the more beautiful.

Mears' Embrace

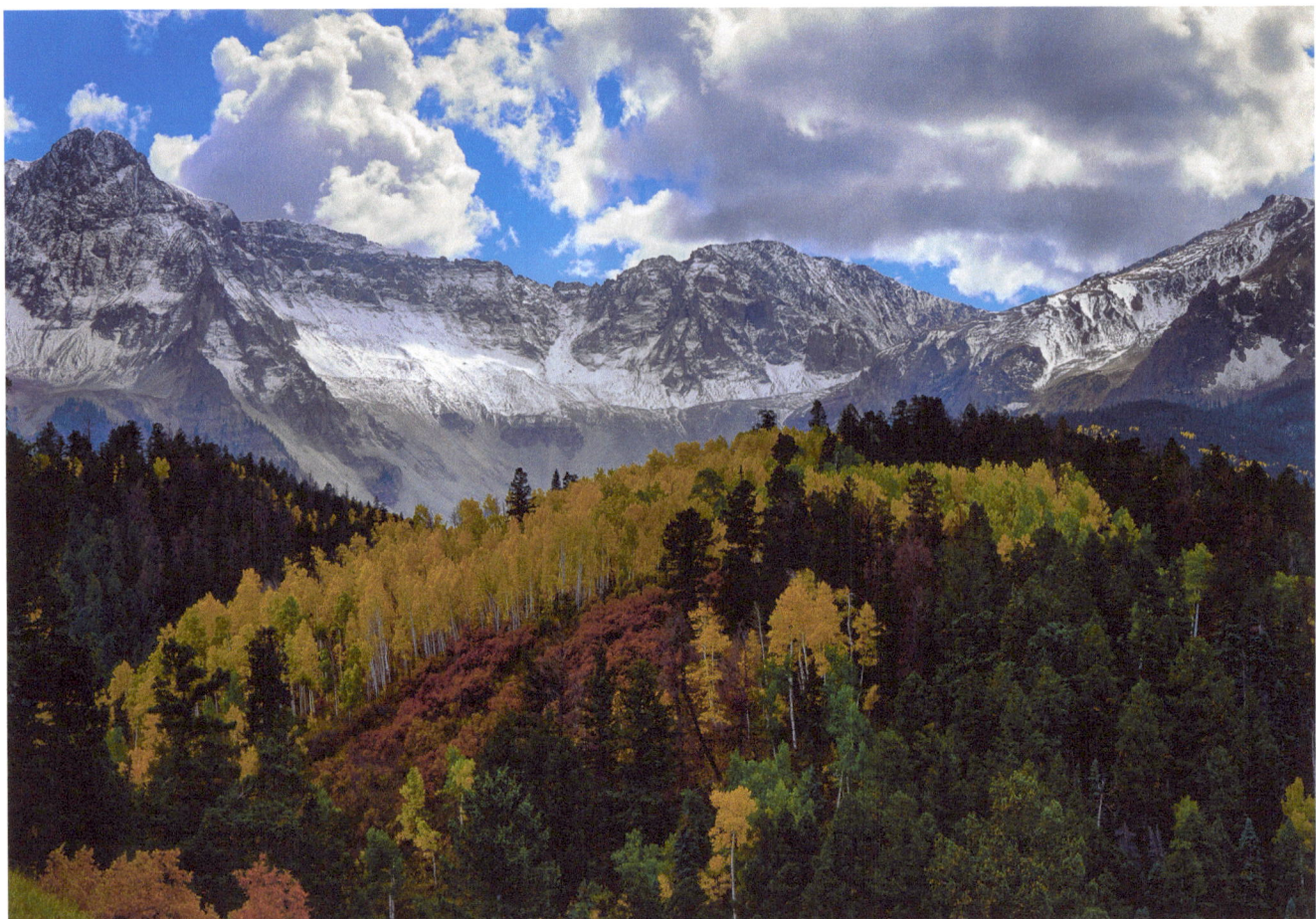

Heading southwest from Maroon Bells, we find another impressive range of the Rocky Mountains: the San Juan Mountains. This area has its fair share of fourteeners and more than its fair share of expansive vistas.

This particular scene showcases Mears Peak, although the peak itself is to the left in this photograph. I really liked how the peak and the mountains are embracing the small hill full of fall colors in every hue. The stand of aspens is the highlight, but the scrub oaks weigh in with their deep, rusty reds that add the perfect counterpoint to the aspen's gold. The evergreens have their say, too, making for a wide variety of colors on the hill. The storm clouds closing in above the mountains add a touch of drama to the scene, but the blue skies behind let us know that the storm isn't very serious this afternoon.

Soon enough the autumn leaves will fall as the breezes knock them off the trees, and soon enough the light snows on the mountains will turn to deep, heavy snows and the San Juans will feel the wrath of winter. Still, they are strong mountains and will weather it as they always do. The hill will return in its glory next spring. Until then, Mears keeps it safe.

The backstory behind this photograph is interesting as well. To be a photographer, you have to wear many different hats. You have to be in the right spot, meaning you have to be knowledgeable about the area you are working in. This knowledge is gained by research and time in the field scouting, which helps you find the perfect location, but location isn't all you need. In addition to the "where," you also need to understand the "when," which is equally as important. For *Mears' Embrace*, I knew the where well enough. I had known about this particular small hill for a long while and knew it would make a spectacular photograph, depending on the when. Having seen the hill in summer, I knew it would be best in the fall, but I also knew that the skies had to be right.

Another hat you have to wear is that of a weatherman, for weather makes or breaks a photograph. Sometimes you want blue skies and other times, you want anything but those blue skies. This photograph, I decided, would look far better in the latter category. I did my research. I looked for an upcoming day when the weather would be dynamic, and I decided that the day I made the photograph would be perfect. Luckily for me, Mary Beth accompanied me on this excursion.

We arrived at the location right on schedule. The hill looked exactly perfect, and I was excited. Unfortunately for me, the skies were clear and blue. Ugh! Everything else was spot on, but those skies would not do. We stood around for a bit, but really, there was nothing for it. I packed up my equipment, hung my head, and headed back down the dirt road to somewhere else. I made it about a mile down the road when Mary Beth caught me looking in the rearview mirror. I kept looking and looking. At the next opportunity, I turned around and headed back. Within the ten minutes we were gone, I decided the clouds would have come in and the photograph would be perfect. In Mary Beth's mind, she knew better.

We arrived back at my spot, and sure enough, the skies were still completely blue and cloudless. She waited in the vehicle, for she already knew what I would do next. Dejectedly, I got back in, and we again headed back off down the mountain road away from what I knew would be perfect, if only I had judged the weather better. She watched me look in the rearview mirror and probably hoped I was also, at some point, looking out the front as I drove away.

We were gone another ten minutes before I stopped again. She asked me patiently, calmly, if I was certain about the weather. I told her that yes, I was really quite certain, but I had been wrong. Gently she reminded me that perhaps I was not so wrong after all, if only we waited longer.

Encouraged, I turned around and headed back to my spot, for it was truly "my spot" by this time, and parked. The skies were clear blue and cloud free. I didn't get out of the vehicle. We sat patiently and let the hours go by. The first wisp of cloud came through after a bit, and I knew then it would all work out. A few hours later, *Mears' Embrace* was made, and I was reminded, again, of a recurring theme in my life. Patience pays off.

Divide's Autumn

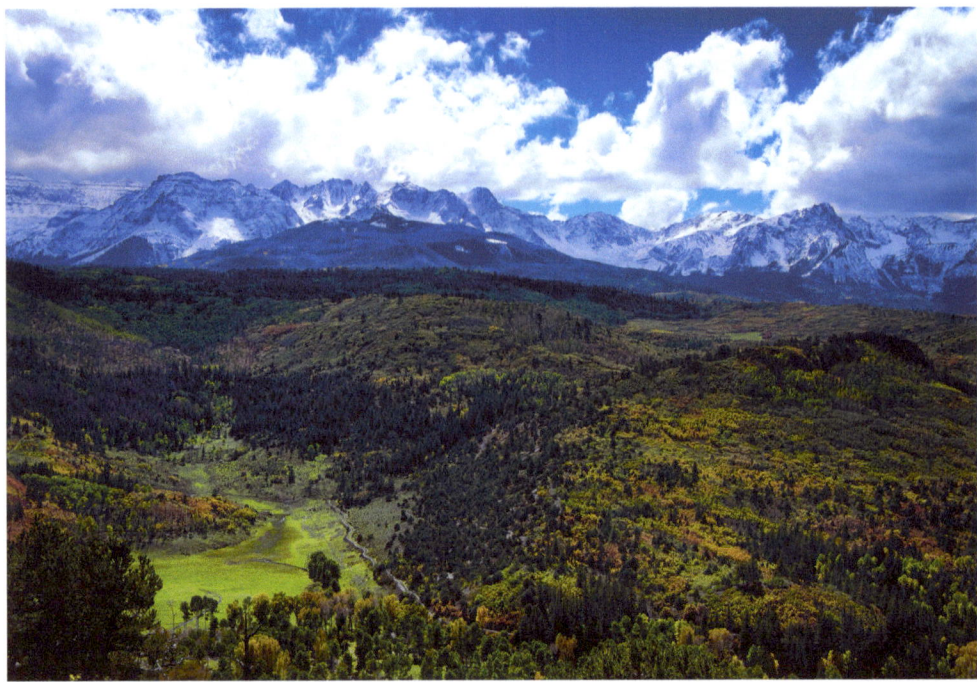

As fall creeps into the Rocky Mountains, the landscape and mountainsides change from their summer greenery to swaths of autumn gold. Swiftly, far more so than it might seem, the color change is complete, and once-green slopes have been completely replaced by fall's golden glow. As beautiful as this sight is, the in-between moment holds my fascination.

The Dallas Divide in the San Juan Range is one of my favorite places. I adore the high overlooks. There, sweeping panoramas culminate in soaring peaks, some of which are fourteeners. Before me small roads creep into the distance, surrounded by fields and forest. Those tiny byways beckon me onto them, calling me, and it was down one of these roads that *Mears' Embrace* was made.

And the trees! Caught here in their transition, every summer and fall hue is on display, adding a contrast and vibrancy to the landscape that one single color doesn't, be it green or gold. Some of the aspens have completed their change and are patiently waiting for winter's cold and ice, while others are still clinging to summer, hoping that by staying green they hold winter's edge at bay. Winter will eventually have its way, but in the meantime, we have magnificent sights such as *Divide's Autumn*.

As inspiring as broad panoramas are, however, autumn also has its more intimate side, as we shall see.

Ashcroft's Window

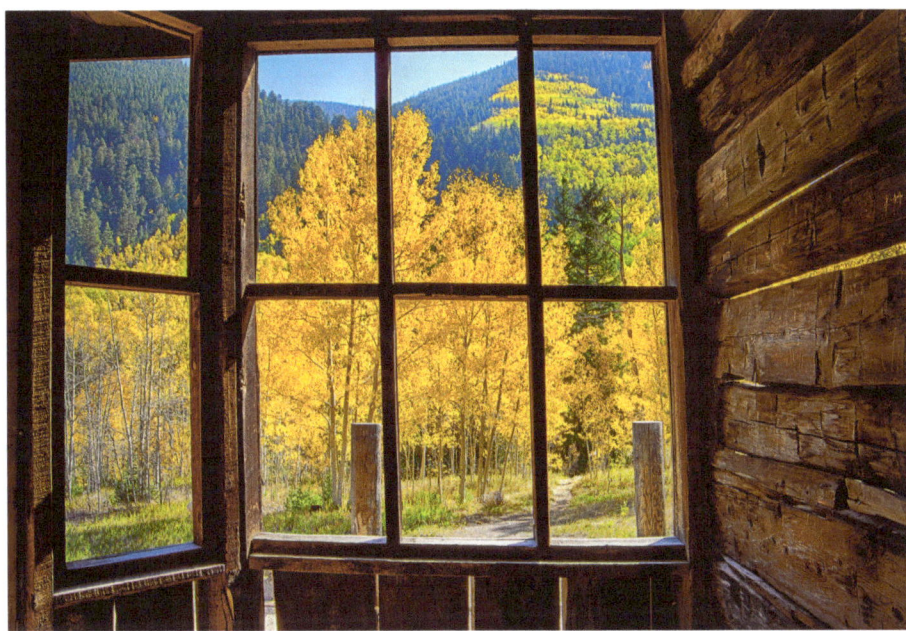

The eyes, it is said, are the window to your soul. Perhaps, then, this window in the ghost town of Ashcroft, Colorado, is the window to its soul as well.

The window in Ashcroft's long-abandoned hotel looks out over a beautiful, though young yet, aspen grove and the mountains beyond. The bay window must have been magnificent back in the day, and looking out of it, you can feel the folks from its past looking out with you. The view to the mountains would have not included the aspen grove immediately out it, as the aspens would come years later.

As I gaze through the window, I see not only today but yesterday, as well. I can easily imagine that I am staying at the hotel on a fall day; the air is getting decidedly crisper these days, and the nights are downright chilly. Outside, the street is busy, for the blue skies won't last much longer before giving way to winter's cold embrace, and the townsfolk are preparing for the heavy snows that are coming soon. People are tending to the last of the summer chores, and the miners are preparing to wrap up work until spring makes its appearance. Off in the distance, children are laughing and playing with the wild abandon that children are known for, for after all, tomorrow is not a concern for them. Footsteps echoing from years gone by are above my head as the guests long gone prepare for their day as well. The travelers spending just a short while in Ashcroft need to continue on their journey.

I stepped outside into the fall day to continue my own journey, the echoes of the past still ringing loudly in my ears and in my soul.

Gothic Fall

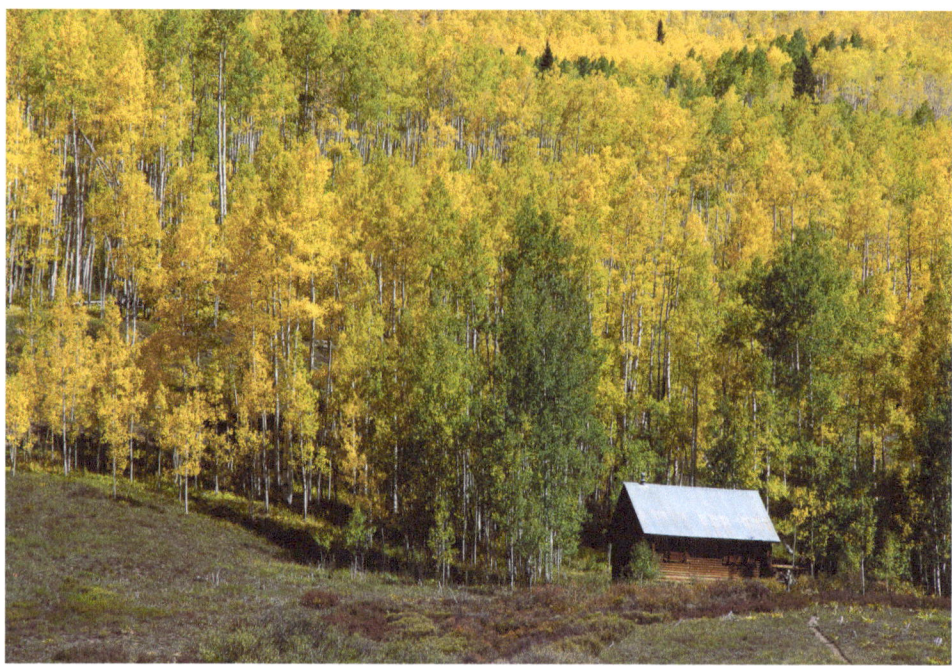

Ashcroft is not the only ghost town to lay claim to autumn, of course.

As summer wanes and begins to pass its torch to fall, the changing of the seasons is celebrated by nature with a display of color. Aspens lead the vanguard of this display. Where one aspen is wonderful to look at, a grove of aspens is breathtaking. Such is the case with this small cabin nestled in an aspen grove in Gothic, Colorado.

Gothic began as the usual mining town. Someone made claims of riches to be found, and the rush was on. The town quickly grew to one thousand residents with the wild abandon that many mining towns saw, and then like most gold rush-inspired towns, it declined just as quickly when the gold and silver played out. Unlike most such towns, however, Gothic was acquired by the nonprofit organization Rocky Mountain Biological Laboratory. The RMBL is dedicated to research and education in the biological sciences, meaning that Gothic is an unusual mixture of a ghost town featuring cutting-edge science. This cabin is not quite as abandoned as it might appear, but in any event makes an incredible scene nestled in the trees.

The aspens, however, are unaware of the history or current status of the town. They simply grow, without any interference or direction by man. They respond to the changing of the seasons and, when fall comes, display their blazing autumn colors for all to see and be awed by.

Oak Variation

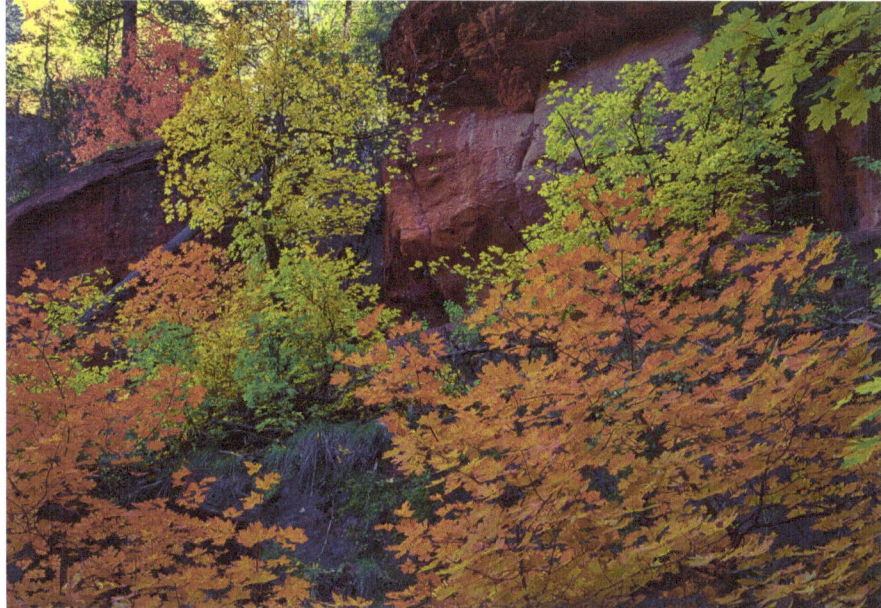

Probably, because of the plethora of photographs I make in Colorado, people tend to think I live there. I don't, but during the fall season, I most likely will be found somewhere in the Rocky Mountains. I adore the aspens that are found there, but they are not the only trees that appeal to me. Another colorful autumn tree is the venerable oak tree, and for those, we leave the state of Colorado.

The oak tree is an amazing tree, when it comes down to it. Easily overlooked in the forest during summer, because, after all, it is "just another tree," come fall it absolutely shouts "Look at me!"

Oaks turn a variety of colors in autumn and provide much of the classic fall color. This scene from the West Fork of Oak Creek Canyon, Arizona, is one of my favorites for the wide variation in color. I was hiking through the canyon on a beautiful fall day, enjoying myself immensely. The day had started out a little crisp and cool, but as the morning progressed, it warmed up nicely. By the time I made this photograph, everything about the day was perfect, including the scenery.

The day was so pleasant that I was becoming inured to the sights around me, and then I looked up. Just when I thought I had seen it all, there was this scene. I was awestruck by the variations in color, all right before me, everything from red rocks to yellow leaves to leaves not yet turned to the classic deep reds, all clumped together. The scene called to me, and *Oak Variation* was made. I think it shows off the progression of fall beautifully, although it is not the only stunning photograph from here.

Contemplative Reflection

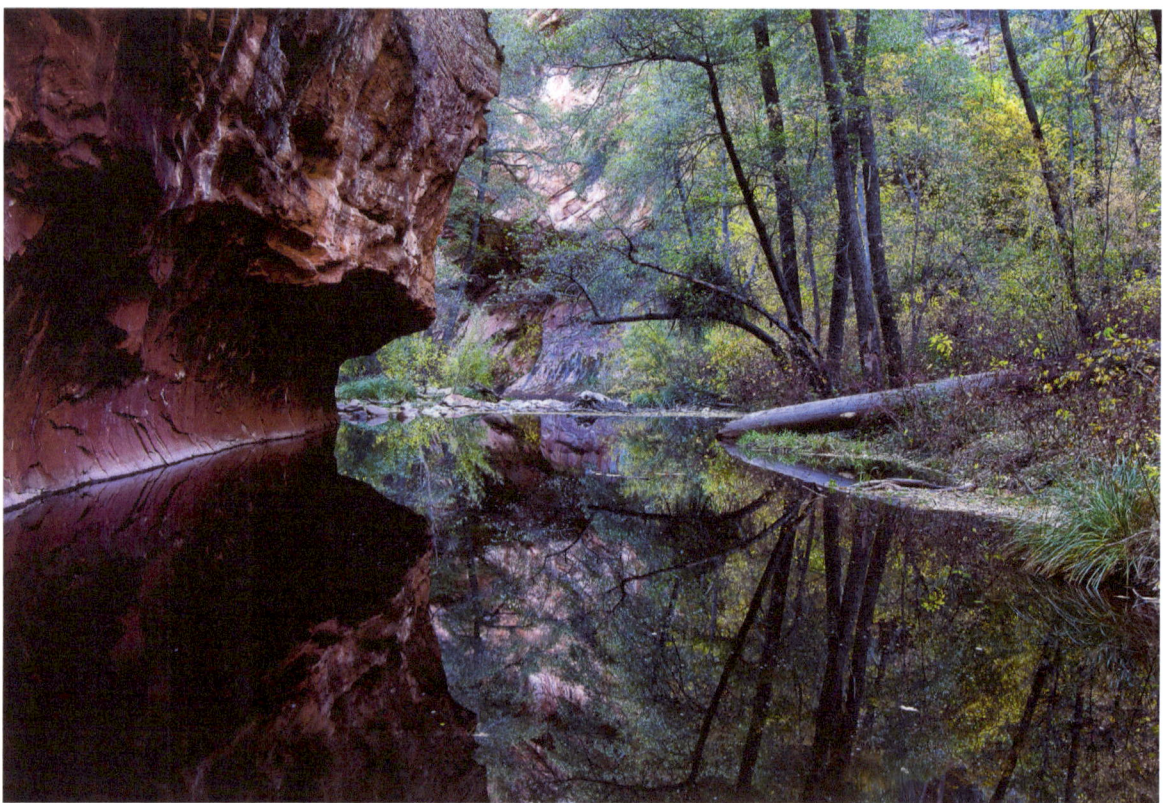

Oak Creek Canyon is a top hiking trail in America, and it is not hard to see why. As the small trail wends it way through the canyon, it crisscrosses the creek, following along it, and never wanders too far from it. The oak trees that line the bottom of the canyon make a perfect counterpoint with the tall red rock walls, and the overall effect is simply stunning. The entire length of the trail is gorgeous, and it is hard to pick a favorite spot along its three-mile length.

In fall this effect becomes even more pronounced, taking one's breath away more often than not. The range of color is extreme, from the still-vibrant greens of summer foliage to the oranges and golds of autumn, with a few trees showing bright red for an extra counterpoint.

Contemplative Reflection was made at one of my favorite locations on Oak Creek, one I visit frequently. This photograph was made late in the afternoon on a stellar autumn day, with the long rays of the sun adding their golden hues to an already golden scene.

Aspens, then, are not the only tree that can lay claim to providing the colors of autumn.

Bosque Afternoon

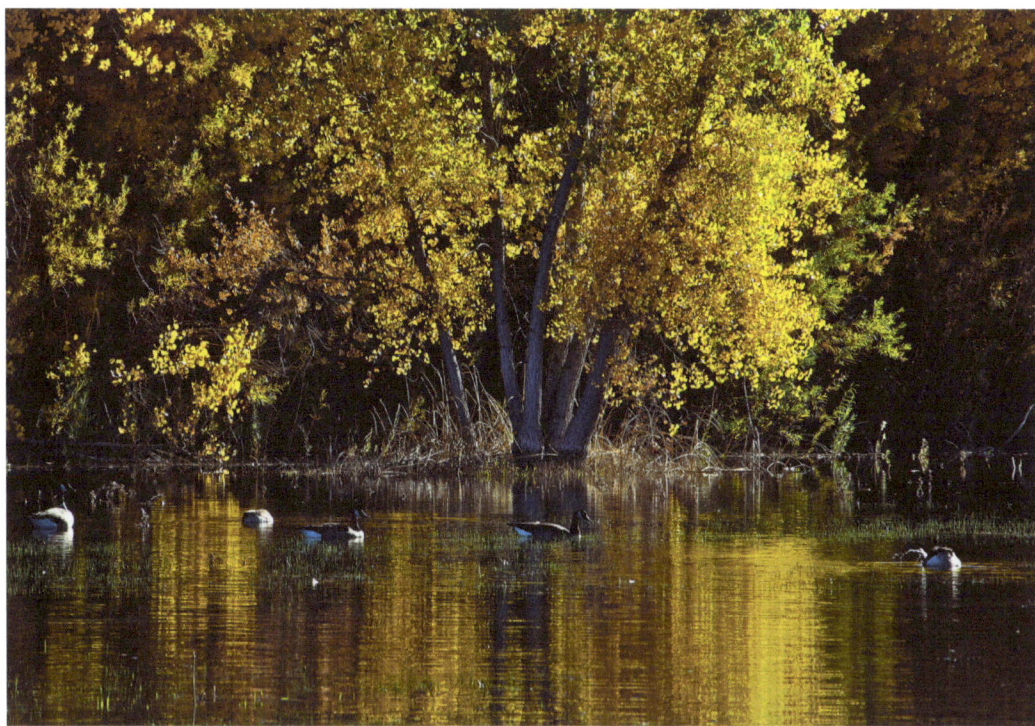

We've seen aspen and oak trees decked out in their fall colors. Let's take a look at the cottonwood tree in New Mexico, which also puts on quite a show. In the late afternoon sun, they glow with an intensity all their own.

It is hard to describe, exactly, how this scene affected me as I made this photograph. I was in the Bosque del Apache National Wildlife Refuge, one of my favorite places to photograph. I find the entire refuge to have a large and diverse range of wildlife in it, and you never know quite what you will see.

This day, however, the refuge was fairly quiet. The inhabitants preferred to stay hidden, and the entire refuge seemed deserted. It was early fall, too early yet for the majority of migratory birds to arrive, so seeing any bird this day was something of a rarity. Still, there was plenty to see, and I enjoyed myself thoroughly.

My trip that day was done, and I decided to sit by the shore of a pond and enjoy the last of the day, for it would be dusk soon. As I sat, I simply relaxed, enjoying the sun, enjoying the day, and mostly, enjoying the few Canada geese at the far side of pond. It was a time of peace, solitude, and reflection. When I look at this photograph I am reminded of that perfect afternoon in the bosque. I hope that you feel much the same, and may the peace of the bosque in fall be with you.

Aspen Road

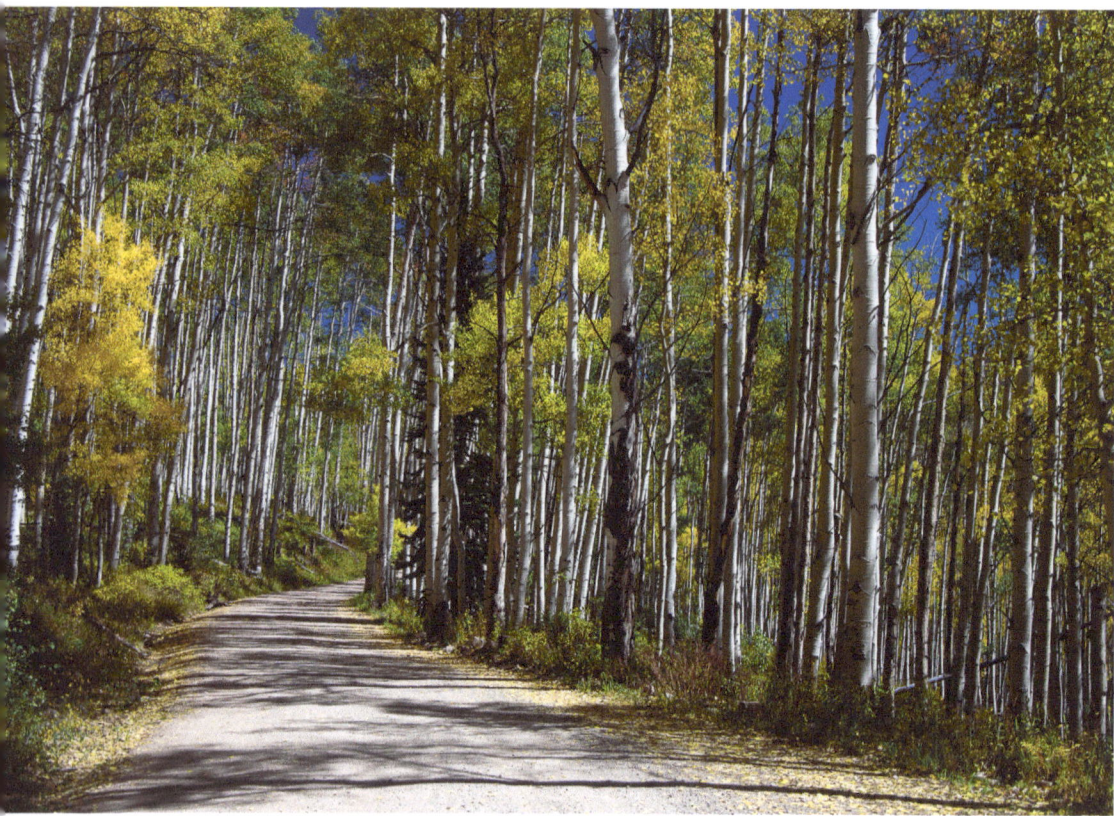

For the rest of this chapter let's head back up to Colorado. Since I live there, or at least people think I do, it seems a fitting way to wind up this section.

The mighty aspen tree holds a special place in our collective hearts. When we think of them, we often think of large stands, grouped together in a forest setting, leaves quaking in the gentlest of all breezes, white trunks holding up the sky, and leaves changing to heavenly golds to mark the passage of summer. We also think of them as peaceful and serene, and just being in the midst of a grove marks a special occasion.

I have spent a fair number of days in aspen groves, looking for the exact moment in the exact location to make the perfect photograph. I've seen them in all shapes and sizes, some small, some monumental, with everything in between. Often I hike through the forest looking all around me. Now and then, though, I am fortunate enough to encounter a road that leads me where I wish to go.

This particular road, deep in the heart of the Gunnison National Forest outside of Crested Butte, was one such road. As I drove slowly along, I was struck by how serene it was to be gliding through the middle of one of the largest aspen stands in North America. The trees surrounded and engulfed me, adding a deep sense of profoundness to my journey and reminding me that time and patience pay off handsomely. The aspen road continued deeper into the forest, drawing me farther in with it. I drove on and couldn't have been happier to drive on into fall.

Snowkissed Aspens

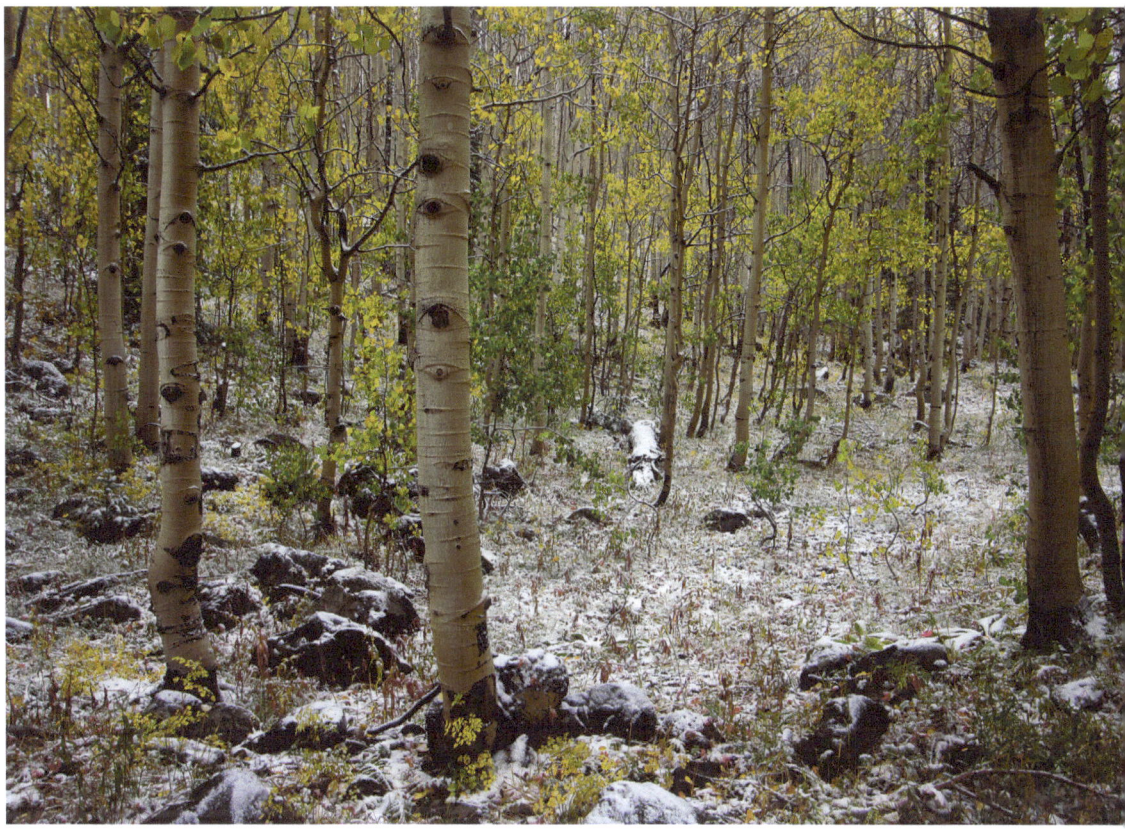

Alas, autumn does not last year round, and the trees change into the fall colors with the pact and promise that winter is not far behind. That bargain always must be fulfilled and fall must step aside. As winter begins to creep in, the changing of the seasons is a time of wonder and magical moments.

The day started out with the threat of snow, and the morning was cold, the kind of cold that seeps right into your bones, further bolstering the snowy possibility. The clouds were low, heavy, and gray, a drab counterpoint to the morning's cold.

Undeterred, I headed up to Colorado's Grand Mesa, a beautiful location on bright and sunny days. Still, I had a feeling about this morning. Even as I went up the mesa and merged into the clouds, I was still optimistic. I soon left the safety of the pavement and headed deep into the forest and up onto the mesa.

The cold and clouds up on top of the mesa hadn't been idle, for they combined for the season's first snow; not a heavy one, but a light and gentle one. I couldn't be happier with the results, and my hunch was confirmed. The snow caressed and kissed the aspens, leaving the lightest of all traces, and it barely covered the ground, a perfect first snow, although later snows would be substantially heavier and much more robust.

I really enjoy the feel of this photograph and the transition it represents. The first snow of the season is a powerful moment, and sometimes, like here, catches fall completely off guard. Being a light snow, it added its touches to the scene, rather than completely burying everything. The snow-kissed aspens didn't seem to mind.

Season's End

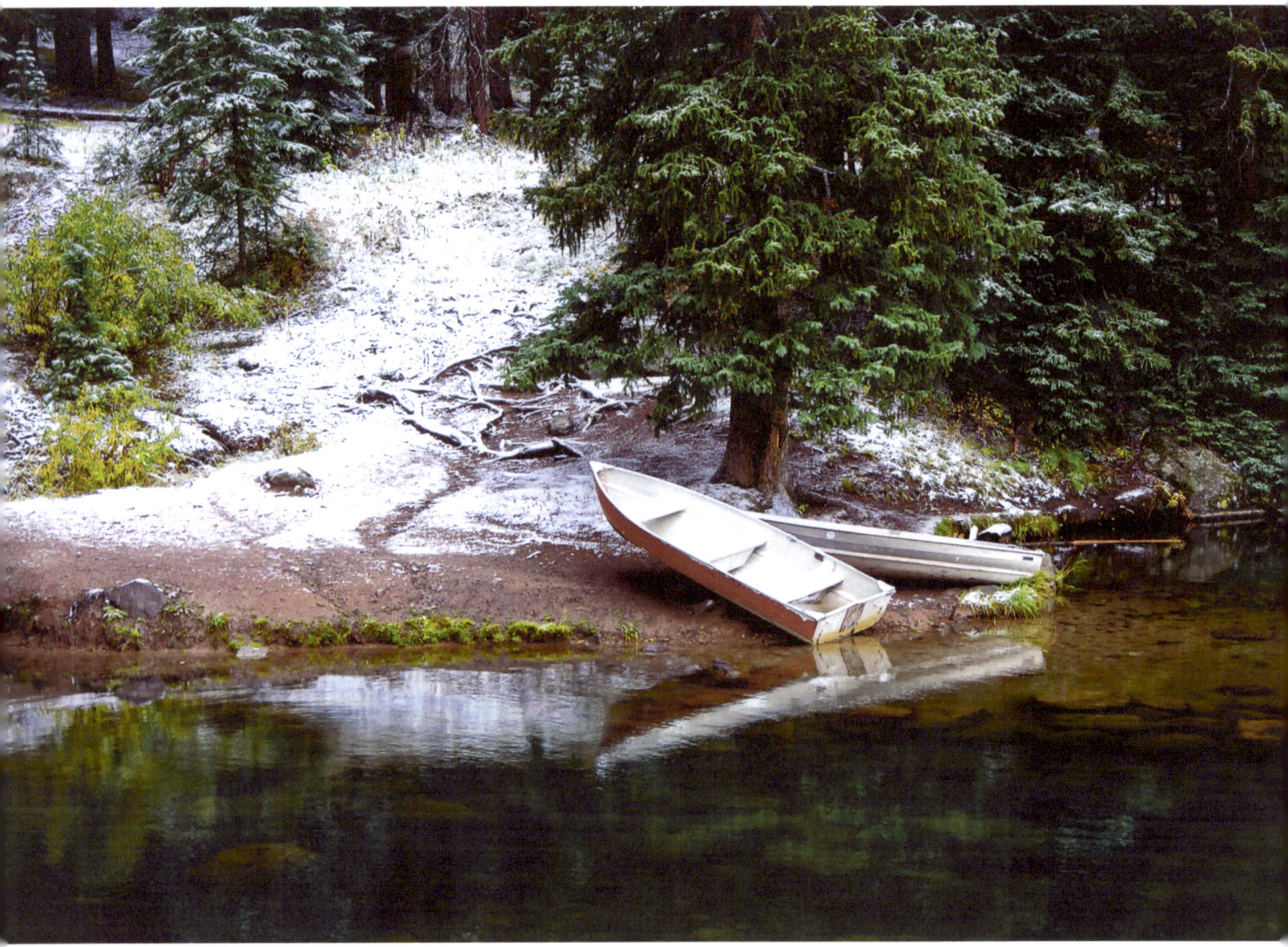

We'll stay in Grand Mesa to usher out autumn and this chapter. This small vignette is one of my all-time favorite photographs, and the moment I saw the scene I saw the finished photograph and knew the story behind it. Here, then, is the tale of *Season's End*.

It had been a good year on the lake; that's for sure. The languid summer days had been idyllic, halcyon even, and the time had simply flown by. The boats stopped to remember the first day they had been out on the water, and it seemed like it was just this morning that they slipped into the clear, crystal waters of early spring. They recalled the lazy summer days drifting, and occasionally being rowed, across the lake; perhaps the fishing was better on the far side, perhaps not, but in any event, it never hurt to find out. They recalled the days when the water had a slight chop, adding a fleeting thrill, and they recalled the days when the mirror surface was broken only by the occasional jumping fish. They remembered each day and shared again the delight of the open water.

At last, however, they finally acquiesced to the season's end, made the final journey to the far shore, and were pulled up on the bank. Their owners trudged up the hill, abandoning the boats to winter. Their hearts were heavy at the moment, but they knew that spring would be back soon enough, and once again they would experience the joy of being out on the water. In the meantime, I simply watched them rest on the shore of a lake, patiently enduring the season's end.

Yesterday's Rails

The railroad was a fundamental turning point in our westward expansion across this great land. I, like many, have a love of the rails, all things connected to trains, and especially steam engines. These stories explore living history on the rails.

Winter's Cut

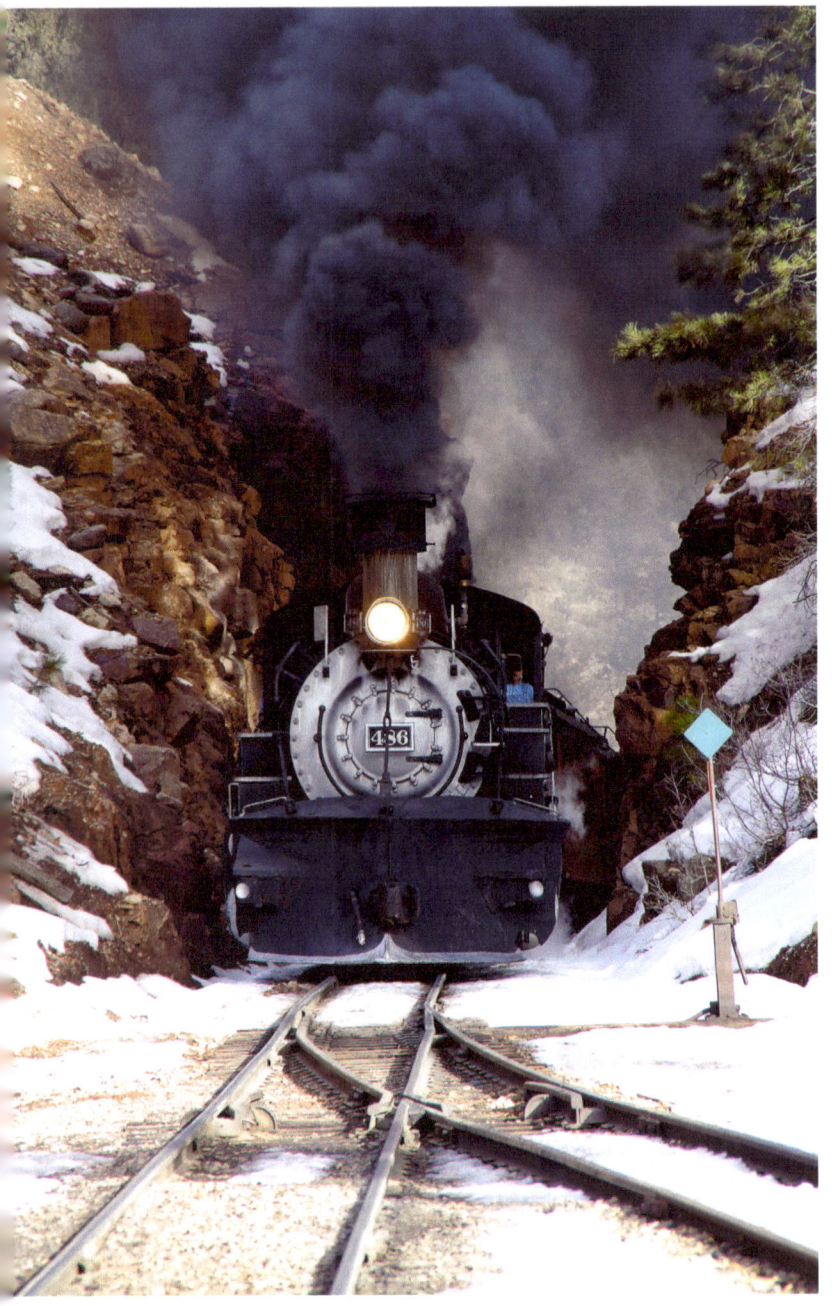

Since we've made the transition into winter, we'll stay there for a few stories. Let's ride the rails of yesteryear and take a trip back in time with the steam engine.

The sound was low, distant, and just on the threshold of hearing. The faint "chug-chug" seemed to be growing louder, but sounds echo in funny ways in the canyons of Colorado's San Juan Mountains, making it impossible to be certain. The cold, biting wind of the winter's day stole everyone's breath, making it all that much harder to concentrate.

After a moment, though, the distinctive whistle of the steam locomotive dispelled all doubt. The low sound was indeed a train, and it was heading this way.

Just like that, Engine #486 came barreling out of The Cut, the name given to this narrow passage through the rock, thick black smoke steaming out behind it as it labored up the hill. The whistle sounded again, startlingly loud this time, and there is nothing in the world quite like staring down an oncoming train. It could have easily been the late 1800s all over again, as timeless as the sight was.

The Durango & Silverton Narrow Gauge Railroad still plies this line, running much as it has for more than one hundred years. It provides an extraordinary opportunity to step back in time and experience the thrill of the mighty steam engines. When the engine roars through The Cut, you relive the power of the locomotive all over again.

Wintery Tefft

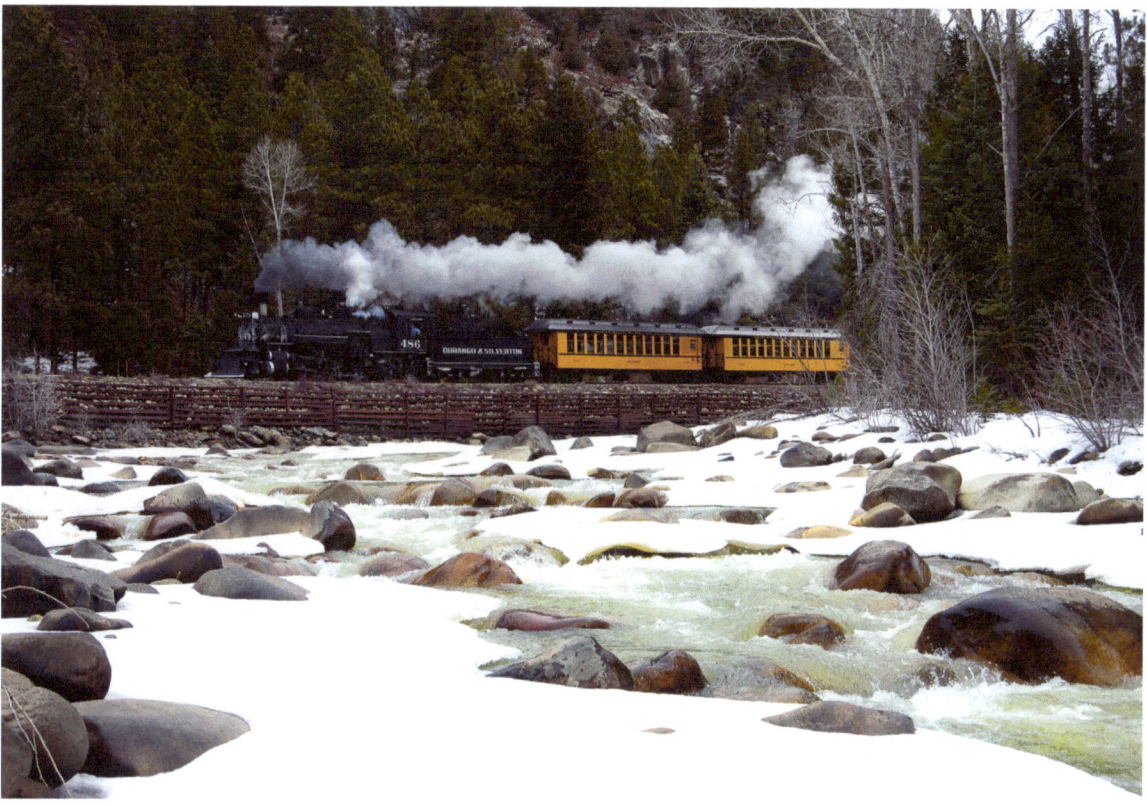

It was early afternoon in Tefft, Colorado, and the train was due in soon. Those who could scurried outside to get ready for it; the rest, the young, sprinted up ahead hopeful they could race and perhaps beat the train as it pulled in. The sharp whistle from the steam engine broke what silence remained, right on time, but when was the railroad not punctual?

As the steam engine crossed the Animas Rover and pulled into the tiny depot nestled high in the San Juan Mountains, a flurry of activity happened all at once. Passengers got off while others hustled to get on. The conductor did a quick inspection of the train while cargo was exchanged from train to depot and depot to train. Before long, the whistle sounded two long blasts and the train was under way, headed back down the mountain to the mining town of Durango.

Although this scene happened in the late 1800s, today the township of Tefft has been forgotten by all but the railroad. As the silver and precious minerals played out, the hardy mountain souls drifted away to the next boom. All that remains of Tefft today is the name and the Durango & Silverton Narrow Gauge Railroad, which still stops there. The railroad is, as always, punctual.

C&TS #484

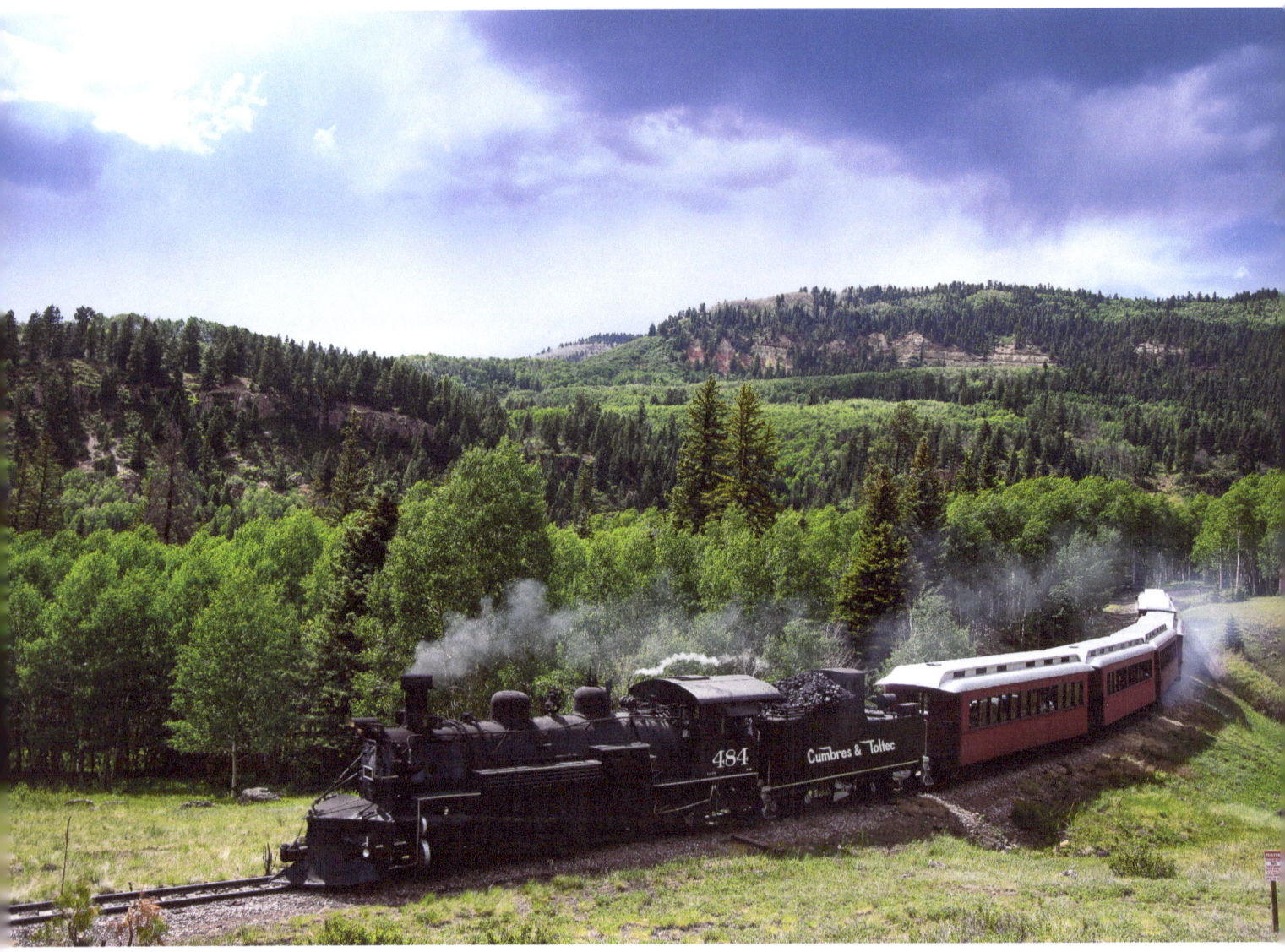

Back in the mining days, there was no more effective way to get your ore from your mine to a processing plant than the railroad. Realistically, you had only two choices: mule and wagon or the railroad. For some mines, the mules to town were the only option, but for many others, the railroad was by far the better choice.

The railroads faced significant engineering challenges in the Rocky Mountains. Out east, with its wide, flat expanses, the railroad could go where it needed, and the labor of hard-working men was enough to build it. In the Rockies, however, almost no amount of manpower was enough to overcome the steep grades, exceptionally tight turns, and engineering challenges. Not to be deterred, the railroad owners tackled these problems with Narrow Gauge Railroads, which are exactly as the name describes: narrower tracks and corresponding smaller engines and train cars. Narrow gauge is smaller than the regular track, but make no mistake about it: these trains are still quite large and are still very powerful. They needed all the power they could muster to tackle the steep mountain grades.

At one time, the narrow gauge system spanned the Rockies, running as the Denver and Rio Grande Western Railroad, enabling the miners, or at least most of them, to get their ore from their mines. As the mines played out, the need for the railroad dissipated in much of the Rockies, and many rail lines were eventually abandoned and removed. One by one the lines disappeared, and sometimes entire towns disappeared along with them.

This history lesson brings us to the Durango & Silverton and Cumbres & Toltec Railroads. These lines used to be part of the larger system. Travel between the cities was as easy as regular service. As the years rolled by, these lines became physically isolated from each other and became islands onto themselves. The individual railroads stayed alive, now running as the Durango and Silverton Narrow Gauge Railroad and the Cumbres and Toltec Scenic Railroad. Today you can ride the rails of both these railroads and ride back into time.

The mighty Cumbres & Toltec Scenic Railroad engine #484 has been a workhorse for almost a century. First built in 1925, this coal-fired, steam-operated locomotive has seen its share of changes during its tenure. First a locomotive for the Denver & Rio Grande Western Railroad hauling freight across northern New Mexico and southern Colorado and later for Cumbres & Toltec carrying passengers between Chama, New Mexico, and Antonio, Colorado, this engine just keeps on going.

The 480 K-36 class Mikados series of locomotives is the last of the narrow-gauge engines constructed in the United States, making #484 a rolling part of history, literally! Manufactured by Baldwin Locomotive Works in Philadelphia, Pennsylvania, the ten 480 series engines were purpose-built for the terrain they ran in. They long-hauled ore, freight, pipe, and natural gas, at least until they were no longer needed. Luckily, however, nine out of the ten engines found new life in both the Cumbres & Toltec and Durango & Silverton scenic railroads. The tenth engine, #485, met its end in 1955 when it fell into a turntable pit near Salida, Colorado.

Today the mighty #484 provides the chance for young and old to experience the incomparable steam engine, a chance not to be missed.

S Curve

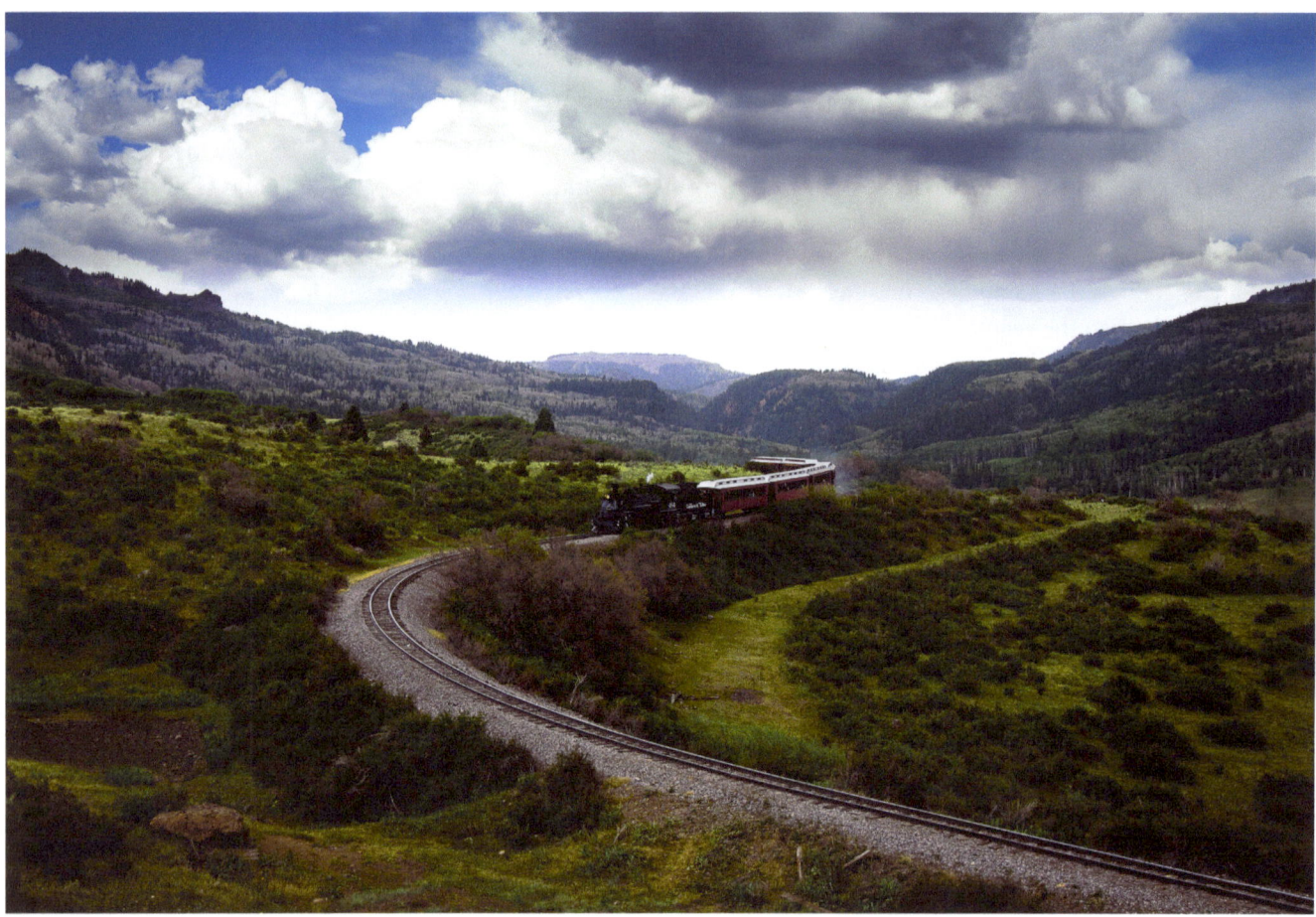

The sight is not often seen anymore, yet if you know where to look, history comes alive. I photographed #484 again as it descended from Cumbres pass on its way into Chama, New Mexico. I am particularly fond of this photograph because I like the power of the engine steaming toward me across the sweeping S curve. It is easy for me to imagine that it was eighty years ago, and instead of passenger cars behind it, perhaps it pulled cars loaded with ore from up north, making its way back into New Mexico. Without the extensive network of narrow-gauge railroads, taming the West would have been a lot more of a struggle.

As it is, though, the power, majesty, and awe-inspiring beauty of the steam engines remain as they still run the rails and keep history in the here and now.

Crossing Chama

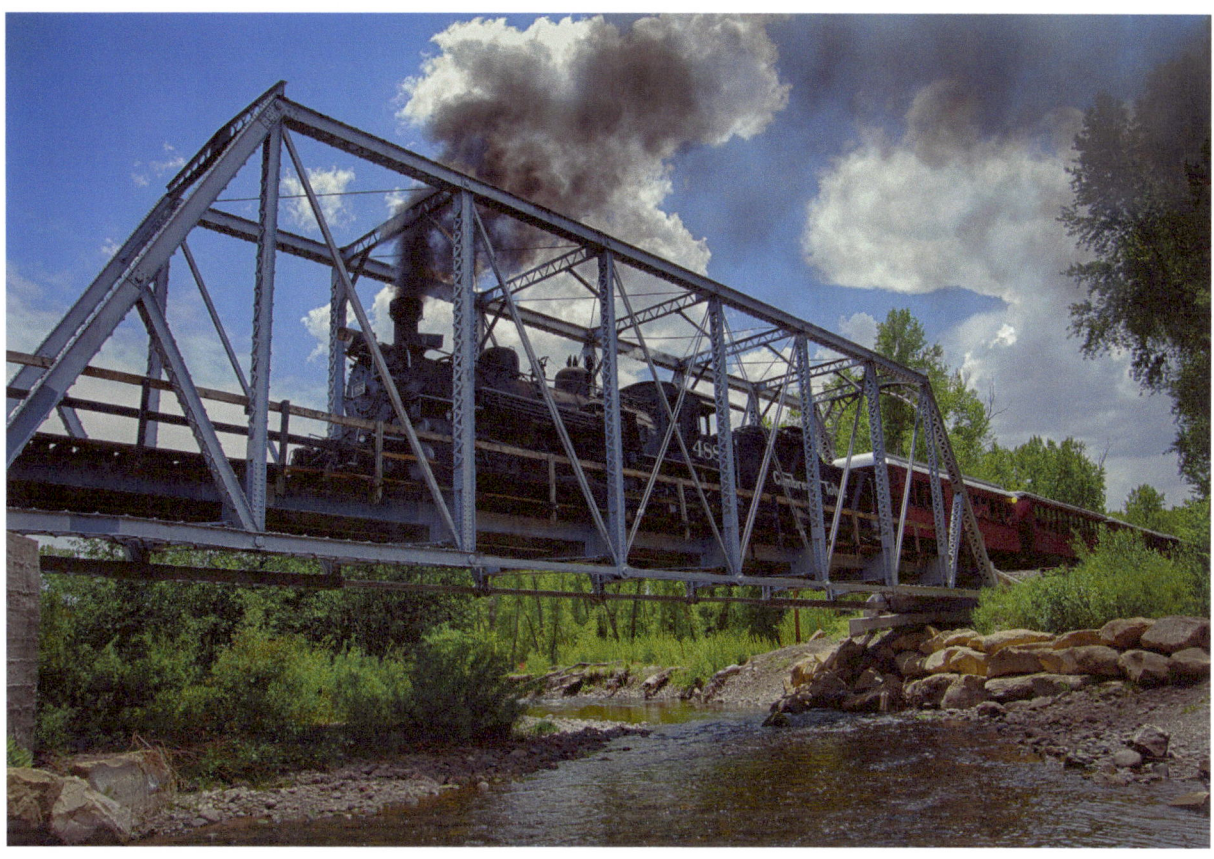

The Cumbres & Toltec train, pulled by the mighty engine #488, pulled out of the station right on time. A late arrival was not acceptable, and the conductor and crew made sure it wouldn't happen. #488 was running well, despite its age, and it easily moved the train down the rails.

It chugged through the outskirts of the small town of Chama, ever so slowly picking up steam. Thick, black smoke belched from the smokestack and then trailed off behind the train.

Down by the Chama River, the day was peaceful and quiet, but of course it was about to change. Long before you could hear or see the train, you could feel it, its power evident as felt by your feet. It wasn't so much as a vibration, but rather just a deep knowing. Suddenly the train was visible as it rounded the bend and steamed over the Chama River Trestle. With a "Toot! Toot!" it was gone as quickly as it appeared, off on its run to Colorado, keeping the pageantry of the line alive.

Free Spirits

The wild horse is a symbol of the Wild West. Even though the "wild" days are behind us, they remain for the horse. These stories celebrate the spirit and freedom of the wild horse; through them, the Wild West lives on.

Stallion's Desert

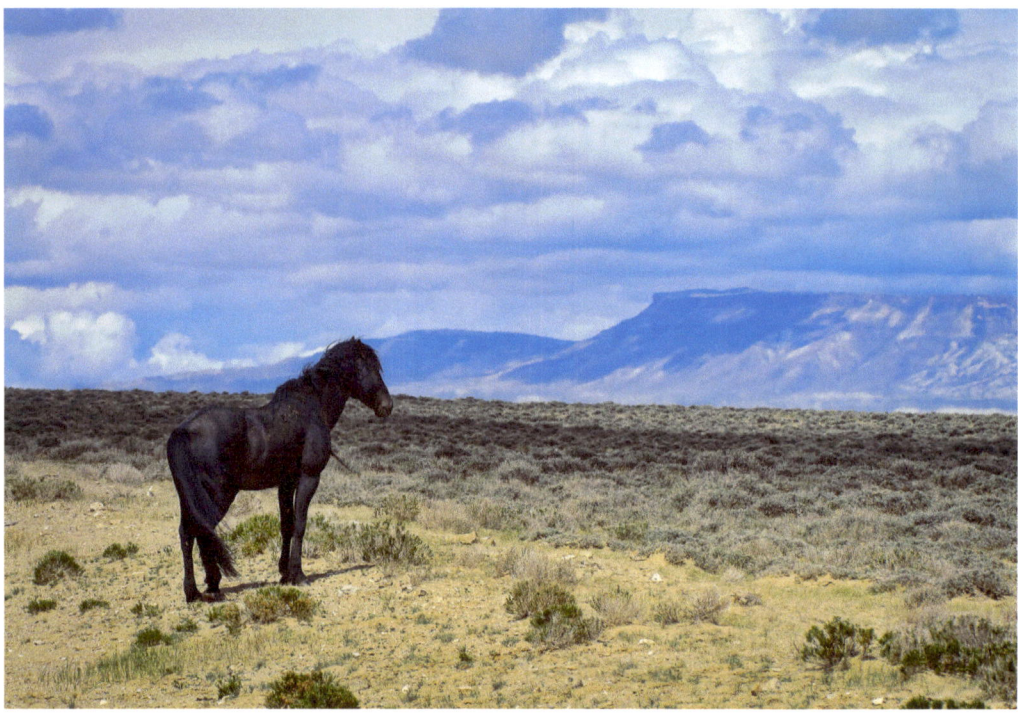

He stood patiently, ever so patiently, surveying the desert before him, perhaps contemplating where to move his band next, and in any event certainly keeping a watchful eye out for anything untoward on the distant horizon. He was in no hurry to move and simply stood, still as a statue, turning his gaze now and then to whatever distant object caught his eye. It is wise to pay rapt attention and be careful out here in the lonely desert.

This proud stallion is in Wyoming's Red Desert, located in the southwest portion of the state, the last high desert ecosystem left in North America. For countless years wild horses have been running free and unfettered in this land, calling it their own, yet living in harmony with it so as to pass it on to their future generations. Small bands of horses roam throughout the desert, living wild, and managing not only to survive, but also to thrive in this environment, which is no easy task. It is a land without fences, but it is not a land wholly without people, and ranchers as well as oil and gas companies make use of this land.

It is important that we recognize the competing interests of people and wild horses, and it is critical that we continue to be excellent stewards of the land. In many cases we need to do what is right for the desert and its inhabitants, rather than seek monetary gain from taking it away from the horses or destroying the land. After all, the wild horses have shown us that all can live in concordance with the land.

Stallion Squabble

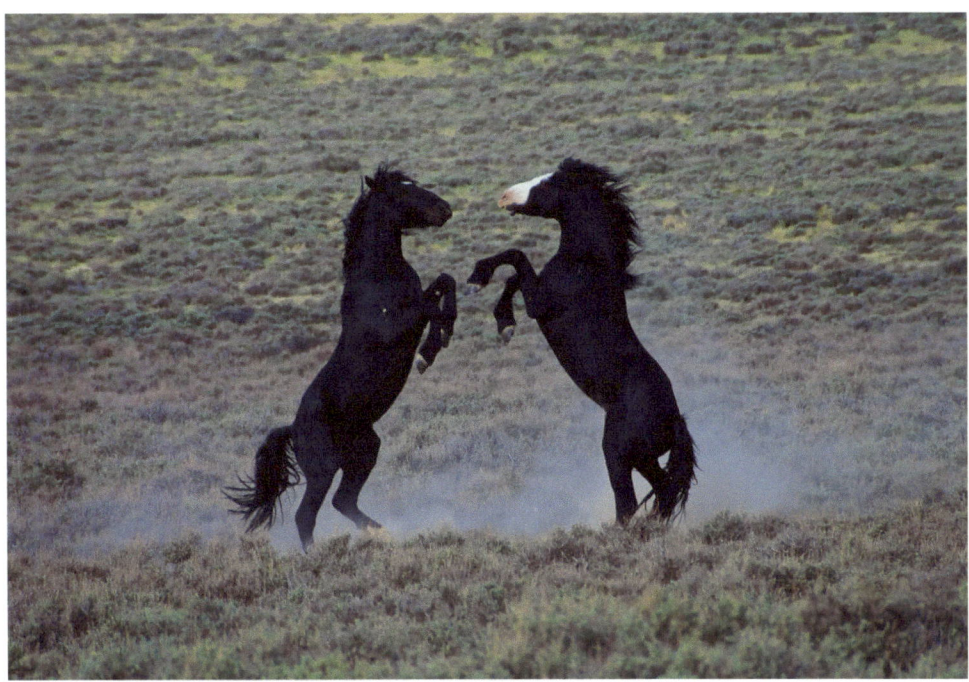

Wild horses have neither the ability or the desire to sit down and talk through their differences. They deal with problems the best way they know how: face to face, with biting, kicking, and pushing each other around. By and large, it works out really well.

These two stallions in the Red Desert illustrate the example perfectly. They are in the same band and are likely father and son. Still, they do not see eye to eye all the time, and when Junior started feeling his oats, Dad took the time to show Junior who was in charge.

Around and around they went in the heat of the afternoon; clouds of dust flew everywhere. They would rear up and slash at each other. I had the impression they weren't out to hurt so much as to make a point. Down they would come, and they would then dance around each other, looking for an opening. Up and down and all around it went. After a lot of pushing, just like that, the squabble was over.

Dad stared at Junior as he pawed the ground over and over. Junior didn't dare move a muscle while this was going on. At the end, they walked away from each other, the horse lessons learned. There was grazing to get back to, and the afternoon wore on.

I feel privileged to have watched this exchange, as well as the next one, which was a far more serious affair.

Stallion Battle

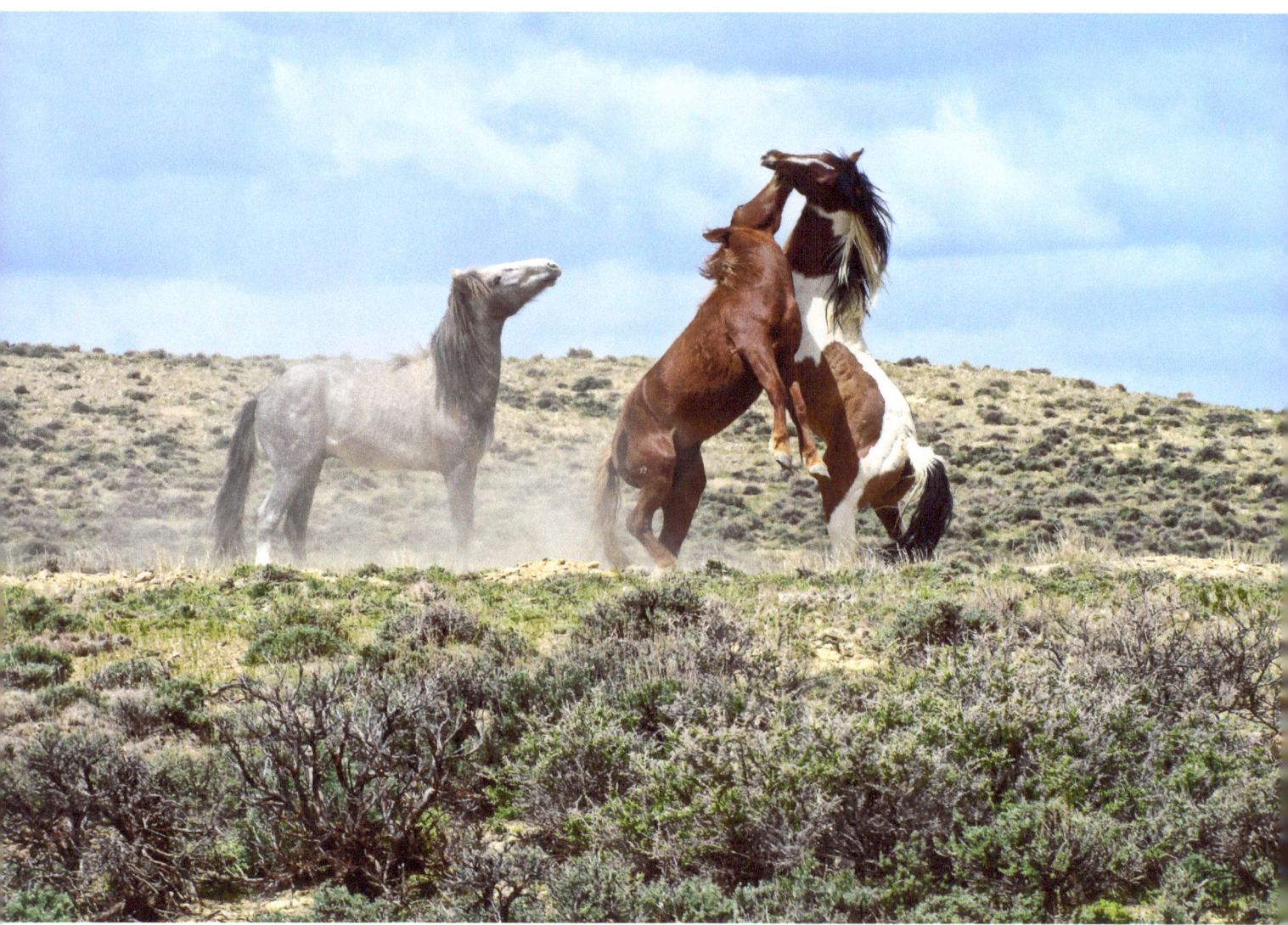

Often we look at horses and think they are gentle animals, and indeed, many times, that is the case, especially when it comes to domesticated ones. Even if we see horses trying to buck off a cowboy or racing across a field, we still think of them as tame animals. When it comes to wild horses, though, nothing could be further from the truth.

This photograph was made in the Red Desert, as all the photographs in this chapter were. When watching wild horses, you might think that they are always rearing up, as seen in this photograph, but in actuality, it doesn't happen often. Being in the right place at the right time to witness the exchange takes an extraordinary amount of patience, timing, and downright luck.

On this adventure I was with my good friend Phil. We had spent some number of days up in the area and had seen some stunning sights, but we were both looking for that one moment that captures the essence of the wild horse. We kept our eyes peeled, for you never knew when the moment would come, and when it did, it would last for the briefest of times. We finally found a set of circumstances that might play out.

A good-sized band of horses was there, led by a paint. The band wasn't in any particular hurry to be in any particular place and was alternatively grazing and moving, slowly making their way across the desert. What was interesting about this situation, however, was the mare in the back, who clearly wasn't all that interested in being part of the band. When the band moved, she moved as well, but she took her time, and if possible, drifted off to the side a bit here and there. Time and again the band moved, and time and again she did her best not to, but she always acquiesced in the end. I knew this situation might become interesting, should something change.

Change did happen, in the form of two young horses way across the desert. A chestnut and a gray popped over a small, distant hill, just the two of them, on their own desert journey. As fate would have it, they spied the band we were watching and read the situation. They changed course and began making their way over to our band.

The mare saw them, and now she had a bona fide reason not to linger anymore. As the band moved one way, she made a long arc in the general direction of the newcomers and then decided to make a clean break for them. Off she wandered, away from the band. This fact did not sit well with the paint who was leading the band, and he too figured out the situation quickly. He wasn't about to tolerate infidelity and everyone was moving on a collision course. Phil and I realized that we had front row seats, because we were almost in the middle of the action.

Sure enough, the horses came together, and before I could blink, the paint and the chestnut reared up in the air, deciding the fate of the mare. Being about a girl, this situation was serious and could have resulted in injury, or worse, to one of the participants. Luckily after a good amount of scuffling, pushing, pawing, and flailing in the air, the two stallions seemed to have sorted the situation out: the mare was now the chestnut's.

The chestnut who won the mare seemed to grow a few hands taller that day. As the chestnut and mare headed off together, close to each other, nuzzling each other, he stood tall and proud, and I could see in his stance how happy he was. What was just as wonderful to see was the mare, who was equally happy to be with the chestnut. We were able to watch them for a while, and they were certainly enjoying each other's company.

As for the paint, he took his band and headed off in the opposite direction, seemingly none the worse for the encounter.

This experience will be with me forever, as powerful as it was. It is amazing to see wild horses being wild horses.

Mustang Moments

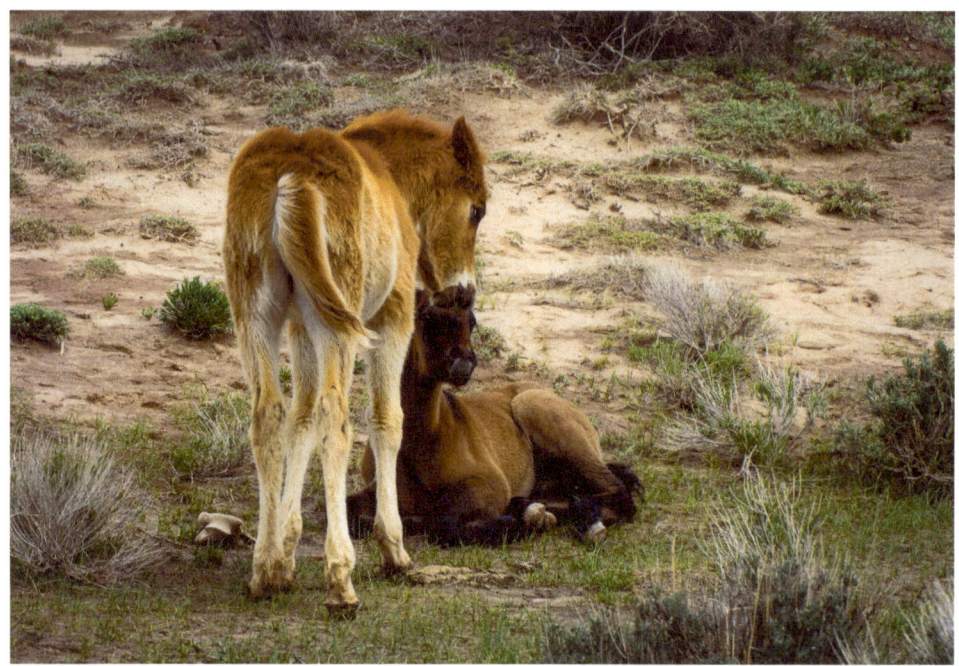

As thrilling as it is to see wild horses rearing up in the air, there are other exceptionally poignant scenes as well. Some of these are the more tender moments, especially when they involve young horses. I was in a different area of the Red Desert when I was able to see this moment in time, and it is just as memorable as *Stallion Battle*.

It is hard work being a wild horse. A day off isn't in your vocabulary, and you are constantly on the move. Your next meal is of the utmost priority, as is making sure you know exactly where, and how far away, the watering hole is. Although there are no predators to speak of, countless thousands of years of instinct say otherwise, and you always have one eye open and are constantly wary.

If you are a stallion, you have all this concern as well as the safety of your entire band to worry about, not to mention the threat of another stallion challenging your position. If you are a mare, you have all this concern, as well as a young foal to watch over and teach.

And for the young foals themselves? Every now and then they do get a moment to themselves. This small, tender moment happened between two young mustangs, one just a few days old, out on the open range of the desert.

It was a tender, sweet, and deeply touching moment. Even in the harshest environment, the young remind us that life is full of love and joy and of caring and sharing, especially if you are a young wild mustang.

Follow Me

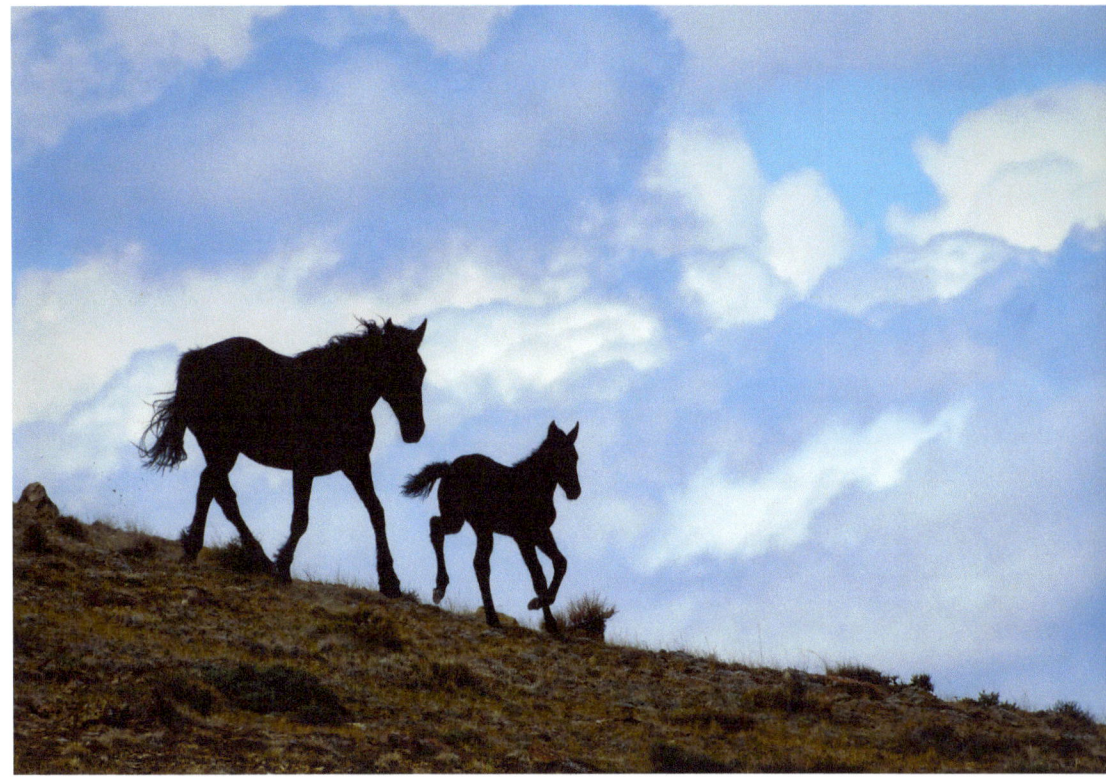

We'll round out Free Spirits with another young horse and another one of my all-time favorite photographs and stories. Although a simple silhouette, it speaks volumes to me and is another story I knew the moment I saw the scene.

"Follow me!" the young colt cried, and took off down the hill.

The mare, being older and wiser, followed after her colt, but not quite as quickly as she might have. She knew she would catch up in short order, and indeed, she did. They continued across the desert at a quick yet easy-to-maintain pace. Up small hills and down, mother followed son.

It was a good day for all concerned. It was spring, and the colt was just a couple of weeks old. Old enough to be well on his way to being self-sufficient, yet young enough that each hill was a new adventure waiting to happen. Recent rains had brought much-needed moisture to the desert, and much-needed standing water here and there, so food and water, perennial problems, were not much of an issue. Temperatures were moderate, winds light, and all in all it was an absolutely glorious day.

The wild horses have been sharing this ritual for as long as there has been time. Free from everyone, they live life on their own terms, wild, strong, and proud. Let's hope that we continue to be good stewards of the desert and let the horses continue as they have always known.

The young colt continued down the hill and into the vast wild of the desert, a free spirit roaming the vast, wide expanse that was his home.

Yesterday's Reflections

Those who came before us left their footprints for us to follow. Even though their time has passed, their spirit, passion, and traditions live on for us to discover and understand. These stories represent a small sampling of what the Southwest has to tell us.

Fiery House

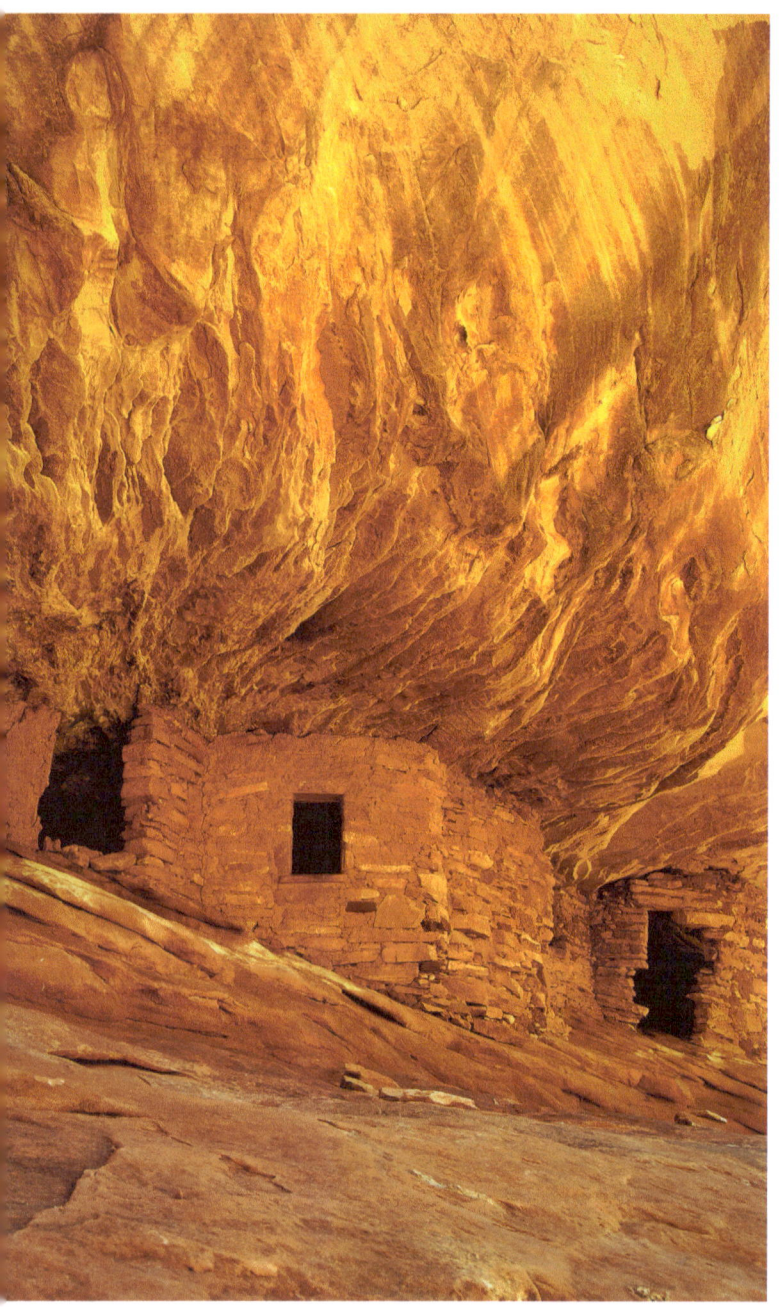

The Ancient Pueblo People, formally called the Anasazi, appeared in the archeology of the Cedar Mesa, Utah, area a thousand or so years ago. They have left lasting marks for those who know where to find them. The Ancient Pueblo People were accomplished builders, and what they built tends to last. They selected their sites carefully, used the best materials available, and built with precision and care. They also built what they needed, no more and no less, a trait that helps their buildings withstand the forces of time.

This small granary, or perhaps dwelling, is located in Mule Canyon. At first glance, there is little to distinguish it from the countless other buildings in the area tucked into the canyon alcoves. A bit of light magic happens here, though, and whether by coincidence or design, it is impossible to say. As the sun rises and light reflects throughout the canyon, this ruin lights up with reflected light, and the ordinary walls above the ruin turn into an extraordinary sight. The very walls themselves come alive, making the walls look as if they are on fire. It is easy to see why this ruin has earned the moniker House on Fire. As the sun continues its journey into the morning sky, the effect fades away, leaving just an "ordinary" ruin.

This is a good time to reflect upon the time that was and the people that built and used this building. They had a hard life by today's standards, yet they not only survived but thrived as a people and as a culture. We should do so well, and we can be hopeful that those who come long after us remember us. We don't know what our ruins will be like, but if we are fortunate they will be symbols and signs representing the best we had to offer, just as this ruin is.

Fallen Roof

The Ancient Pueblo People were master builders, and they often built their buildings into the alcoves of canyon walls, often far up from the floor, seemingly defying gravity. Their stonework is impressive even to this day, and they built with care and precision, allowing many of the works to remain looking like they were just finished yesterday.

Although the buildings have withstood the ravages of time, the same cannot be said of some of the canyons they chose. These small granaries tucked into Road Canyon were probably unremarkable when first built; however, since part of the alcove roof has fallen, leaving a dramatic and impressive design in the new roof, that's changed. Add in some reflected light, and the ruin known as Fallen Roof takes on a mystery and magic all its own.

The Ancient Pueblo People built to last, and today it is not always easy to see their ruins, cleverly situated in the natural surroundings, and getting to them is often another story entirely. Still, they serve as excellent reminders of the spirit of these proud people.

As a side note, Road Canyon is an interesting canyon for what it later becomes. In the Cedar Mesa area of Utah, Road Canyon is fairly steep and narrow, where one could throw a rock from one side to the other. Road Canyon continues to travel southward, however, widening and flattening out as it does. Just before it crosses the state line, it is wide enough that monolithic buttes jut out of the landscape. At this point we call these monuments. The first named area in which the monuments appear is called Valley of the Gods, which we learned about earlier. The canyon continues to widen, and as it crosses southward into Arizona, we call it Monument Valley. Road Canyon, from start to end, is full of significant features.

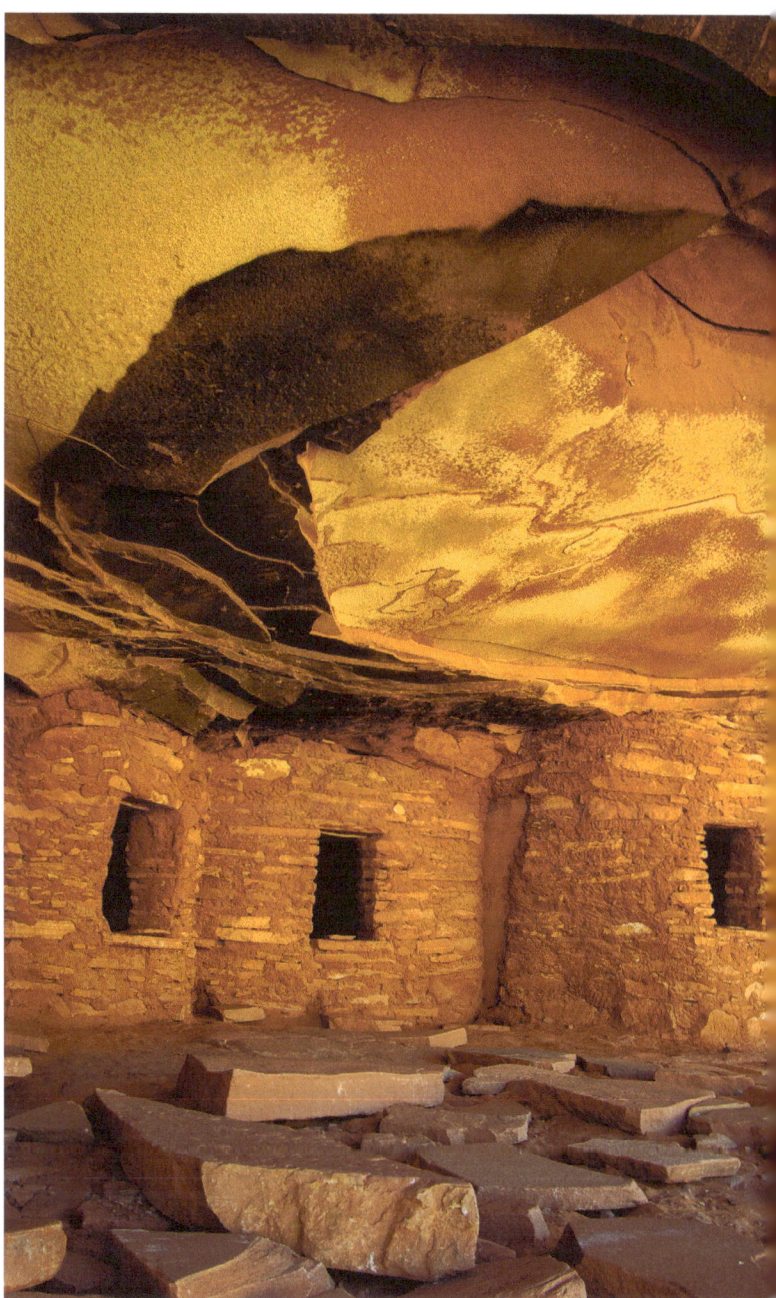

Yesterday's Tower

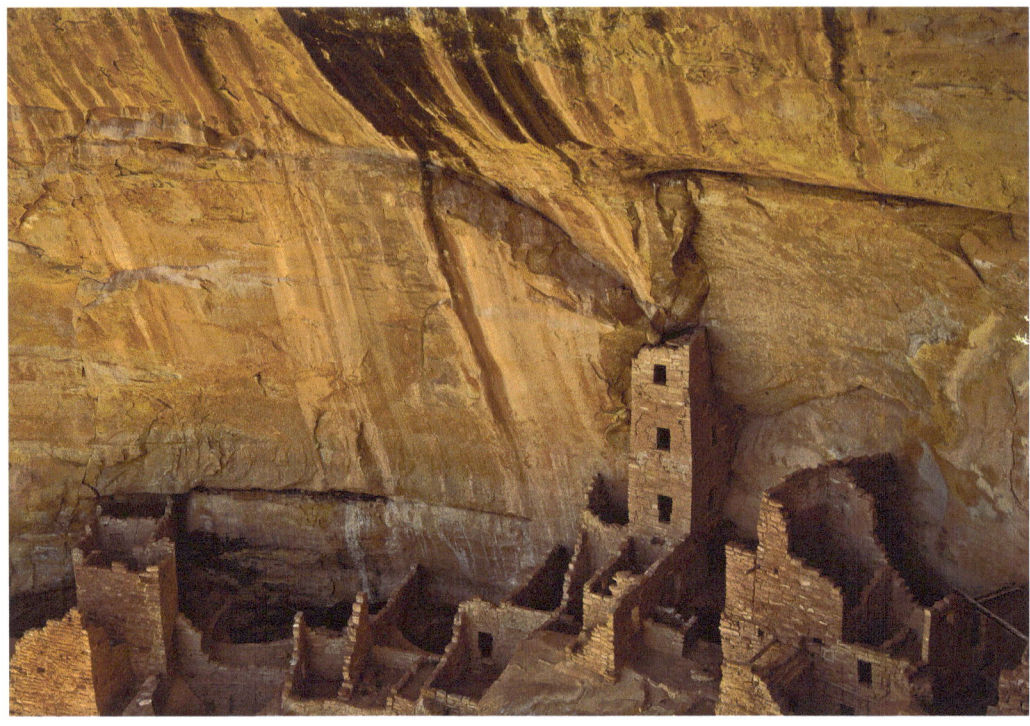

Yesterday wasn't so long ago, really, when you come right down to it. If you measure it by a wristwatch, yesterday was just a few hours ago. If you measure it by a more subjective term, it was longer ago. And if you measure it by the ceaseless rhythms of the Earth, "yesterday" was just a thousand years or so ago.

It's good to step back from time to time to remember yesterday and especially those who have gone before us. They paved the way for us today, and reflecting upon their works is a fitting tribute.

Our next stop is Square Tower House in Mesa Verde National Park, located in southern Colorado. Although the area has been occupied for an exceptionally long time, the Grand Pueblo Period of the site saw the construction of its cliff dwellings probably around 1100 to 1300. It was one of the last major construction projects in the Mesa Verde area and today is considered one of the great antiquities in North America. In fact it has such significance that it is a World Heritage Site. It wasn't occupied for long, a mere blink of an eye in the grand scheme of things, yet its impact is profound.

Mainly known for their cliff dwellings, the builders of Mesa Verde were accomplished. Some of their works fit together so well that they have survived for more than a thousand years and will likely survive another thousand or so. Comprising sandstone blocks with adobe mortar, these buildings are excellently constructed. Some structures have been stabilized to help preserve them, but by and large they are still quite sound.

Those who built Mesa Verde were not confined to the area. They spread throughout the Four Corners area (Colorado, New Mexico, Arizona, and Utah), building other sites and refining their techniques.

Casa Blanca

Deep within Canyon de Chelly lie the ruins of Casa Blanca—the White House, as it is sometimes known. It is a proud and iconic place, with its history dating back to approximately 1075. It derives its current name from the Navajo appellation *Kiníí' Na'ígai*, or "house with white streak across," which is about as literal as a description as you can possibly have. This location holds deep significance to the Navajo and holds supernatural powers. It figures prominently in the origin of the Nightway Ceremony and possibly others as well. The Nightway Ceremony may well be the most sacred of all Navajo ceremonies. Difficult and demanding to learn, it is composed of song, prayer, and sand paintings, all of which combine to create the ceremony. The ceremony is a healing ritual, but it heals more than sickness, for it also addresses the balance of relationships within the Navajo pantheon.

Although it was not built all at once, the White House was steadily expanded upon over the years until its eventual abandonment. It shows several styles of architecture and construction, spanning from very early Navajo to later Mesa-Verde and Chacoan-style techniques.

This photograph shows one of the classic views of this location. The orange and red tones change throughout the day as the sun transits the canyon walls. Today the ruins stand as you see them here; the echoes of the past swirling around and through them and onto us today. Preserved and protected for all to see, Casa Blanca stands as a testament to our early beginnings as well as the necessity to retain order and balance. It is an exceptionally good location for reflection.

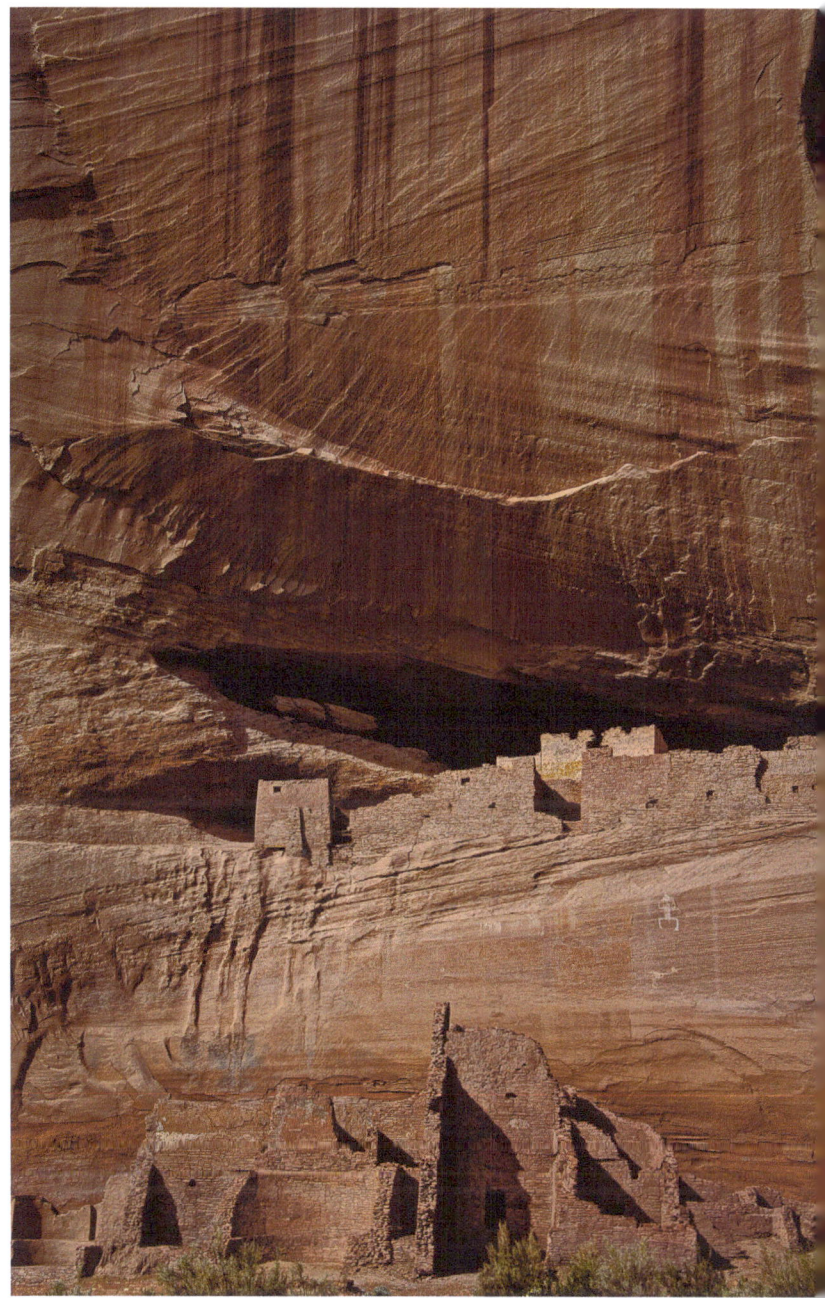

Hovenweep's Lookout

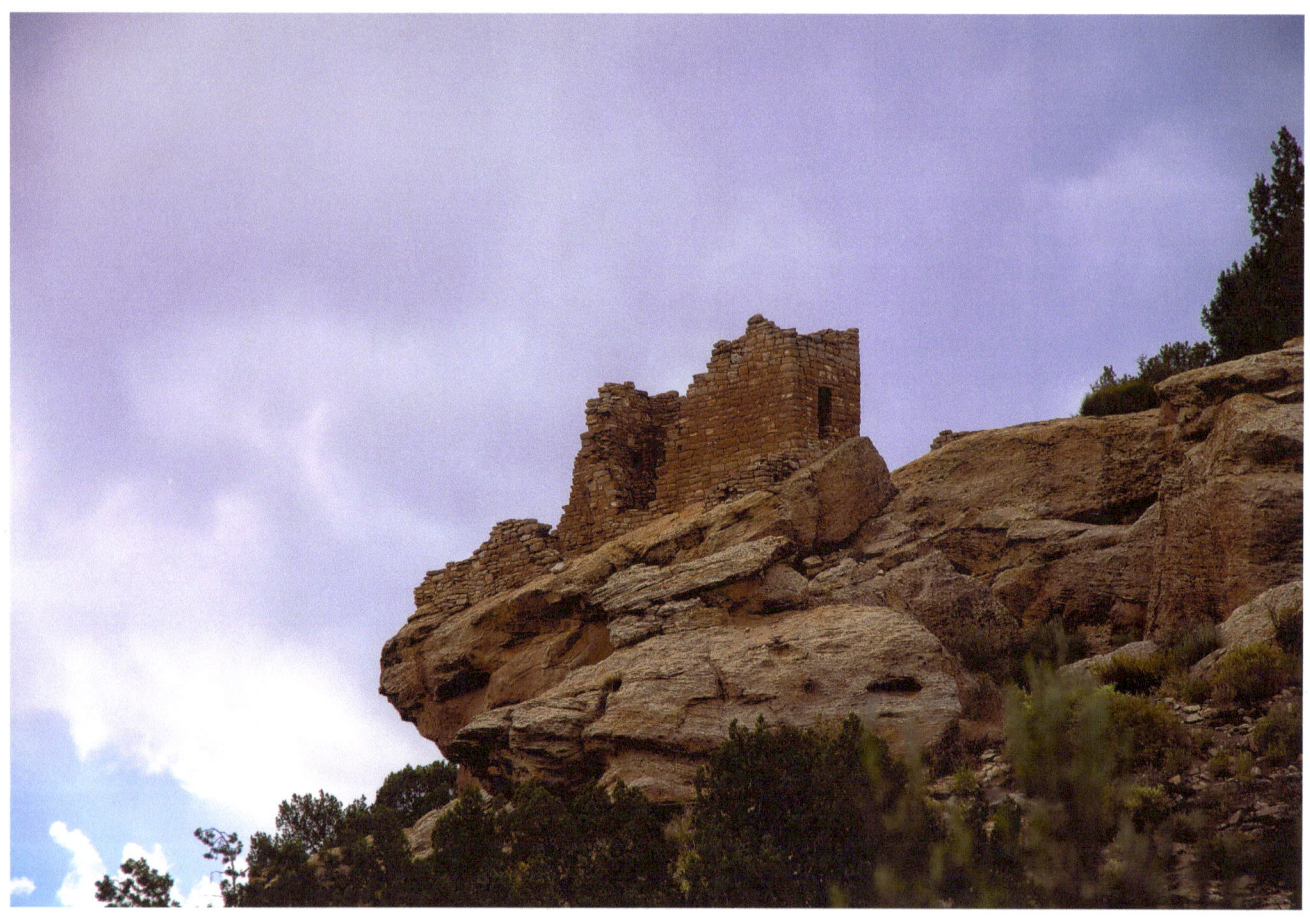

Hovenweep, although a National Monument, is not nearly as well known as some of its neighbors, but that doesn't mean it isn't important. It too deserves reflection and appreciation for those who made their home here.

Hovenweep started to come into its own somewhere around 900, and by 1100 it was in full swing. With solid influence from Mesa Verde, Hovenweep's architecture reflected some of the same styles as Mesa Verde. Structures tended to be built up on the top of canyon walls and possibly served as lookouts.

This structure, perched precariously on the edge of a cliff, fascinates me. The color of sky made a striking contrast to the building itself, and I like the feeling and imagery that this photograph evokes.

The ancient peoples who lived in the Southwest left more than buildings for us, however. They also left writings.

Abo Mask

Outside of Socorro, New Mexico, tucked away in a field, are a small set of pictographs. It is hard to see or find these, as their location is not well known, not marked in any meaningful way, and although archeologically cataloged, they have not garnered a lot of attention. No one knows for sure who left them, and, as with all rock art, no one knows exactly what the meaning is.

What is known, though, is that these pictographs are done in the Abo style, which is characterized by masks such as the one here. Distinctly they tend to have flat tops, and quite significantly, these are polychromatic, meaning painted in different colors. We're not sure how old this mask is, other than "very, very old," quite possibly dating to before 1 BC. It is amazing that such art has survived so long, and this site does because of a very fortuitous geologic location, protected from the elements by a well-positioned alcove and modern-day obscurity.

This mask fascinates me, because it looks at me from depths of time. I don't know the message or what it means. I don't know if it is a message for good, a message of warning, or whether it marks a significant event or location, yet my lack of knowledge doesn't lessen the fascination as it gazes through the years at me, trying to tell me something important. That I don't understand it causes me to ponder it that much more.

This is not the only writing in the Southwest.

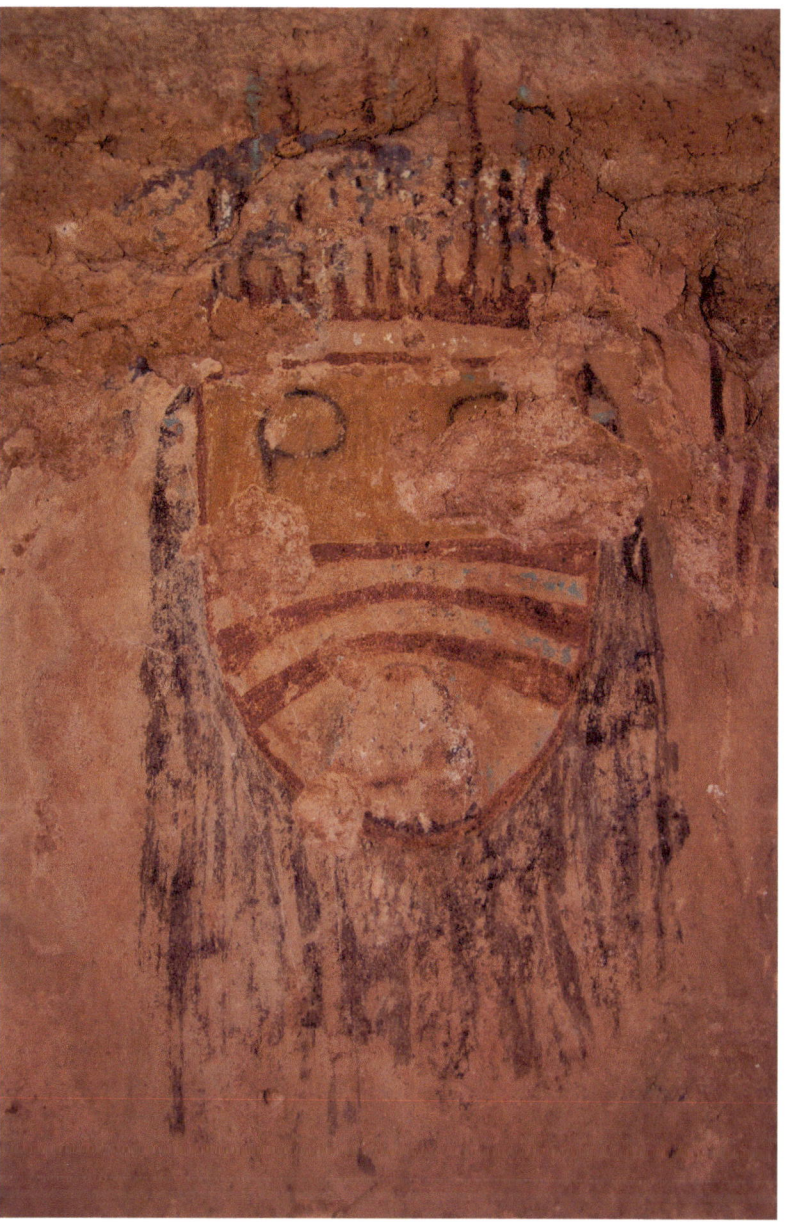

Abo Panel

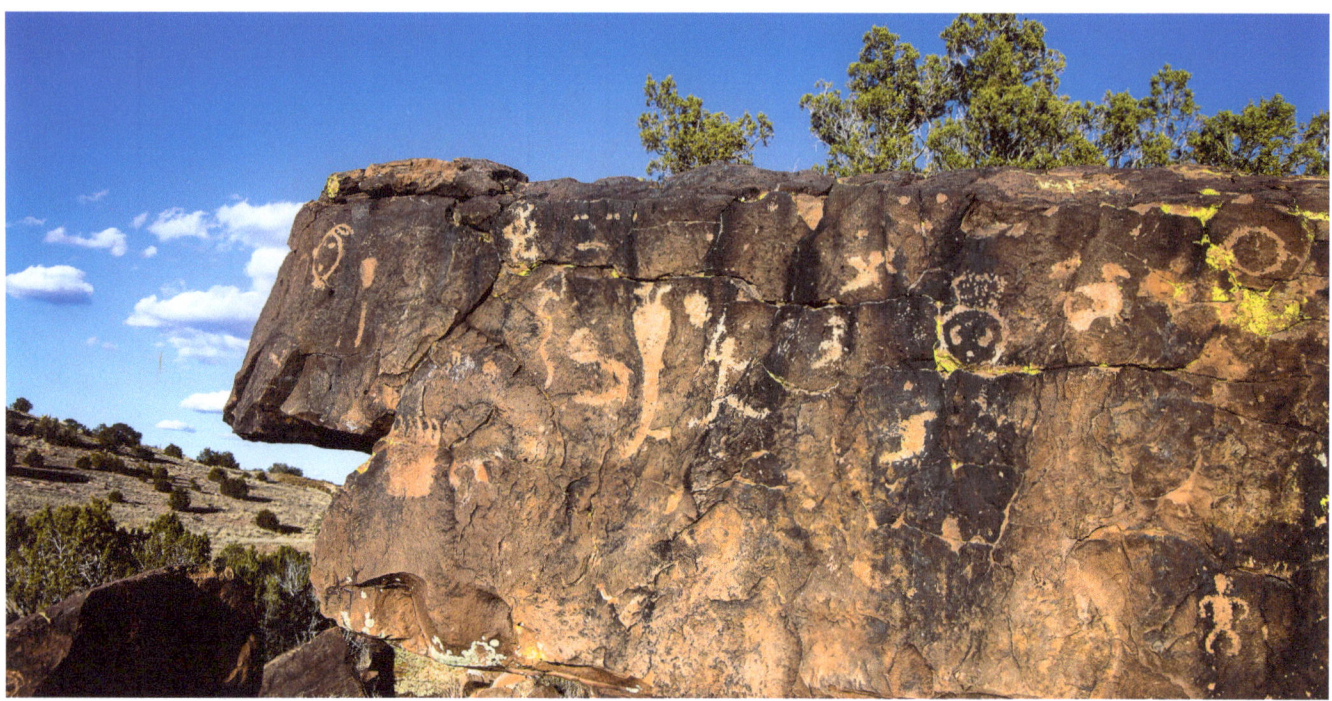

Not far away from *Abo Mask* is a small panel of pictographs, or drawings, etched into rock. This panel is a different style, possibly from a different culture in a different time, but as with *Abo Mask*, the exact meaning of each glyph is lost in the mists of time.

What does it mean? What message, or messages, are encoded in the rock? Who left these figures and why? The answer today is that no one knows.

As an interesting side note, some of these pictographs decorate the Grand Canyon's Desert View Watchtower. Some of the Abo pictographs were documented by Herman Schwizer, who was from Albuquerque, which is near this location. Mary Colter, who designed many significant and historic buildings in the Grand Canyon National Park, heard about these pictographs and arranged to have a reproduction of them placed on the ceiling of the watchtower. Just like times of old, the sites of today are interconnected in strange yet significant ways. Although *Abo Panel* may be a little visited site, millions of people each year gaze upon copies of these pictographs and ponder their meaning.

Petroglyph's Alien?

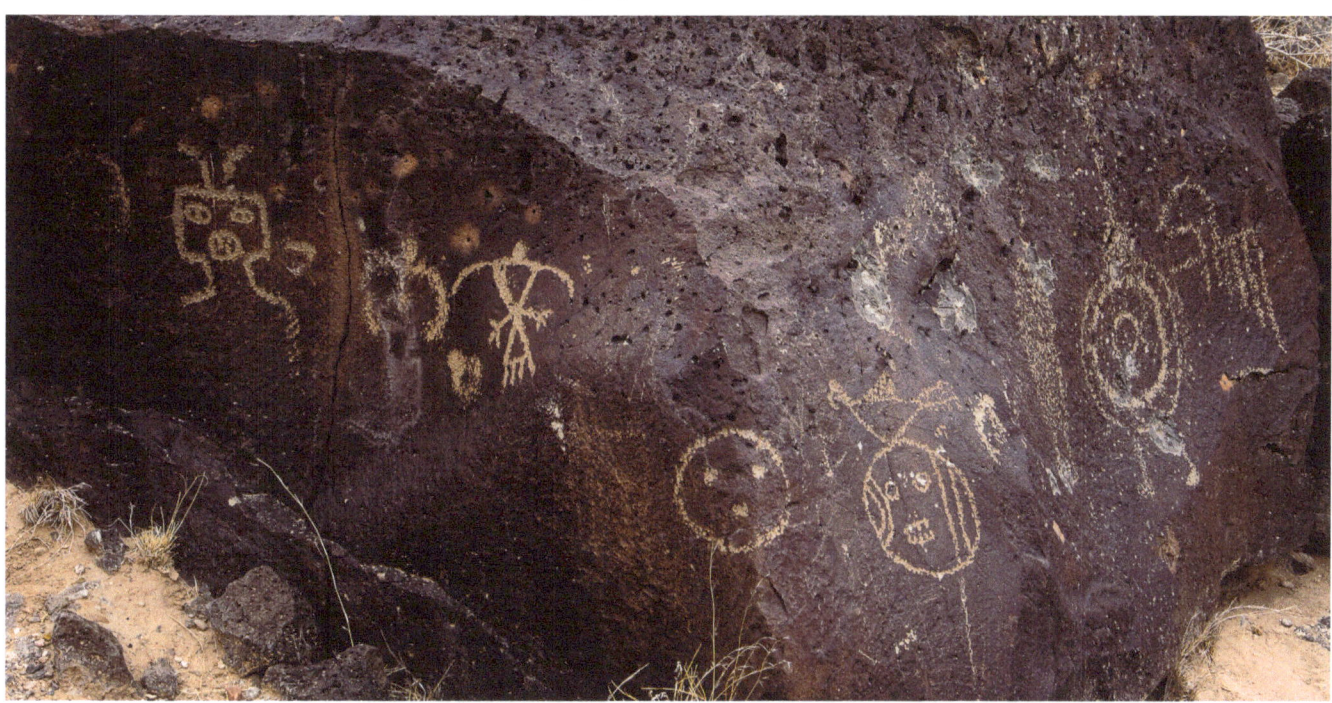

When the meaning of the petroglyphs is lost, it is tempting to attribute modern-day interpretation to ancient symbols. There is no right or wrong answer, but since we're on the topic of ancient writings, I thought I would present this image for your consideration.

I made this photograph in Petroglyph National Monument, New Mexico. The National Monument encompasses thousands upon thousands of petroglyphs that cover the area. Most of these drawing are on boulders, easily accessible, in low washes. They are old; of this there is no doubt, and like all such petroglyphs, the meaning has been lost to us. In and among the petroglyphs, a few stand out, such as the ones on this rock. Many people have speculated that the image on the far left represents an alien, for although we have plenty of examples of heads that are properly rounded, we have but a few examples of ones that are square. Surely, some people speculate, this image represents an ancient traveler to our planet. Of course not, others say, for it is of this world; we just don't know what it means.

The truth of the image and the purpose for which it was left is long gone, leaving us only mystery. I present the image here in situ with the rest of the panel on the boulder and invite you to find your own interpretation.

Newspaper Rock

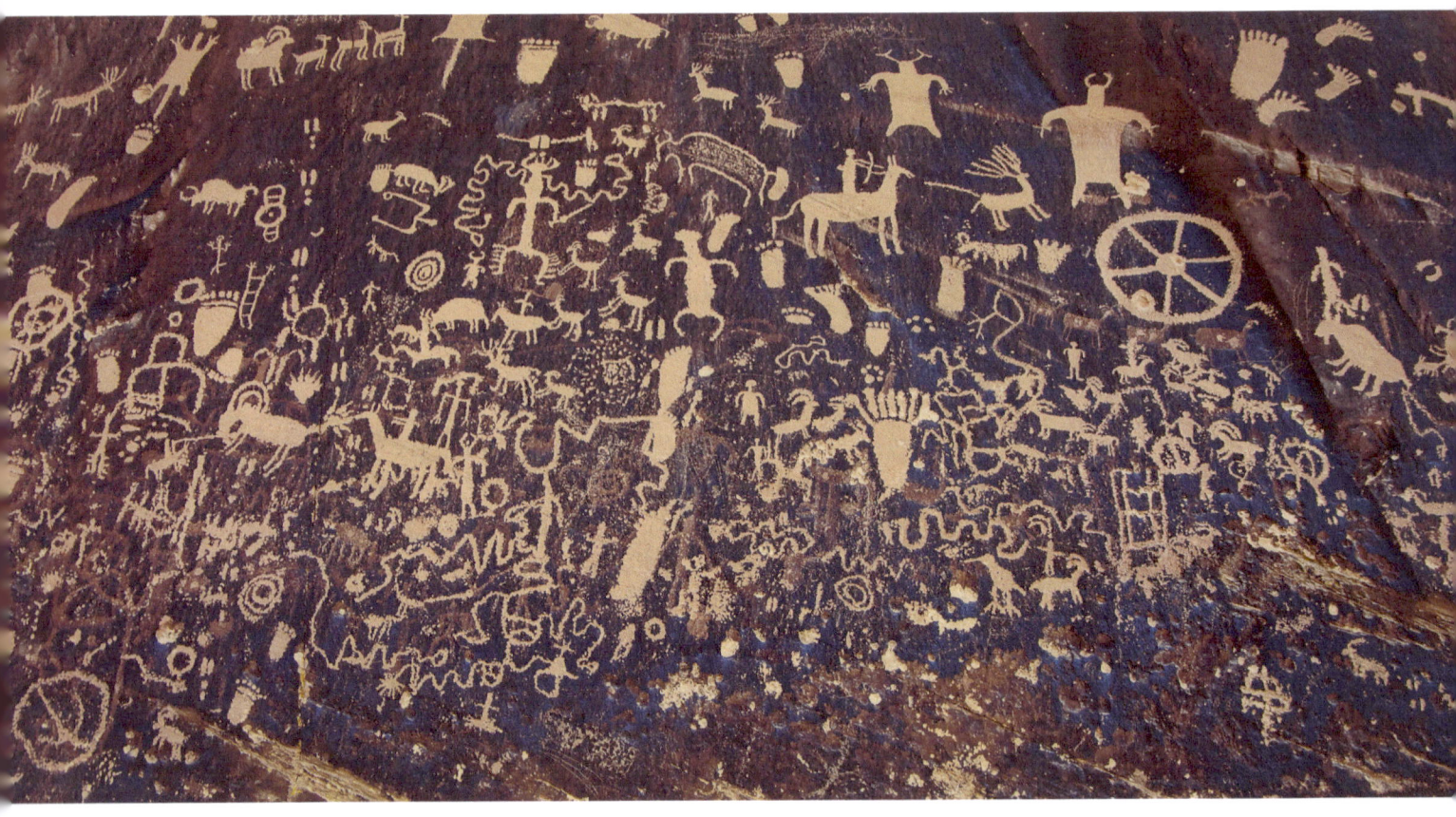

We'll leave behind yesterday with one of the best panels in the entirety of the Southwest: Newspaper Rock.

Newspaper Rock, or *Tsé Hone*, as the Navajo named it, is a rock that tells stories in southeastern Utah. These stories, though, are somewhere around two thousand years in the making and told through petroglyphs. People from the Archaic, Anasazi, Fremont, Navajo, Anglo, and Pueblo cultures have all added their carvings to this rock, covering an extraordinary time scale. We know that the prehistoric Archaic culture is there, and we know that some of the story was told after the Spanish arrived, and every time in between.

As with most rock art, we are not sure what is actually being said. The meaning of rock art is, by and large, dependent on when, where, and importantly, by whom it was created as much as what the figures actually are. Context is important. We are fairly confident of some symbols and their meaning, but even then, there are doubts. Perhaps this is best, for it gives us a chance to interpret the stories for ourselves.

As you look at this panel, one of the most extensive collections known, you'll find a broad range of stories waiting for you to read. I hope they speak as strongly to you as they do to me. I like to look at the ladders with hands in the left center of the photograph and wonder what that might mean. I see the wheel on the right side and wonder if it was influenced by the Spanish wagons, and then I look at the humanoid figure to the immediate left and wonder who it represents. I see hunting scenes, some from horseback. I see big game, maybe. I even see what appears to be a cross in the lower center left and wonder if a cowboy or ranger left that for us.

In any event, *Newspaper Rock* is a perfect end to Yesterday's Reflections, so let's get back to today and head off in search of some wildlife.

Running Wild

The Southwest has more than extraordinary landscapes, and folks who live within it have equally compelling stories. These are a few stories of some of my favorite wildlife encounters, all of which were breathtaking to witness and have the privilege of documenting.

Elk's Paradise

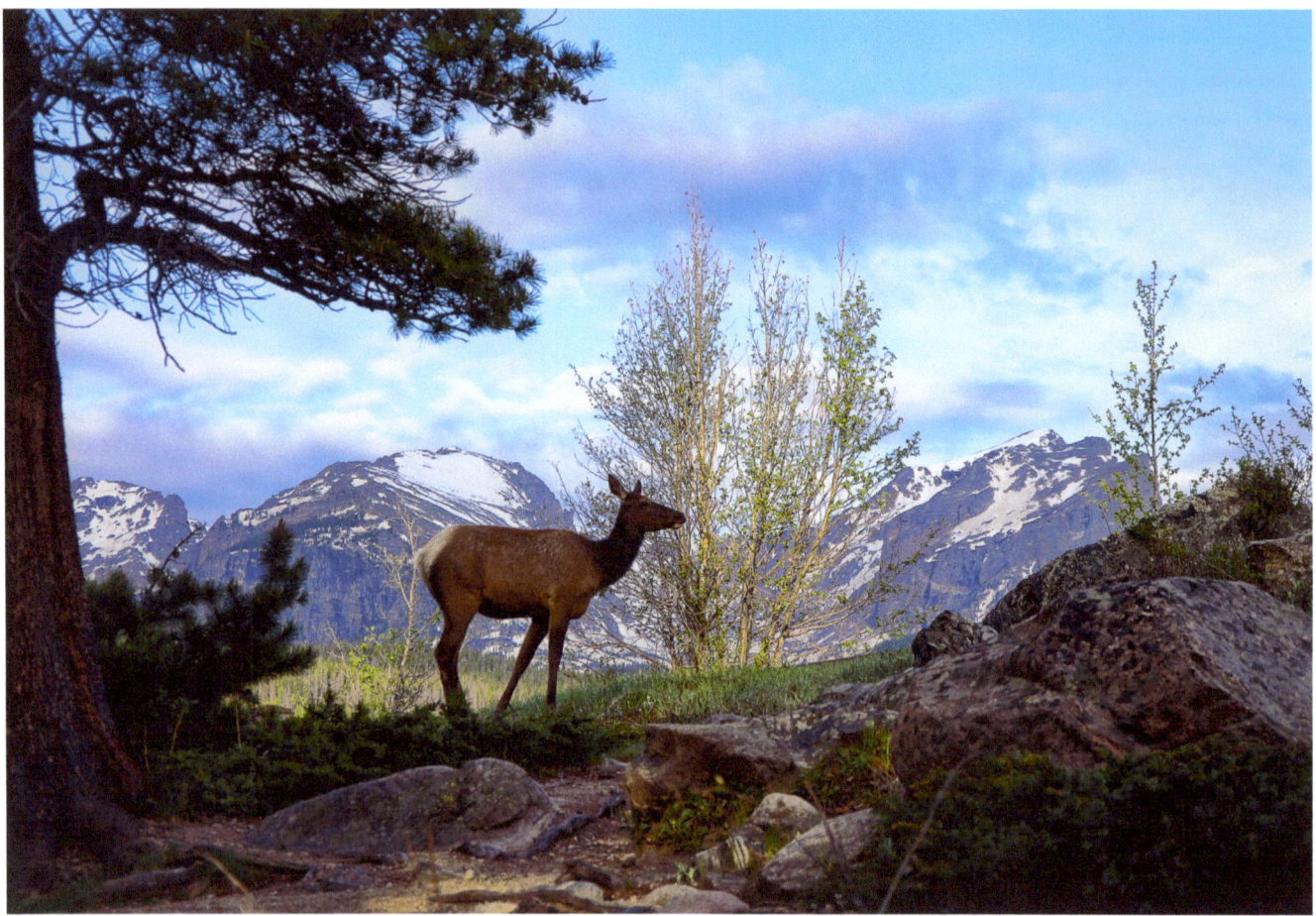

The spring morning was cool and calm, and the day ahead held considerable promise. The previous days had seen a little rain, and the forest was a little brighter, a little greener, and definitely more vibrant than normal. The snow-capped mountains reached for the rising sun, eager to shed their winter's burden while high above them the clouds lazily drifted by, indifferent to the mountains or anything else below. The elk simply stood at ease, gazing out over her paradise. It was going to be a very good day.

This tableau happened in Rocky Mountain National Park, Colorado, where both human and elk consider it a paradise. There is something deeply profound about sharing such a moment with nature; I was there with the elk, enjoying the morning. Elk and human, while not side by side, stood together looking out at the glorious, perfect morning, each lost in thought. It seemed to me that this moment lasted an eternity, and I am glad that it did, for I wanted to soak up every little detail. I will remember it forever.

Eventually the moment passed, and it was time for us to part ways. We did so, each acknowledging that this interlude in paradise was extraordinary.

As is often the case when photographing wildlife, the final photograph was not as simple to create as might be imagined. The morning was certainly an excellent morning; the kind of perfect morning that you can see coming from first light. The skies were filling with color and clouds, and would make for beautiful photography. Even the temperature was nice, not too hot or cold, making for a comfortable excursion. Everything was lining up.

I saw the elk not far from Sprague Lake, off in some scrub brush, and decided to watch her for a while to see what she did. My hope was that she would go up and by the lake, and I figured that scenario would make an interesting photograph. I sat quietly, patiently, some ways away, watching her forage. There was no need to be any closer, not only because this is a large wild animal and thus not entirely predictable, but also because her location was anything but photogenic. The rangers had clearly been working in the area, making piles of brush and weeds, plus the ground was torn up, and the elk was in shadow. Nothing to do but wait. I "hid" behind a tree, although the elk knew full well I was there. At least I felt like I was hiding.

Over my shoulder, the day continued to be spectacular. If I thought it was good before, it was becoming excellent. Still, the elk continued to forage and generally mind her own business, exactly in a location where it was not photogenic.

This tableau continued for the longest time, almost an hour. I was becoming quite impatient, for the morning was extraordinary, and although I had the perfect subject, there was little I could do about it except hope. This is another lesson for me in patience, but it was not a lesson I appreciated learning at the time. Still, having nothing to show for it, I continued to wait.

Eventually, after an eternity had passed, the elk looked up and decided that the forage was better elsewhere. It was a fifty-fifty chance which way she would move, either deeper into the woods or out to the lake. I held my breath. And was rewarded.

Sure enough she moved toward the lake. She came up the edge, right underneath a pine branch, and … stopped. She just stopped and stood completely still. I quietly, carefully stepped out from behind my tree and made this photograph. It was almost as if she knew, too, for when the photograph was made she resumed her journey around the lake and into the morning.

Elk's Paradise titled instantly, and to this day I believe she knew what she was doing and made sure that my patience was rewarded on that phenomenal morning.

Rocky's Newborn

As majestic as a full-grown elk is, and standing next to one of this incredible animals, you learn just how big they are. On the other end of the spectrum the newborns are equally majestic. There is something powerful about watching life beginning in the animal kingdom.

Mary Beth and I were fortunate to witness and document the first difficult journey of a newborn elk in Rocky Mountain National Park. Over the course of an hour, we watched a mother and baby elk, just after it came into the world. Life will always find a way, but not always without peril.

Mid morning on a splendid June day in the park, Mary Beth and I were at the far end of Moraine Park, an excellent place to watch the elk. It was a time of calving, and we were hoping to see a baby elk or two. The best way to do that is to find a likely spot and simply wait, so that is exactly what we did. We were almost immediately rewarded.

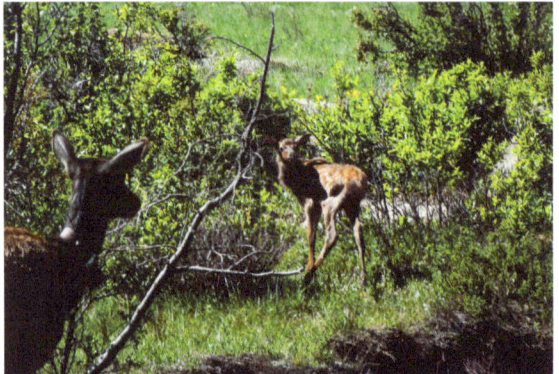

Photograph #1

We noticed the action begin on the far side of the Big Thompson River. This area is the headwaters of the river, and here it is not wide, sometimes as narrow as ten feet in places. The water is unexpectedly deep, though, and it flows quickly for such a small river. The mountains ringing this area of the park feed this river, and it packs quite a punch for such a seemingly tiny river. A mother elk was calling, but we couldn't see the reason at first. After a moment, a baby elk stepped into view. It had to have been born a short time before, because it was still learning how to walk. It was highly unsteady on its feet, quite wobbly, and was clearly in the process of learning how to walk.

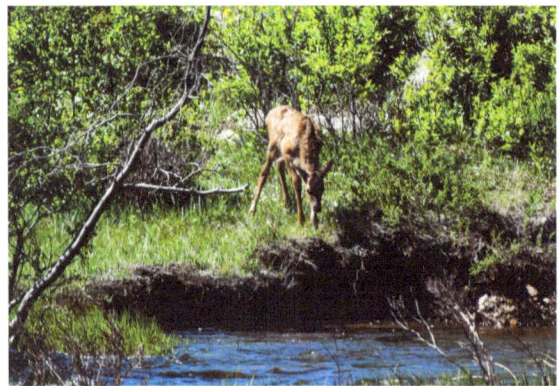

Photograph #2

Mother elk took a last look at her baby and immediately swam across the river. Even for her, a full-grown elk, the crossing was not quick or easy, and she fought against the strong current. She made it to the other side and then stopped and waited for her baby. The drama began to unfold for us. We pick up the photograph sequence here, with *Photograph #1*. Mother elk is across the river, calling to her newborn. It sees its mother, but it also senses the danger the river poses. Forty-five seconds later, in *Photograph #2*, the baby has come to the edge of the river and realized that the crossing would not be easy. Mother elk continues to call to her baby.

In *Photograph #3*, thirty seconds later, the baby has found a low spot and has committed to the crossing. Both Mary Beth's and my hearts stopped, and we didn't draw a breath.

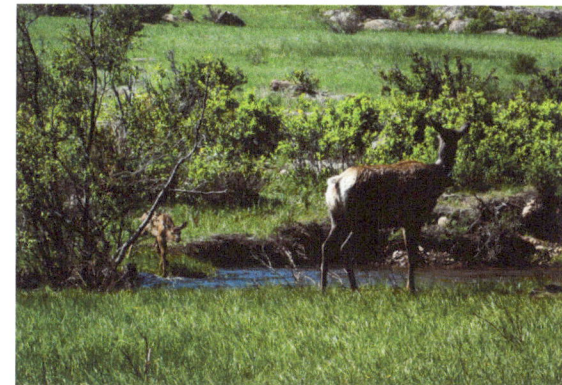

Photograph #3

In *Photograph #4*, six seconds later, the baby has taken the first tentative steps into the river and discovered, the hard way, that the water was moving with quite a bit of force. The baby paused and bleated, only to have an answer from Mom. It had to have been encouragement. We waited, still not having drawn a breath.

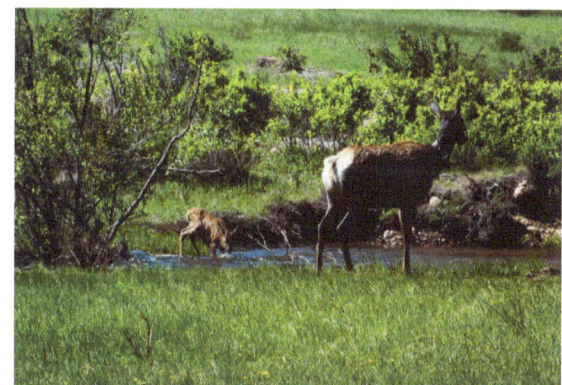

Photograph #4

The moment of truth was upon the baby elk. Three seconds went by, and the baby charged headlong into the water in *Photograph #5*. It was all or nothing, and there was no turning back.

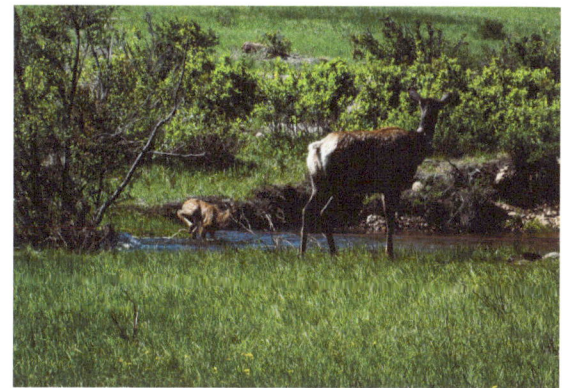

Photograph #5

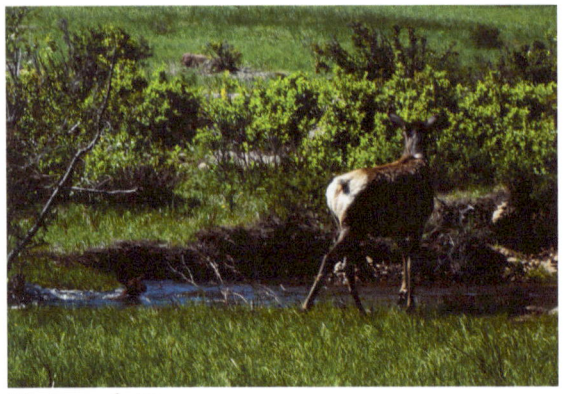

Photograph #6

A mere two seconds and all of eternity later, in *Photograph #6*, the baby elk was in the river and swimming. Unfortunately the swift current was pulling it quickly downstream. We were not sure if the elk would survive. Its head went under the water, only to instantly surface again. It was mere seconds that the elk was in the river, but time stood still.

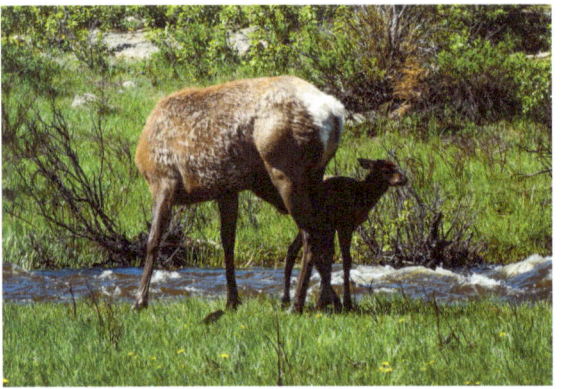

Photograph #7

Before we even realized it, the baby made the crossing. Clearly exhausted, it pulled itself out of the river on highly unsteady feet and hobbled over to its mother. *Photograph #7*, made about a minute after *Photograph #6*, shows Mom carefully inspecting and cleaning the newborn. Our own hearts had begun to beat again, unsteady at first, and then finding the correct rhythm. We were astounded at what we had witnessed.

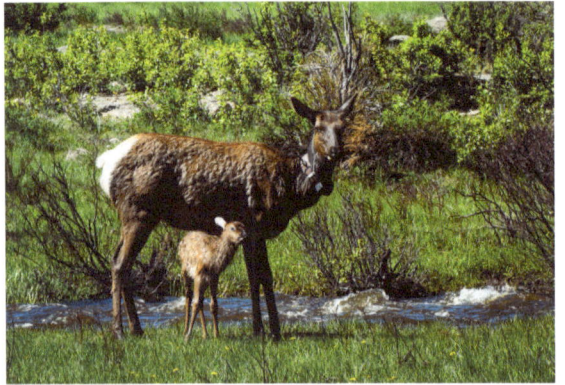

Photograph #8

For a few minutes after that, Mom carefully tended to its baby. In *Photograph #8*, they both looked up, inspecting their surroundings.

A couple of seconds later, in *Photograph #9*, Mom decided on a course of action and began moving toward a brushy area. She had just given birth, and she was hungry; it was time for her to eat. Foraging with a newborn, however, was not possible, so she needed a safe place for it. The brushy area she had spotted seemed like an ideal location.

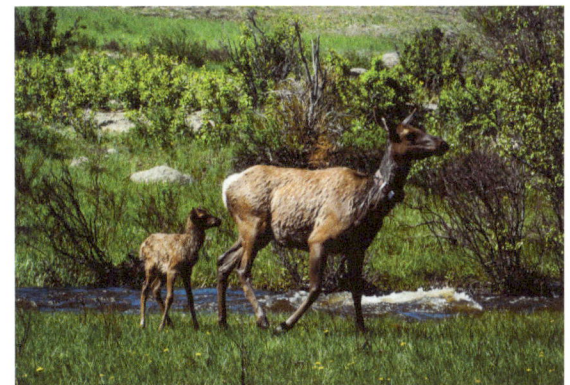

Photograph #9

In *Photograph #10* she inspected the baby again and the spot she selected. All seemed well. The baby curled up safe and secure under the bushes, and Mom headed off for a well-earned meal.

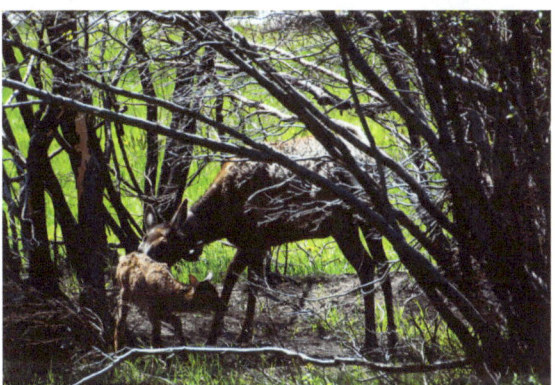

Photograph #10

Mary Beth and I continued to watch the baby for the next hour. Mom eventually came back, inspected the baby again, and together they headed off deeper into the park. We had seen one of the true miracles of life as it happened. It wasn't a made for television show where you knew that everything would be okay at the end. We had no idea at all how it would turn out, but you can be sure we were rooting for that baby. We were so excited when it made the crossing that we each had tears in our eyes. To see and behold such a small but momentous moment puts everything in perspective.

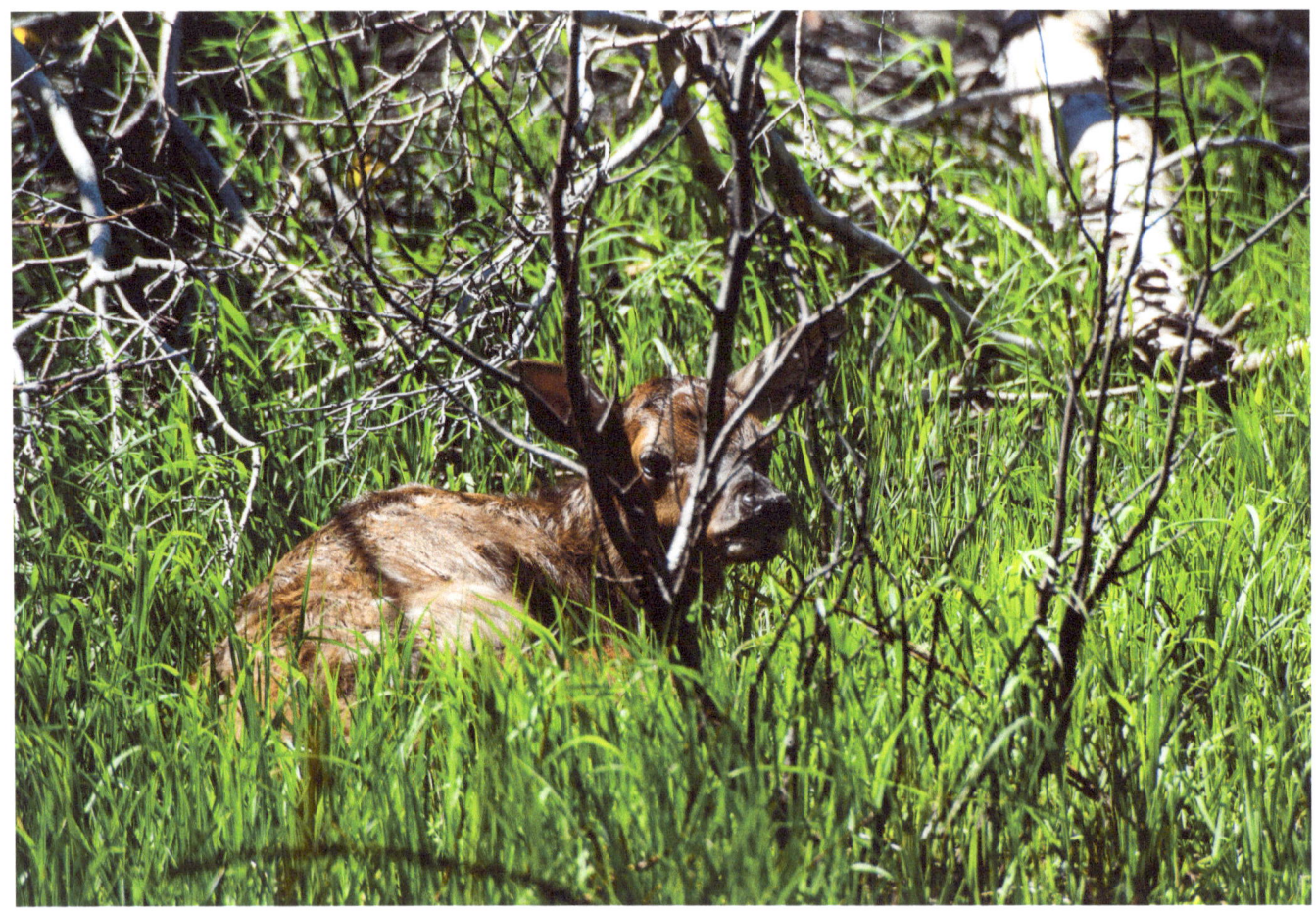

The last photograph, *Rocky's Newborn* is the final photograph from this encounter. I made it a good bit after Mother Elk had left and everything was calm. It means a lot to us, and we hope to you as well.

A few final thoughts are in order in this story. Mother Elk is wearing a radio collar. Ongoing research in Rocky Mountain National Park tags a few elk with collars. These elk are then tracked over time to study their range and habits, providing valuable data on the elk population to the researchers. Also, Mary Beth and I were a very long way away from this action, so as not to disturb anything. I used an exceptionally long telephoto lens to provide the close-up images, but I was out of sight, very far out of the way, during this event. The elk never knew I was there.

Moosen Flower

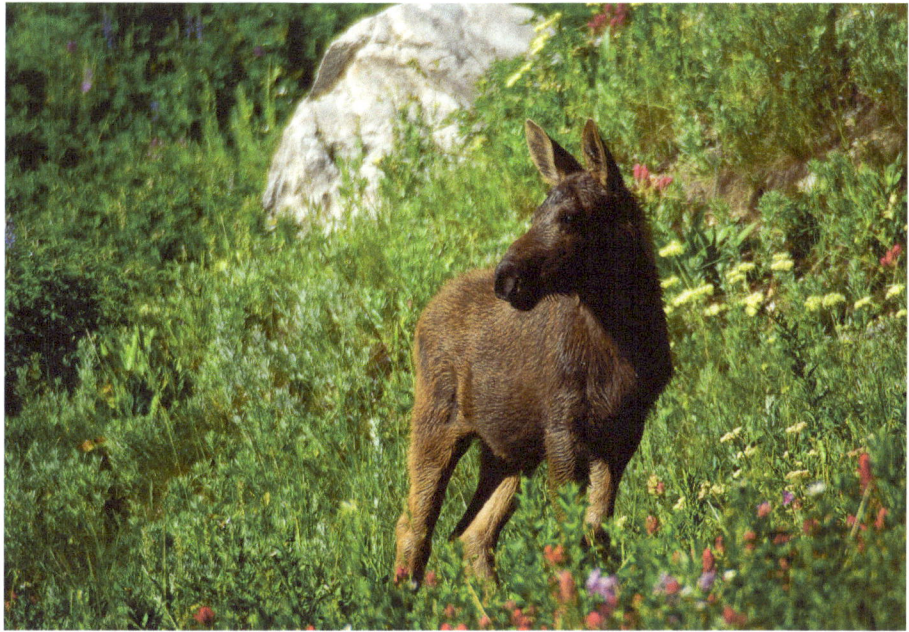

After the drama of the last story, let's stay with a baby, but dial back the intensity. We could both use the break, and why not relax with a baby moose in a field of flowers?

There is something so precious about new life. I am forever awestruck when I encounter newborn wildlife and never forget how important those moments are. From seeing the first steps to watching babies learn the ways of the wild, the privilege of seeing nature's newest additions is not lost on me.

I first saw this young moose high up on a mountain in the Wasatch National Forest in Utah. It was close by its mother, following in her footsteps, doing as she did, and learning what it meant to be a moose. It was raining, and as I watched, quietly and unseen, the rain increased. The three of us were soaking wet. Moose, however, are not bothered by the rain, so they continued foraging. I, too, am not bothered by the rain, or at least I pretend to not be bothered, and continued after them.

We went ever up the mountain, the three of us, each of us hunting, although for entirely different things. Eventually the rain passed and the sun broke through the clouds. Mom was a little way off, and the baby stood for a moment looking after her. This photograph was made at exactly that time. The baby moose stood still as a statue in a field of wildflowers on a perfect summer evening.

I eventually dried out, and I am guessing that both moose did as well.

Bighorn Flock

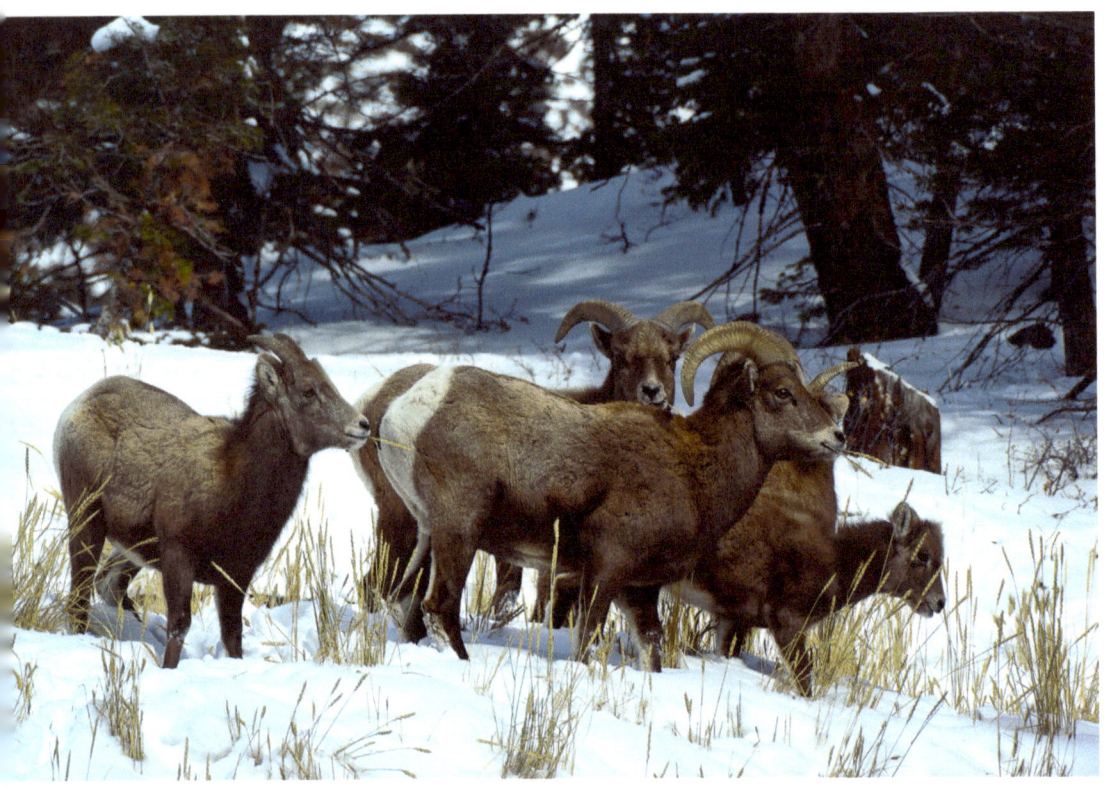

I especially enjoying finding groups of wildlife. Mom and her baby is always one of my favorite subjects, but when I find a family, I also get excited. One winter day (ironically, for me, it was a temperate winter day; imagine that) I was up in southern Colorado. Out of the corner of my eye I spotted movement. Turning quickly, I saw that it was an entire family of bighorn sheep up on the mountain above. What an experience it was to observe nature in her finest!

The family moved along the mountainside on a chilly winter's day. Actually it wasn't all that cold, considering, and the snows were not terribly deep yet, mostly because the worst of the winter hadn't arrived. This time of year suited the flock of bighorn sheep perfectly, since the foraging was still easy, and they could take their time in any one area.

Mom, Dad, and the kids moved together, generally staying close to one another. When it was time to move and one of the little ones was not ready, Dad would simply come up behind the reluctant one, lower his head, and tenderly, lovingly, and with some degree of force head-butt the kid. The kid would startle, jump, and then move along. This process played out repeatedly throughout the afternoon. Nature finds a way, every single time, to get her point across, no matter if you are bighorn sheep or not.

The bighorns stayed on the mountainside for most of the afternoon. The sun came and went from behind the clouds, making for the most delightful play on light and shadows; the bighorn sensed this, too, for they often headed into the sun. Eventually the afternoon wore on and it was time to go. It had been a productive afternoon for the bighorn flock and for me as well.

Squirrel TV

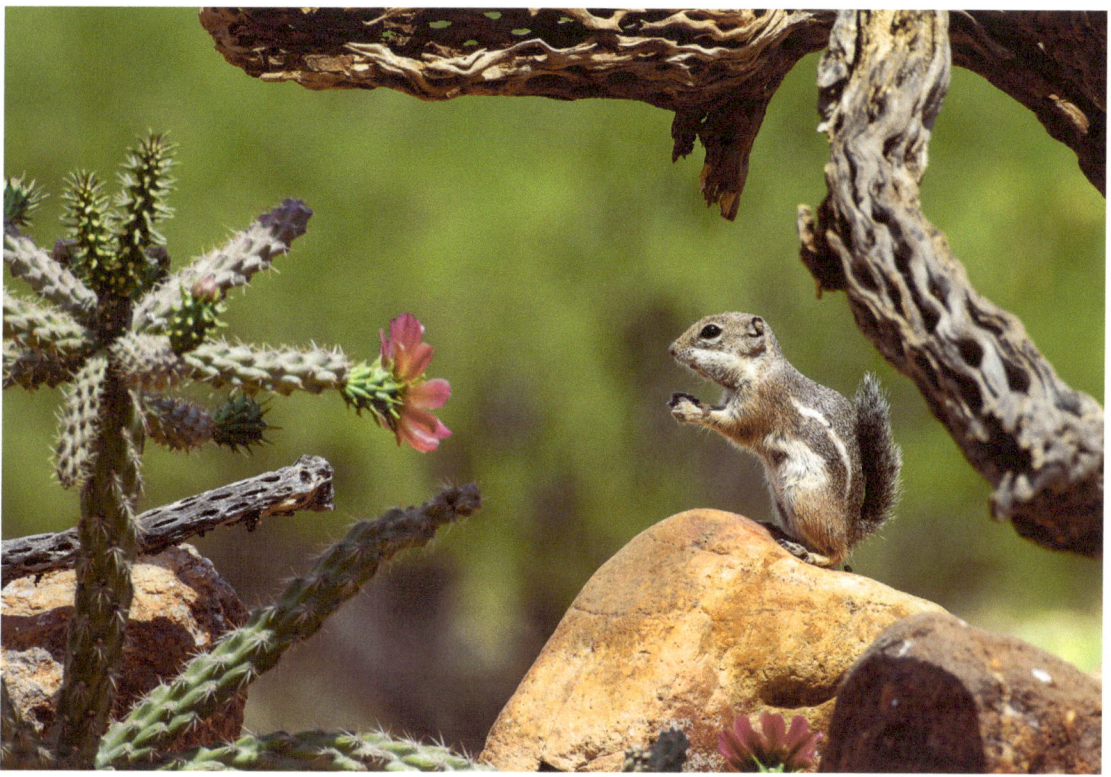

The larger mammals aren't the only ones that attract my attention. Sometimes even the smallest of creatures put on the biggest show. Take for example this particular antelope squirrel.

Eating a meal in front of a television is a very common thing for people today. Some go so far as to eat almost all their meals with a TV on. We don't think much about it, and whether or not it is good is a moot point, since the practice is here to stay.

But what if you are, say, a squirrel? What do you watch while you eat your meal?

The answer is simple: you "watch TV" with a flower. Flowers are beautiful and entertaining. They are about as pleasing as you can get in the animal kingdom. Just ask this squirrel, who is clearly enjoying a meal with flower TV. Best of all, he never has to fight over the remote control, worry about what is on, or even wonder if what is playing is worth watching. A flower is always worth watching.

Perhaps we could all learn something about squirrel TV.

Life Unbounded

From time to time I breach the boundaries of the Southwest. As much as I love the desert, oceans also hold a powerful sway over me. Their endless waters stir something deep within me and are a source of boundless fascination. These stories range from coast to coast, with some interesting points in between.

Swell Shells

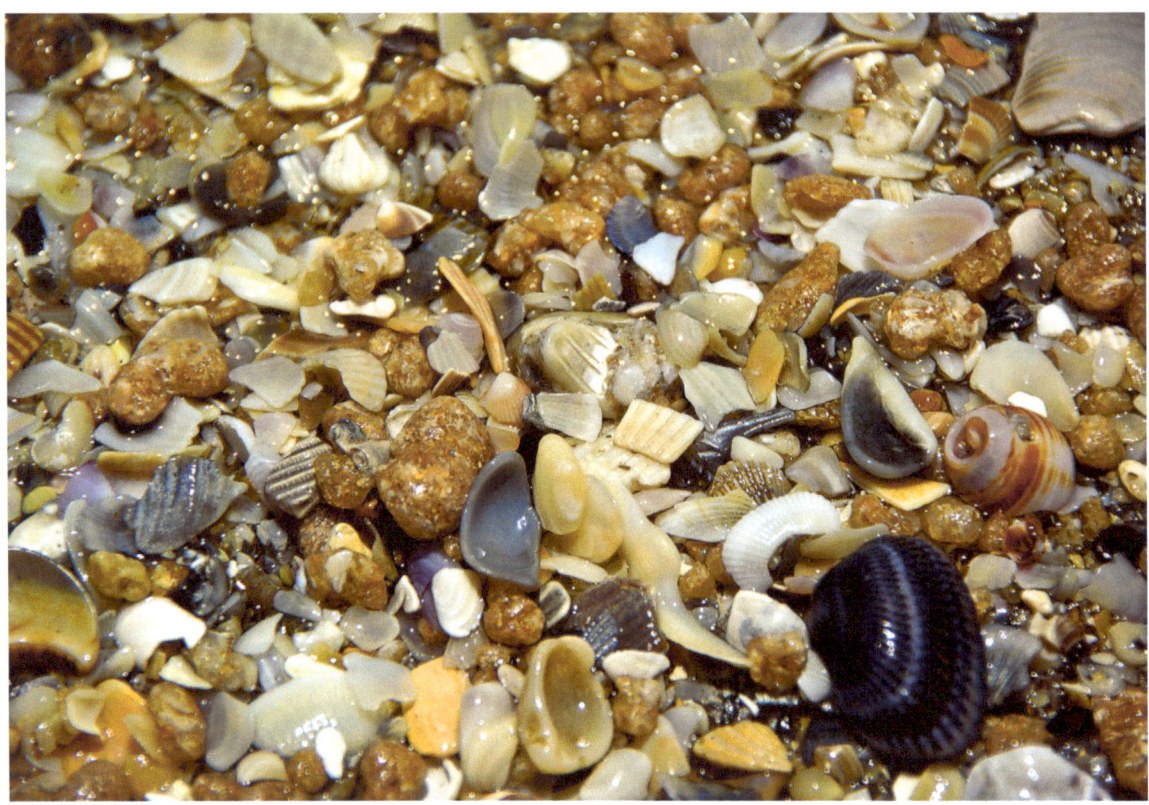

We'll begin this portion of our adventure on the far eastern coast of Florida, on Satellite Beach. While it is true that I adore the Southwest and all that it contains, I also have a strong affinity for the ocean. I make my pilgrimages to the oceans just to check in with them and make sure they are still there. They always are, which I find comforting and reassuring. The sheer enormity of the ocean is compelling. Standing there, gazing out to the horizon that stretches forever, I am reminded of all the possibilities that are yet to come. I am also reminded to keep my eyes open, and looking down at my feet I see a small, yet amazing sight there.

Satellite Beach has a diverse collection of shells that tend to accumulate right on the tide line of the shore. Jumbled up, placed there by the tides and the waves, they collect day after day, year after year.

I have always liked this photograph; I made it just as a wave was going out. The receding water revealed the collection of shells to me, each one wet and glistening in the bright Floridian sun. Although few are complete shells, that's okay, for the pieces make a comprehensive portrait as assembled by nature.

Point Sur

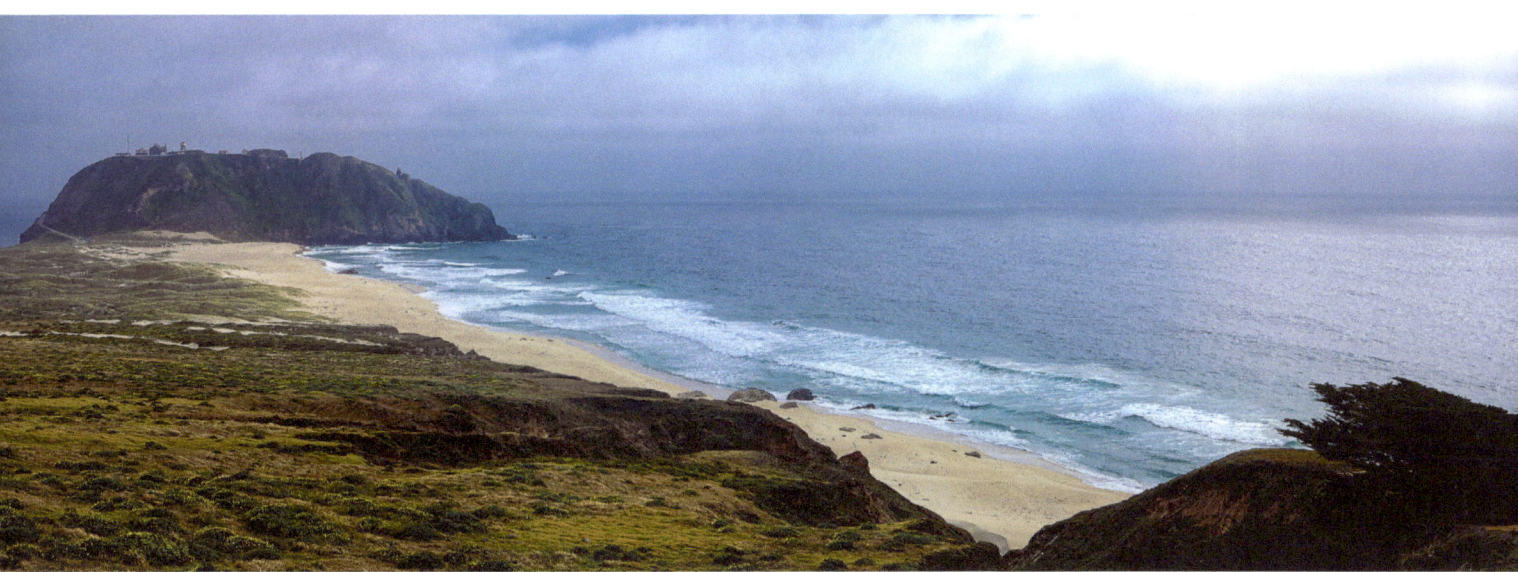

Let's head west for 2,462 miles as the crow flies to Point Sur Light Station, south of Monterey, California. Sure, it's a big jump, but since we're unbounded, we can make these kinds of leaps. The contrasts between the coasts is worth noting.

Point Sur is a working light station. Located on a small hill above the Pacific Ocean, this light station guides and warns ships away from the deceptively treacherous coastline. In the dark of a moonless night, or when the fog rolls in, mariners are beyond thankful for the warning.

This scene reinforces the power and the majesty of the ocean. The small, yet mighty, light attempts to stave off the entirety of the Pacific Ocean. Reaching out into the sea, whether the sea wants or not, it guides ships well and safely past the shoreline. Through sunny days and fierce winter gales, the light station continues its vigil, holding out hope to all who need it. Today the weather is relatively calm, although a storm is just beginning to think about brewing off the coast. Point Sur pays it no attention and will ride through it, should it dare to come this way.

The lonely, empty beach stretches away from the light station, further underscoring the solitude that the light keepers must face. Windswept trees bent backwards by a lifetime of strong winds keep those who walk its sands company. The ocean rolls on forever, and the light station keeps watch over it all.

McWay's Paradise

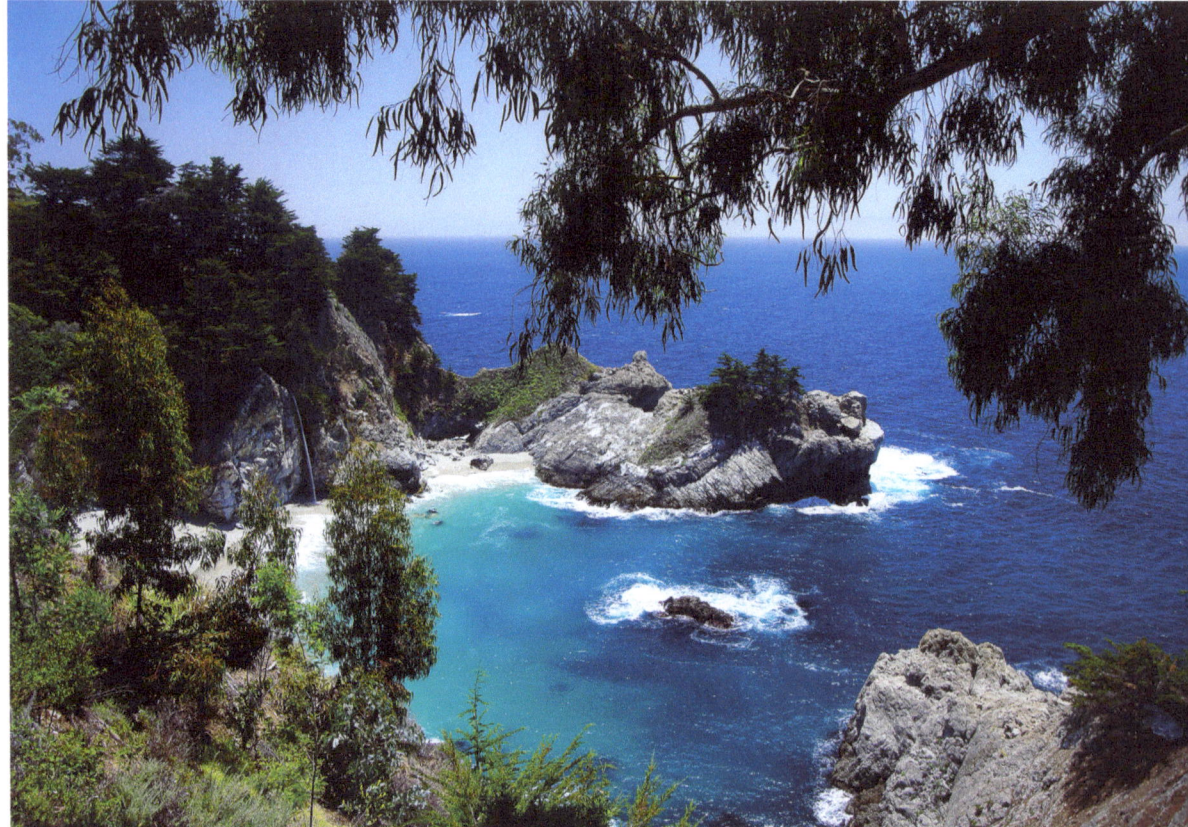

Places of extraordinary beauty are tucked into the most unexpected places, if only one knows where, and sometimes when, to look. I seek out these places and spend countless hours doing the research necessary to find them, yet I am not oblivious to the more well-known locations. McWay Falls falls, no pun intended, somewhere in the middle of blindingly obvious and maddeningly obscure.

This eighty-foot waterfall is exceptionally beautiful; McWay Creek, a small creek, flows languidly down from the surrounding mountains, headed toward the sea. Suddenly, and quite abruptly, it plunges over a cliff and onto a small and inaccessible beach. Before 1983 it plunged directly into the ocean, an even rarer occurrence, but fires and landslides created the modern-day beach below it.

In any event, looking through the portal created by an overhanging eucalyptus tree gives the effect of peering through the trees into a lost paradise beyond, and it is this idea that caught my attention. Considering that no humans actually go to this particular beach, the lost paradise idea isn't as far-fetched as it seems. The beauty of the falls, the white sandy beach, and the turquoise waters reminds us that beautiful and serene places are all around us, and finding them always brings a thrill, rush, and excitement of adventure. McWay Falls is a paradise that isn't lost, but finding it is still quite exciting.

Foggy Fishing

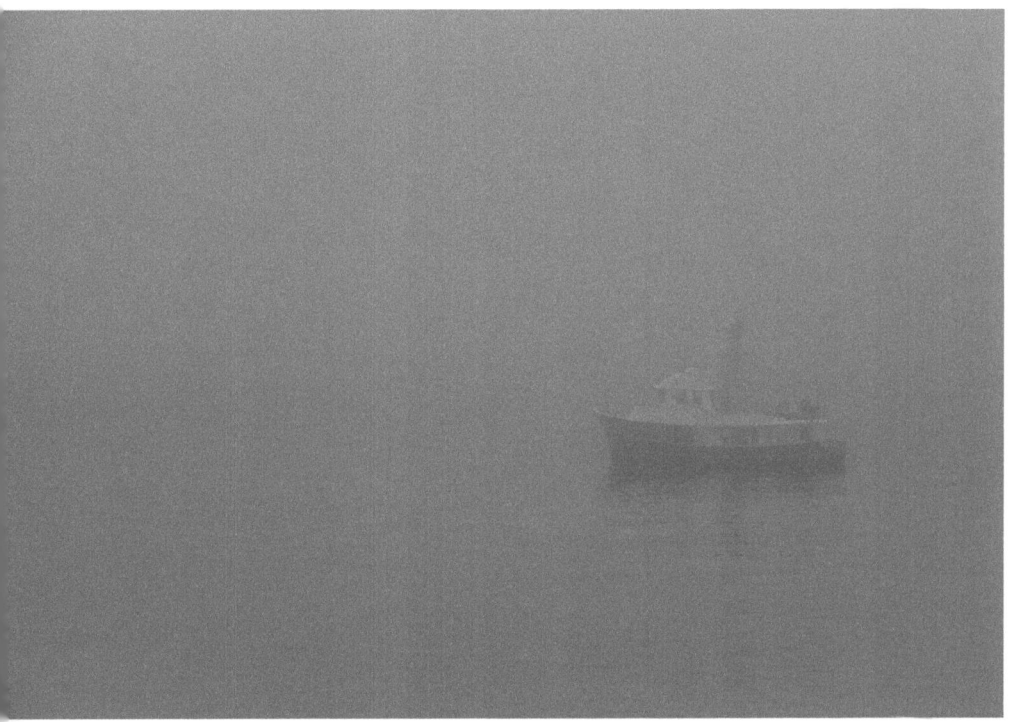

One more West Coast story, and then we're heading back east. This photograph is another one of my personal favorites. California is renowned for its fog; fog rolling in or out is interwoven deeply into a myriad of stories. The story of this particular fishing boat, just off the coastline of San Simeon, is one of those.

It was early morning, and although the sun was making its journey into the sky, it was invisible to the fisherman. The heavy blanket of fog lay over everything, obscuring the landscape, and for that matter, everything beyond a couple of feet. Just beyond the bow of the boat it was nearly impossible to tell where the water was, and the difference between air and sea was narrower than at most times. The fishermen, however, were used to these circumstances and rigged the boat for its journey.

With not even a whisper, it glided through the still waters; the fog stole whatever sounds the boat dared to make. Creeping its way forward, it kept on a heading that would take it out to sea and its fishing grounds, although anywhere out of the fog would probably be just as fine.

After a few moments the boat was swallowed by the fog, making me wonder if it was ever really there for foggy fishing, or if it was just another foggy story.

I was happy to have encountered this vignette on my travels; it was a fortuitous set of circumstances that brought the story to me in that it was foggy at the moment I made the photograph and the boat was in the right spot at the right time, at least from my viewpoint. This is another story that was written in my mind as I made the photograph; they materialized together, in this case quite literally. The mystery of the sea swallowed by the fog enchants me, and adding the barely visible vessel adds the perfect counterpoint.

As promised, let's head east again.

Glade's Mill

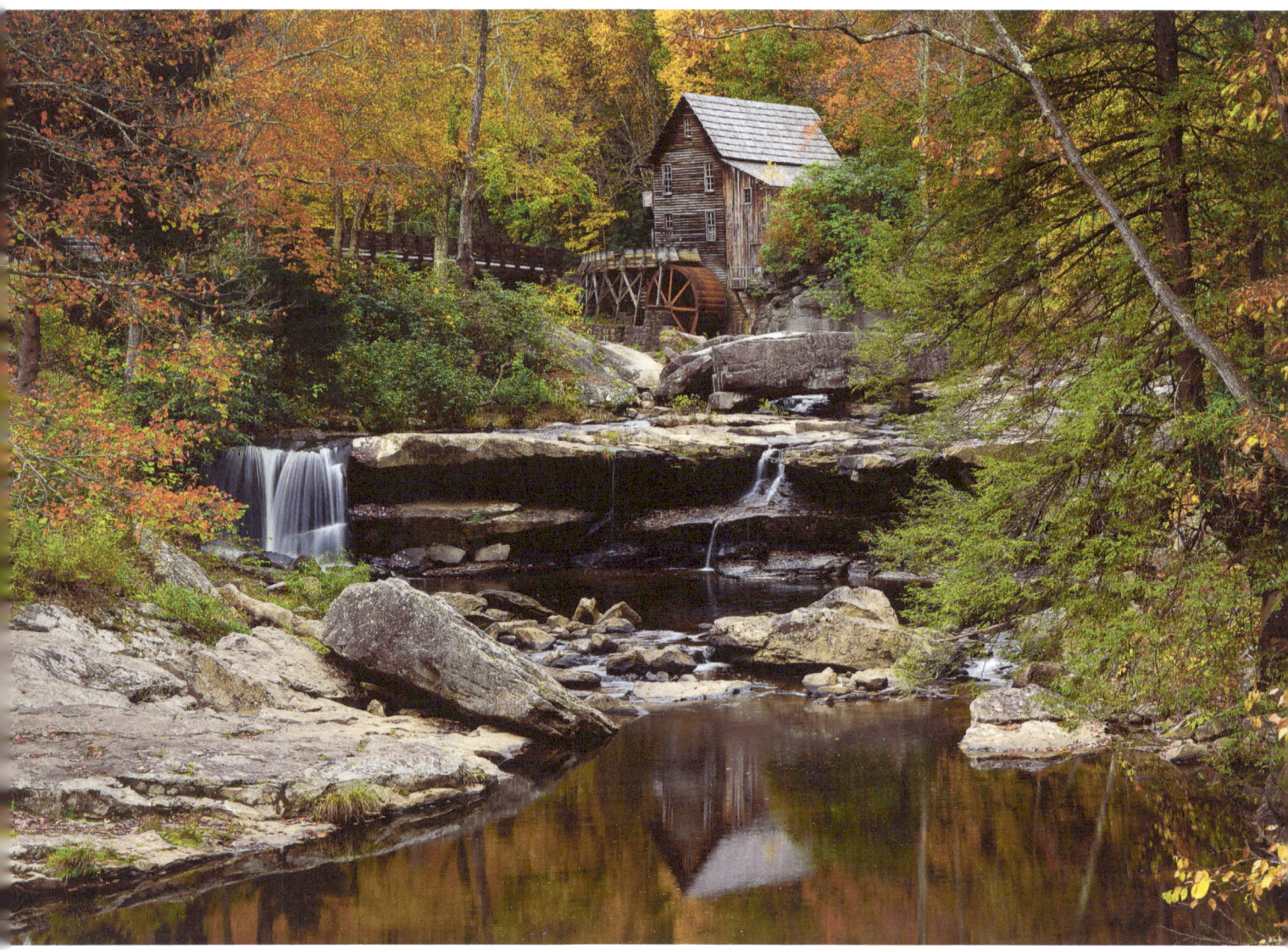

There are some locations that I have known about for a while and have yet to visit. Some of these are close by, and I am waiting for the correct timing to make my way there, but I can reach them when that happens. Others are quite a bit farther afield, making the logistics more complicated. Glade Creek Grist Mill is one of those locations. Nestled in West Virginia, it is not at all close, but despite that, I knew I needed to journey there.

One fall day I received word that the mill, and more specifically, the leaves surrounding the mill, were looking exceptionally good, and now, right now, was a good time to be there. I hurriedly packed up and took off in my vehicle for West Virginia. It was only twenty-seven hours of driving time from the house, so I figured I would be there the next day if I hurried, didn't bother to stop, and didn't sleep much along the way. The trip would be no problem, I reasoned.

Indeed, the first seventeen or so hours were not a problem at all. I made excellent time, although I had forgotten about the words "rush hour." I needed to go through several larger cities along the way, and rush hour took on a frightening aspect. I managed to dodge most of the traffic, but I was slowed down. I had also neglected to think about the words "road construction," but fear not. The various state departments of transportation had remembered for me and put plenty of signs and lane closures along my way to remind me constantly. I had also not counted on weather, as in heavy rain, along the way, which slowed me down. Still, I drove on, and despite the obstacles made excellent time. I stopped briefly for a few hours of rest partway, and then continued.

The next day, late in the afternoon, I made it to the mill. I was bone weary and tired beyond belief, but I was thrilled at the time I had made, and looked around anxiously to see if I had made it in time and if the leaf reports I was hearing were accurate. Not only did I make it in time, but I also made it right on time. Even better, the weather reports had gray skies and light rain for the next couple of days.

Normally gray skies are the bane of my existence. I can handle almost any kind of sky for my landscape photography, but flat gray skies are seldom photogenic. In this location and this time, however, the skies were exactly what I was hoping for, along with the rain. Here, at Glade Creek, the dull skies allowed me to create a very even exposure between the mill, the mill roof, and the leaves. The even exposure was critical, for it meant that all the details, and especially the shingles in the roof, were easy to see in the finished photograph, and it looked encyclopedic. Because of the light rain, which is no problem to operate in, the leaves were wet, further reflecting the evenly exposed light. It was a dream come true, and I couldn't have asked for anything more. I spent several days at this location over a variety of conditions; I had made it just a day before the leaves began to fall, so the timing all around was incredible.

As I was preparing for the actual photographs, I stood back from the mill, no camera in hand, gazing at the scene before me. You see, Glade Creek Grist Mill is one of those transcendent places that can transport you from the hustle and bustle of the modern day world to a different time entirely. As you stand there, you can feel yourself fall effortlessly back into the late 1800s, and it is quite easy to imagine that era. I fell back into that time, and the sights and sounds of yesterday sprang to life.

The clear, crisp autumn day has been a little warmer than the previous ones, a welcome, though brief, respite from the encroachment of winter. The farmer brings his wagon to a halt at the mill; his horses, having hauled a load of fresh grain from field to the mill are more than happy to oblige. The farmer greets the miller, and the old friends catch up on the local news and events, for these trips provide the opportunity for more than just milling. Eventually they tackle the task at hand, the actual milling, although while doing so they continue to catch up and talk as old friends do. Despite the hard work, many hands make it easier, and they put their backs into it willingly. The sluice is opened, the water flows over the water wheel, the milling stones grind against each other, and grain is slowly turned into much-needed flour. The farmer can already taste tonight's fresh-backed bread; so can the miller, for his payment is a portion of the flour. The flour is loaded onto the wagon, and once again the horse and farmer start the short journey back to the farm. The forest quickly swallows them up, and the mill stands silent until the next load comes its way.

Today the mill stands as testimony to a time long past, yet it provides us a with a bridge to that past and helps us remember those times and stories.

Despite how perfect and pristine the mill looks, this mill isn't the original one, and it isn't in exactly in same spot where it started. It is a combination of several mills from nearby, lovingly, carefully and accurately restored to what its original condition would have been, had it been a single mill. Part of the restoration goal was to bring it to a working state, and that goal was met. Glade Creek Grist Mill is a working mill.

Originally there was a mill just across the stream from the present location, but time eventually won over it, and it began to fade into oblivion, just as many of the mills across the country were. Progress had come, and progress did not favor the mills. One by one they were abandoned, since they had no customers. This particular one, however, was special, and every effort was made to preserve it. It was moved across the creek to its current location. Since 1976 it has stood proud once again, milling grain using nothing but the power of the small stream that flows over its wheel.

We're lucky that this restoration was accomplished for us to marvel at, and we're lucky that we have such a tangible connection to our past. The mill continues into time, bridging past and present for all to visit and admire.

Shaking myself, I returned to the present and the task at hand. With those thoughts in my mind on an absolutely perfect autumn day, *Glade's Mill* was made.

Alas, it was time to leave this mill, but my mission was more than accomplished. There is, however, another significant mill in Virginia that we will head to next.

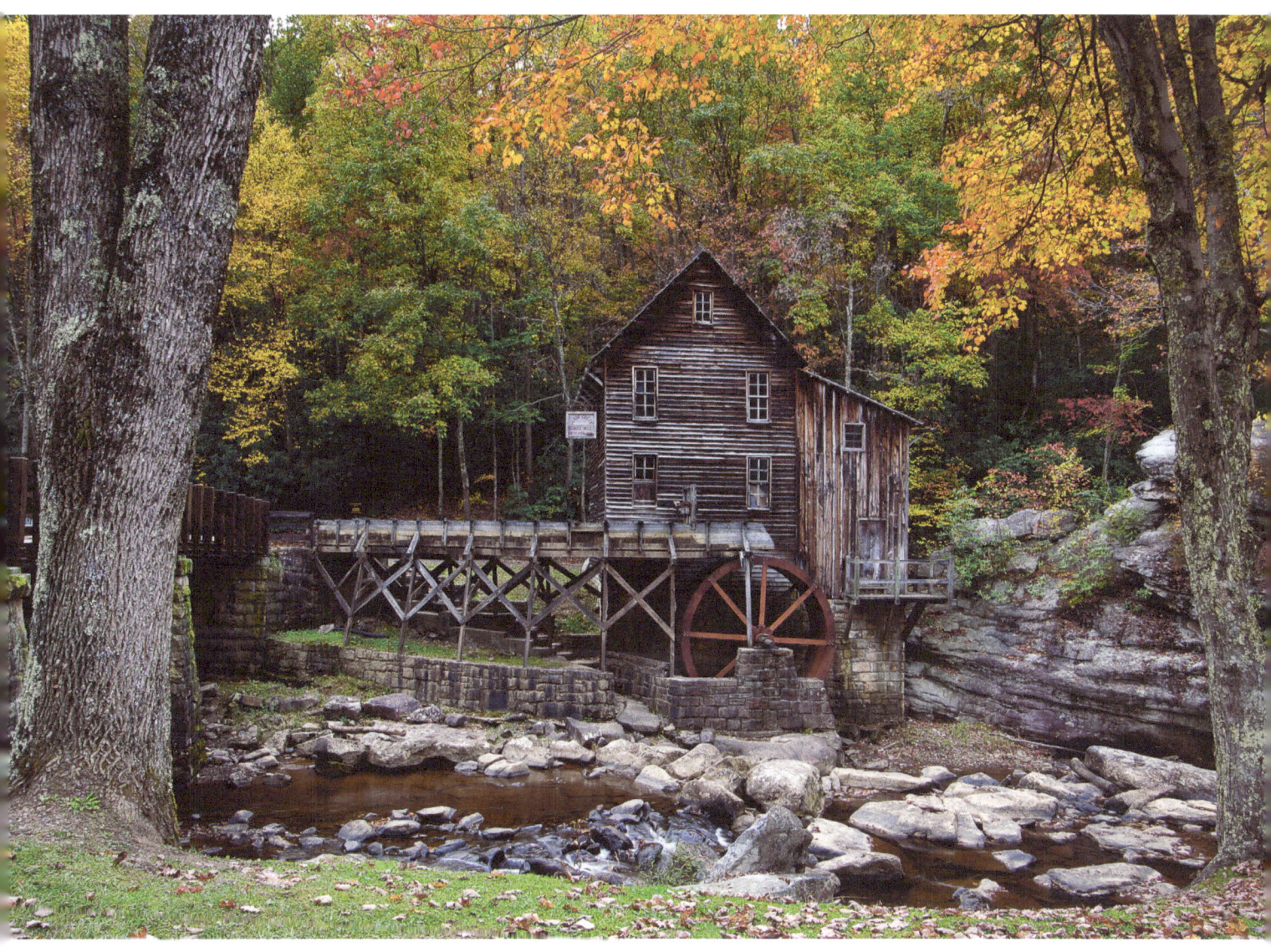

Mabry's Days

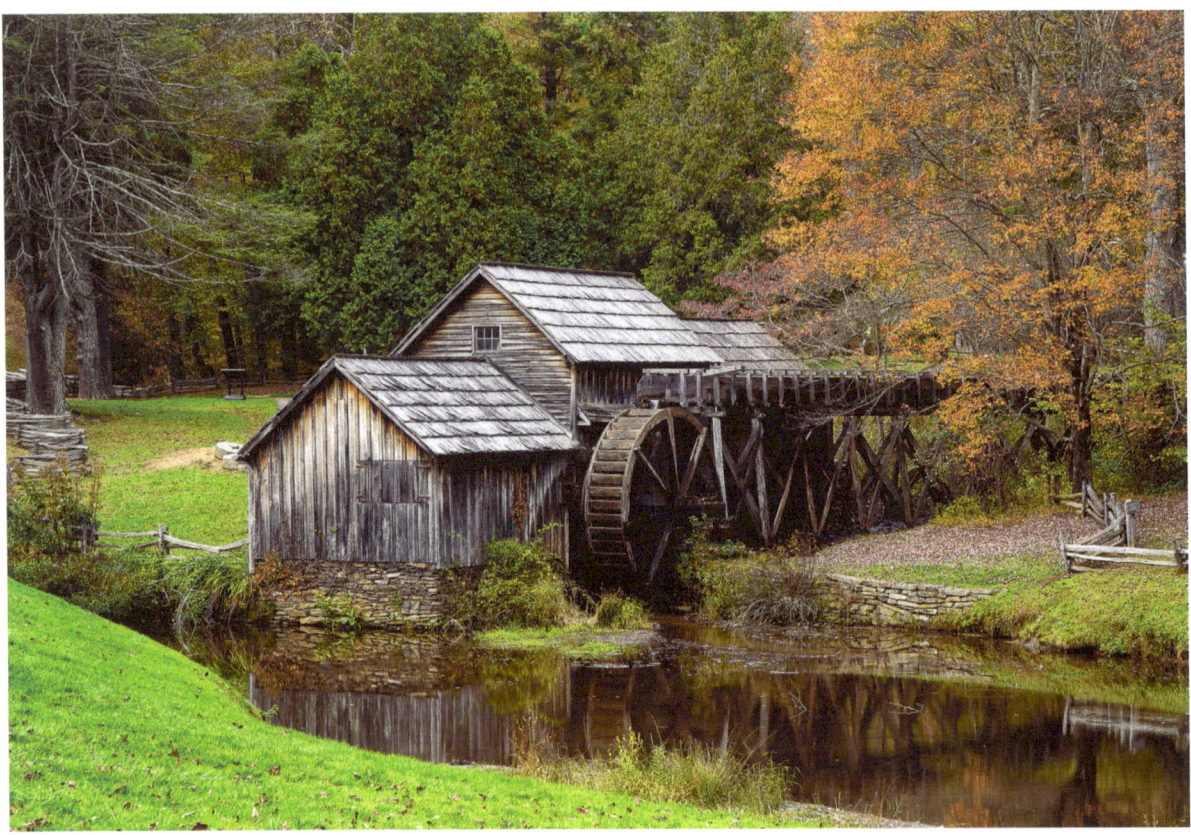

Edwin Mabry, sometime back in 1903, decided that he could best serve his community by building a mill. We don't know how or why he came to this decision, but we do know that he acted on his idea and constructed the mill he envisioned, and we do know that it took a few years to realize his dream. He did a superb job, and when the mill was fully operational, it served as a blacksmith shop, sawmill, and gristmill, all powered by a small stream he diverted for this purpose.

Mills at the turn of the century were important to the community they served, for there was always a need for a gristmill and sawmill. When they were the same structure, so much the better. Local trees were turned into planks and boards necessary to continue building, and crops were ground into flour for baking. Edwin's mill quickly became a community hub in Meadows of Dan in western Virginia.

His mill was a labor of love as much as anything else, and through his hard work and dedication, Mabry Mill served the local community well.

Mabry Remembered

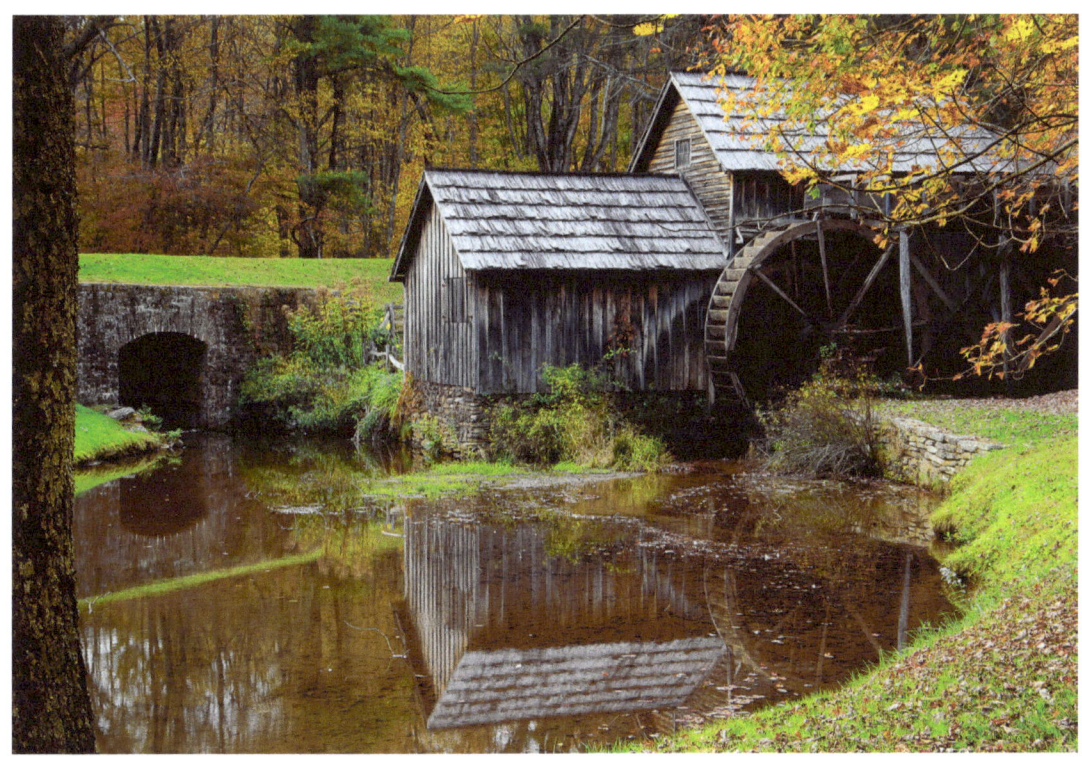

Alas the wheels of progress, as they always do, slowly but surely turned, and in so doing ground out the need for small local mills. Mabry Mill fell into disuse and was eventually abandoned. It was a shame that the mill was no longer needed, but with the advent of modern, convenient transportation and the resulting grocery stores that were turning into supermarkets, it was no longer necessary. The elements would eventually reclaim the mill, and like many others around it, it would fade to a distant memory, and after that, into nothing at all. The lifeblood of the community would fall prey to inexorable progress, yet there was nothing to be done to stop it.

In 1945, however, Mabry Mill was saved from oblivion, and the National Park Service restored the mill to its current condition. This mill was deemed significant enough to save, luckily for us. The Blue Ridge Parkway is nearby, and the mill is a worthy stop. Tourists from all over visit the mill to learn about the history of the region and the mill, ensuring that it will live on in our hearts and minds. The National Park Service continues to make routine restorations to the mill, ensuring it will stay with us.

Today we can gaze at the mill as it was more than one hundred years ago and remember Edwin, his mill, and his enduring testament to a time that was.

Falls Display

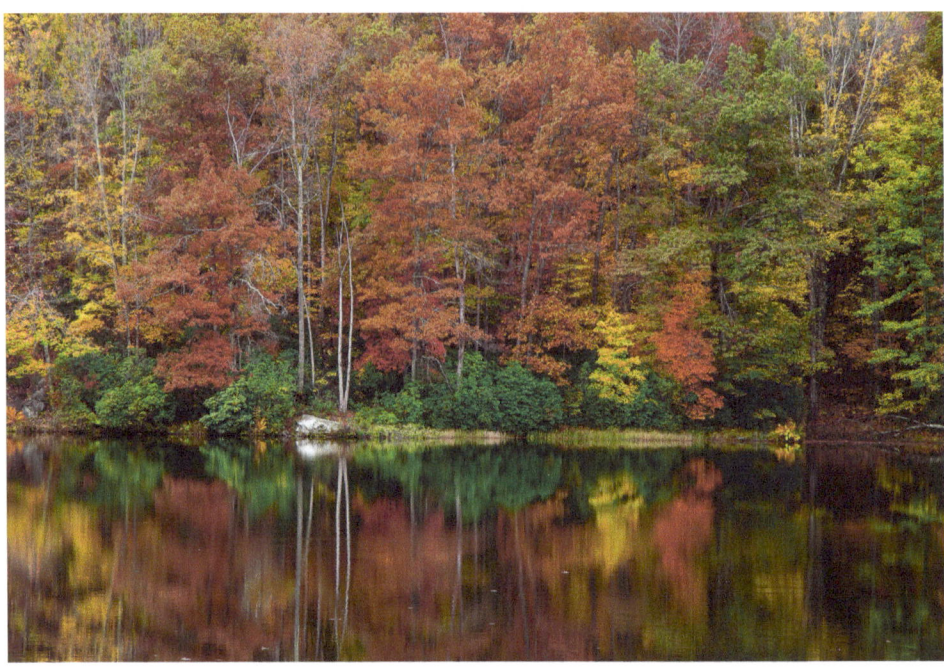

As long as we are in the area, it is worthwhile to note that the Southwest and its glorious aspens do not have the only magnificent fall display. Fall in the East is equally vibrant. When the oak, poplar, and maple trees get into the act, fall erupts with color.

The morning was cool and crisp, in exactly that cool and crisp kind of way that said fall was at its peak and winter would soon enough storm into the mornings. Still, for all that was about to come, it was a gorgeous morning. The air was still; warmth was just beginning to find its way into the day, and the sun was just beginning the daily journey into the sky. Winter would have to wait its turn.

This small lake is located in West Virginia although really, it could be about anywhere. The riot of colors from the oak, poplar, and maple trees reflecting into the warm morning hues of the lake attracted my attention immediately, and I was captivated by this scene. How could I not make a photograph of it?

I especially like the progression of fall—greener on one side than the other—and I like how it tells the story of fall's display.

The sun rose higher into the sky, delivering promised warmth. Fall could not hold on forever, though, and one by one the leaves fell. Winter would have its way in the end.

Heading Home

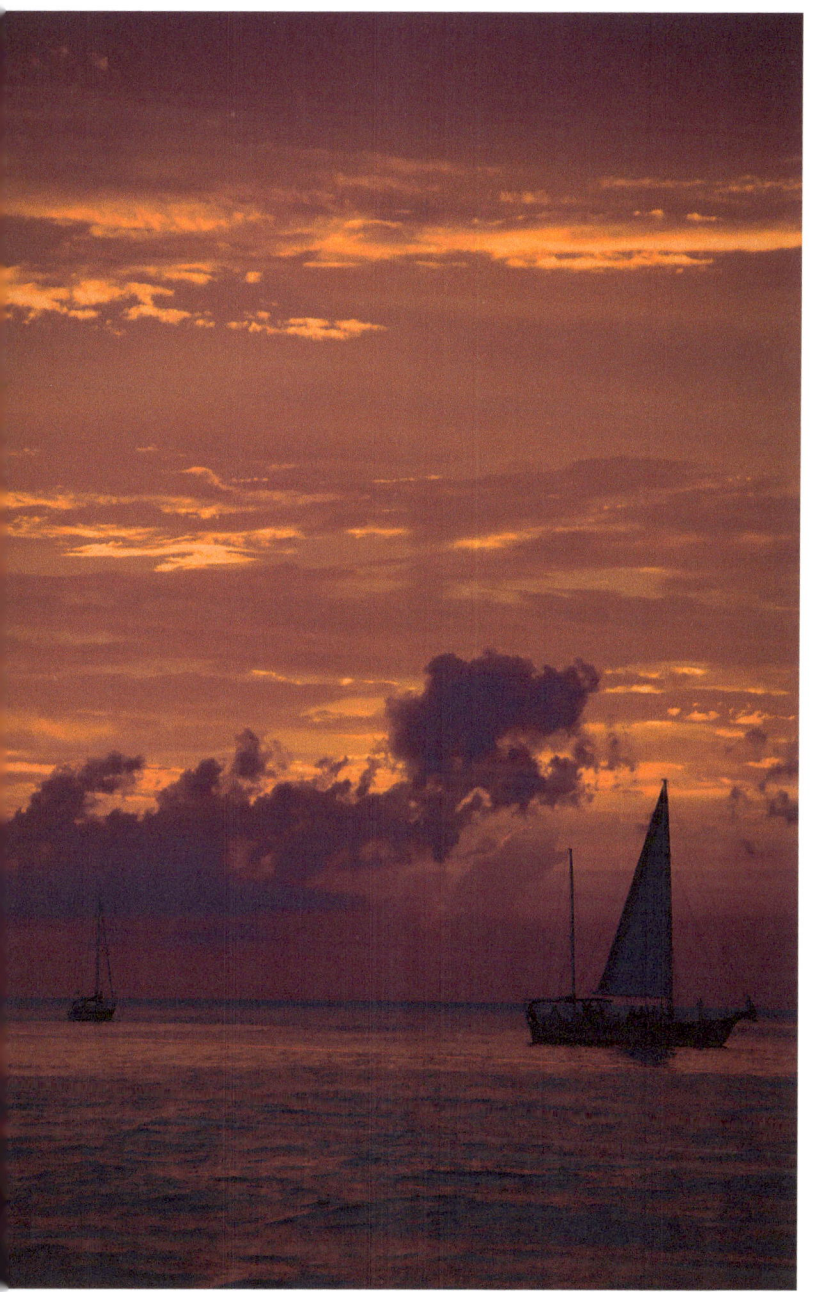

We'll leave our unbounded chapter where we began: Florida. We'll head to the southernmost tip of Florida for this story, which would be, of course, Key West. The name alone conjures up images of the carefree life of sun and surf, of halcyon days out of the office, and relaxed night life spilling into the wee hours of the morning.

In many places, day's end is just that: the end of the day. Not so in Key West, though, for there, especially around the Mallory Square area and Duval Street, the party is just getting started when the sun goes down. This fact does not mean that everyone is starting their day out, though. Far from it.

These sailors had been out on the ocean for the day, and as the sun set, their day was drawing to a close. Chasing the last rays of the sun across the open ocean waters, they were making for safe harbor, which, as it turns out, was just to the right of this photograph.

One of the great things about Key West is that some days, just as the sun dips below the horizon, the most surreal colors spring to life, if only for a moment. This image is exactly in the middle of one such moment. I loved the deep, rich tones of the sky, the sharp contrast of the clouds that had been lingering throughout the day, and the faint reflections of the sun on the water, even though the sun was below the horizon. It was a beautiful sight and one I will always treasure.

The sailors made it home safely and probably set sail again the next morning for parts unknown.

Water Power

Water, be it flowing, rushing, falling, or even standing calm and serene, creates a compelling subject and story. These photographs record some moments that transfixed me as I listened to the tales the waters whispered to me.

Zion Serenity

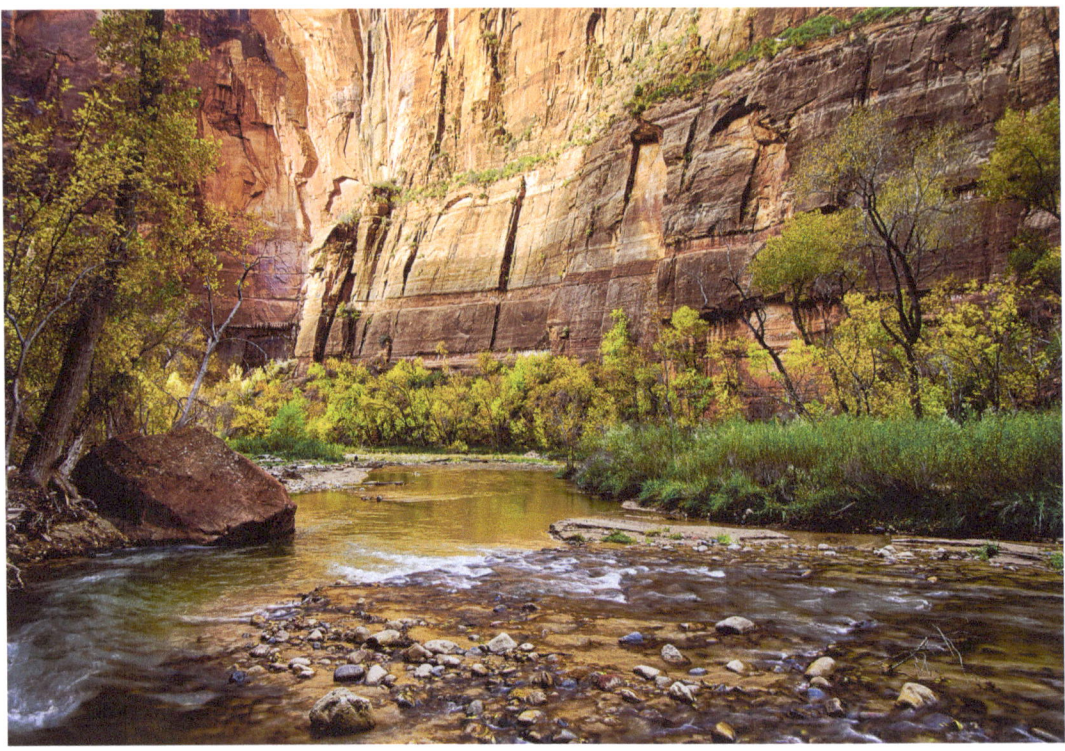

The mild November day was still and calm, a welcome change from the colder temperatures of the previous days. All too soon winter would come barreling in and steal the warmth away, making this day all that much sweeter to enjoy.

The Virgin River flowed stately and serenely through the canyon in Zion National Park, Utah, blissfully unaware of the changes that would come, or perhaps not, for the river would flow through the deep of the winter as well. The cotton-woods lining the bank were enjoying the moment, and their fall colors glowed all that much brighter in celebration of the day. As the sun rose higher into the morning sky, the canyon walls lit up with their own joy, adding even more life to an already extraordinary scene.

I stood drinking it all in, enjoying the moment. It was peaceful; the summer crowds had long since departed, and it seemed that the entire park was mine alone. For all practical purposes, it was. The stillness of the morning was broken only by a deer foraging with her baby. We looked at each other, and then they moved on in their leisurely way. The sun continued its journey into the sky, the river flowed on, and the day was, all in all, serene. Zion National Park is a favorite haunt of mine, especially when I have the park to myself. It doesn't always happen, so I cherish the moment when it does.

Rifle Falls

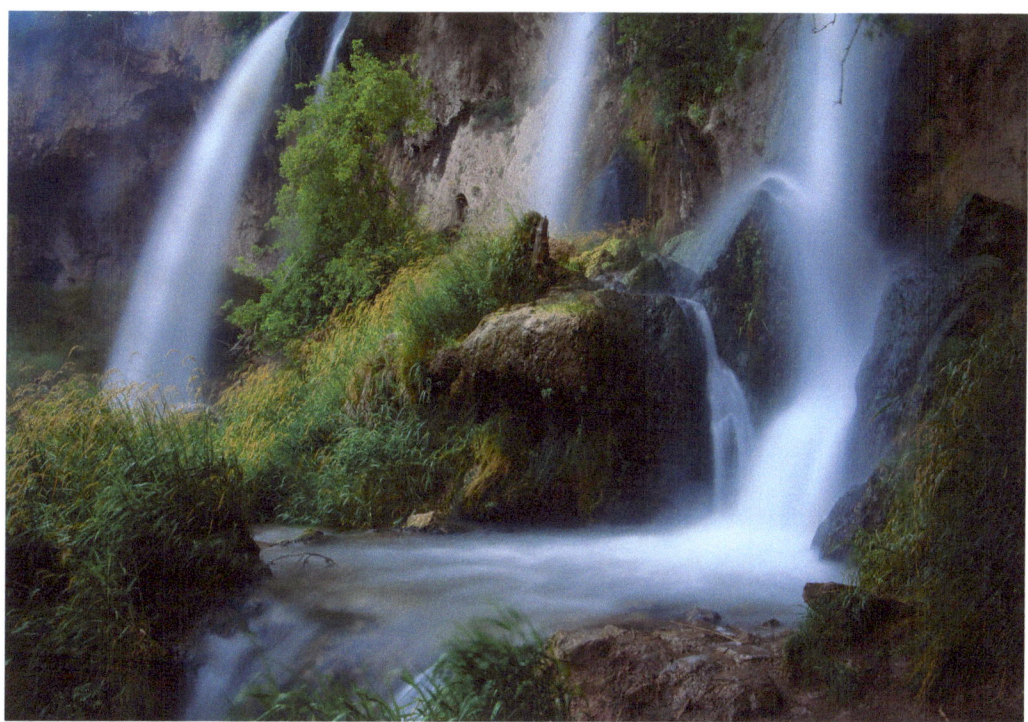

The Southwest has a few significant waterfalls, in addition to jewels such as the Virgin River. The pouring water often has a deeply hypnotic effect as it tumbles endlessly, ever moving, ever falling. Being there in the moment is much like being in a dream, for your entire attention is drawn to the falls and the constant, ever-changing spectacle of the water falling, pooling, coming back together, and continuing about its way. The falls fall on, holding you, entrancing you, and captivating you.

This triple waterfall is Rifle Falls near Rifle, Colorado, and the water source is East Rifle Creek. Although the location is unassuming, these falls are a mesmerizing spectacle. Unexpected, at least to me, is the sound of the falls. Although I have presented the scene here as a tranquil, dreamy scene, which matches how I view the falls, the falls themselves are loud. From a height of seventy feet, the water comes crashing down, and it is hard to hear yourself think. The roar makes it perfect, though, for as you gaze at the falls and are drawn into them, thinking about anything else just doesn't seem important.

There is something magnificent about this scene. The power of the falls giving way to a tropical-feeling environment below and then fading away into the creek again gives me a sense of wonder as well as a never-ending sense of peace. The water flows endlessly into endless tranquility.

Ice Lake

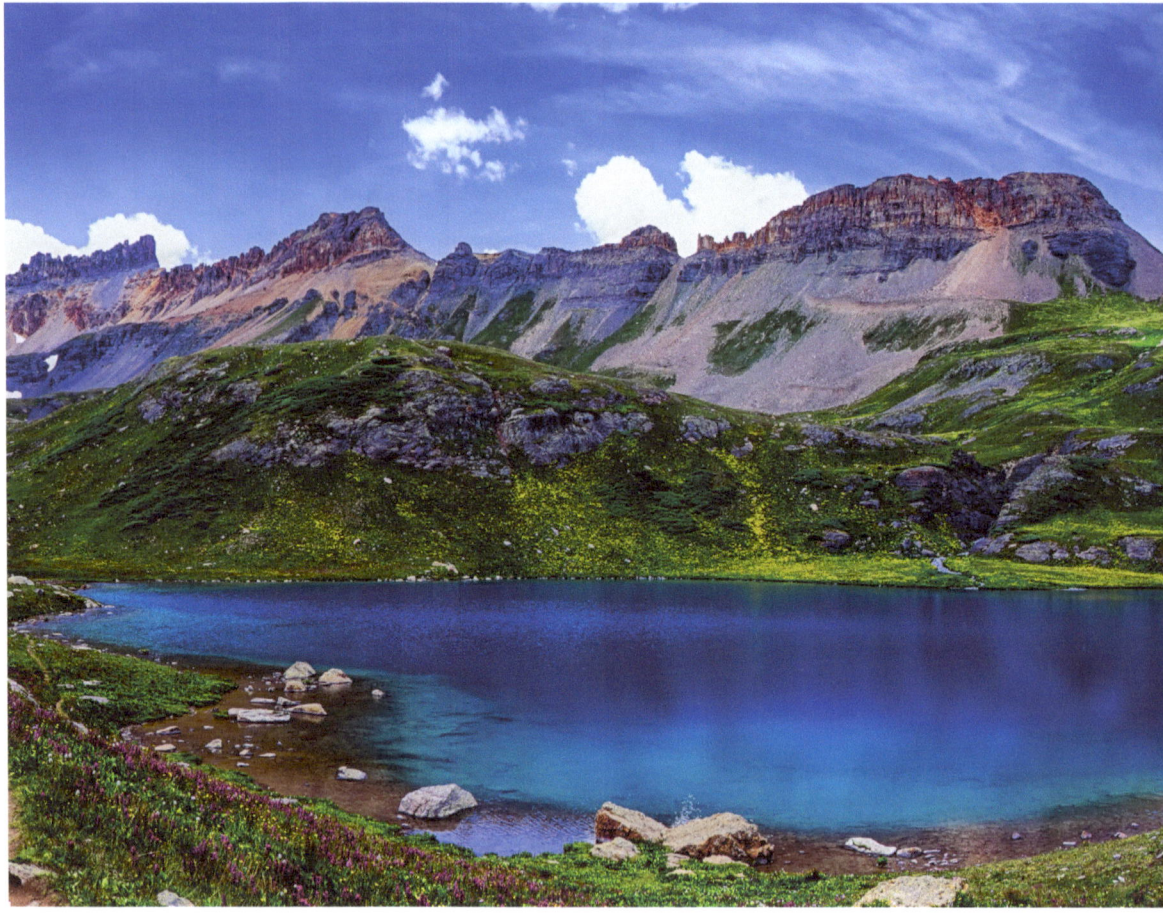

The Southwest is well known for its deserts, and in the case of Colorado, its mountains. There is water here, and some rivers, such as the Colorado, are powerful, able to carve out canyons such as the Grand Canyon. Other bodies of water, such as Lake Powell, are destinations in themselves. Small pockets of water, however, possess extraordinary qualities that take your breath away. Ice Lake is one of these.

Ice Lake isn't exactly unknown, but neither is it extremely popular. Nestled in a shoulder high in the San Juan Mountains, it is one of the few blue lakes. Blue lakes are exactly what the name implies: blue. Not your everyday, ordinary lake that is your everyday, ordinary blue, but a blue unlike any other blue. As are most glacial tarns, Ice Lake is compact, but what it lacks in size it more than makes up for in raw beauty.

The hike to Ice Lake is three miles, all of it straight up. There is a three thousand foot elevation gain over these three miles, which is quite a grade. Snaking through woods and then over rocky scree and then up the sides of mountains, the hike is challenging, yet rewarding. As you near the top, for what the elevation of twelve thousand feet doesn't take out of you, the grade and distance will, you wonder if the trail ever has an end. Just as think you are hopelessly lost and attempting to hike forever upwards, you crest a small rise and there, before you, is Ice Lake.

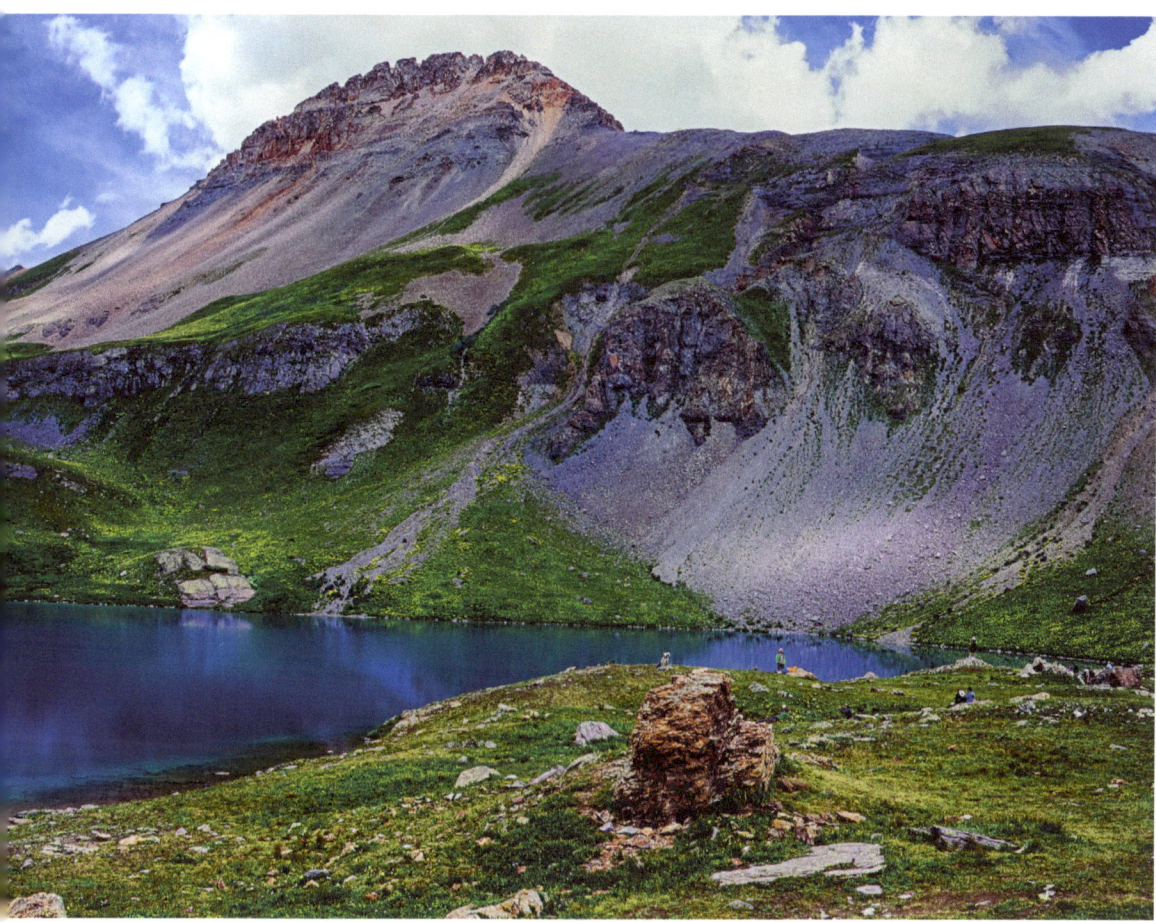

I watched a few other hikers after me top that rise, and each one did exactly the same thing: we stopped in our tracks and tried to comprehend the beauty before us. What little breath we had was ripped away.

This view of Ice Lake is the one that I treasure the most and is one of my first views of this gem. Tucked among the verdant hills of a wet Colorado summer was the small tarn glowing almost a mystical shade of, well, something. The color defies description, and the color changes subtly as the sun shifts. The wildflowers lining the bank in neat rows completed the tableau, and the result is this moment frozen in time. A few hikers were lounging on the shoreline, but the silence was absolute. No human word could ever top the sight before us.

What makes up the hue of the water? The color comes from the water itself, which contains a high concentration of glacial flours created from glaciers grinding down the bedrock into a fine powder. This flour is suspended in the water column, giving the lake a cerulean color.

What an outstanding place!

Brush Creek

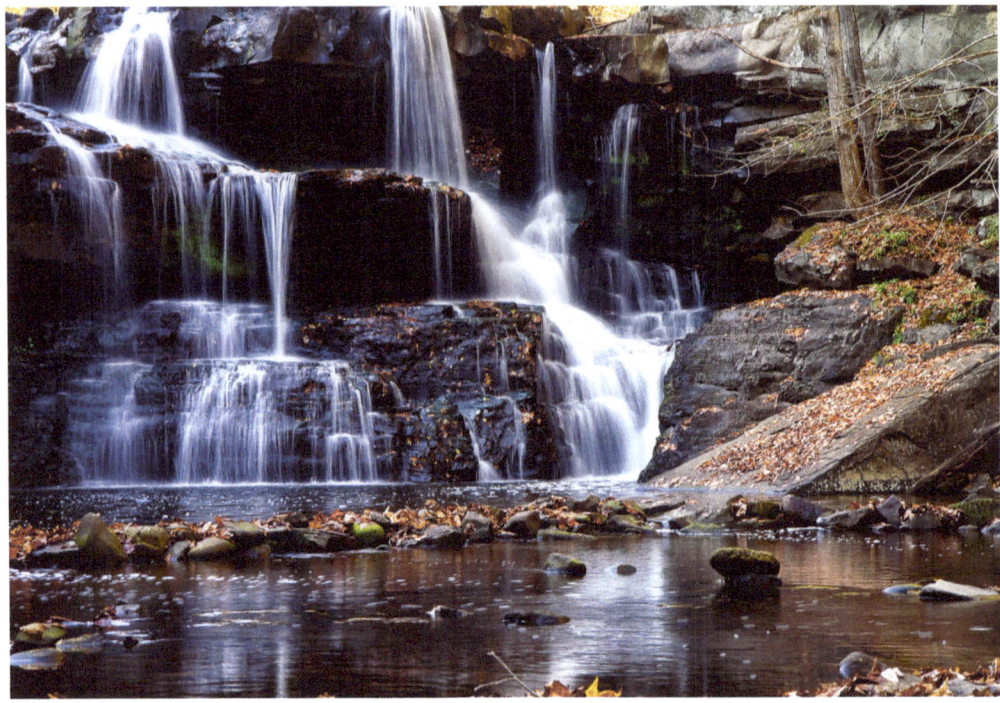

Small things, given the right circumstances, can become great things. We'll briefly head back to West Virginia for a waterfall and autumn scene that I find relaxing and tranquil, to explore the concept of small waterfalls that look stunning.

Applied to photography, even the smallest, unassuming creeks can become powerful images, provided one knows where to look. Take for example Brush Creek, which flows in southwestern West Virginia. This small creek meanders peacefully enough through forests. It isn't the largest creek by a long shot, and the moniker "river" isn't even in the equation. The creek is as unpretentious as they get and is largely unassuming. In most places you can walk easily through the creek and in several right over it without breaking your stride. The creek is gentle, quiet, and peaceful, a perfectly well-behaved creek.

That is, until it comes to one section. Here the ground abruptly falls away, leaving the creek no choice but to cascade over the fissure, creating a waterfall. Instead of simply pouring over the drop off, the creek decided, instead, to show off for everyone, creating a beautiful streaming cascade that is beyond stunning. Add the taste of fall into the mix, and this powerful scene is created.

Small things can indeed become extraordinary.

Quiet Creek

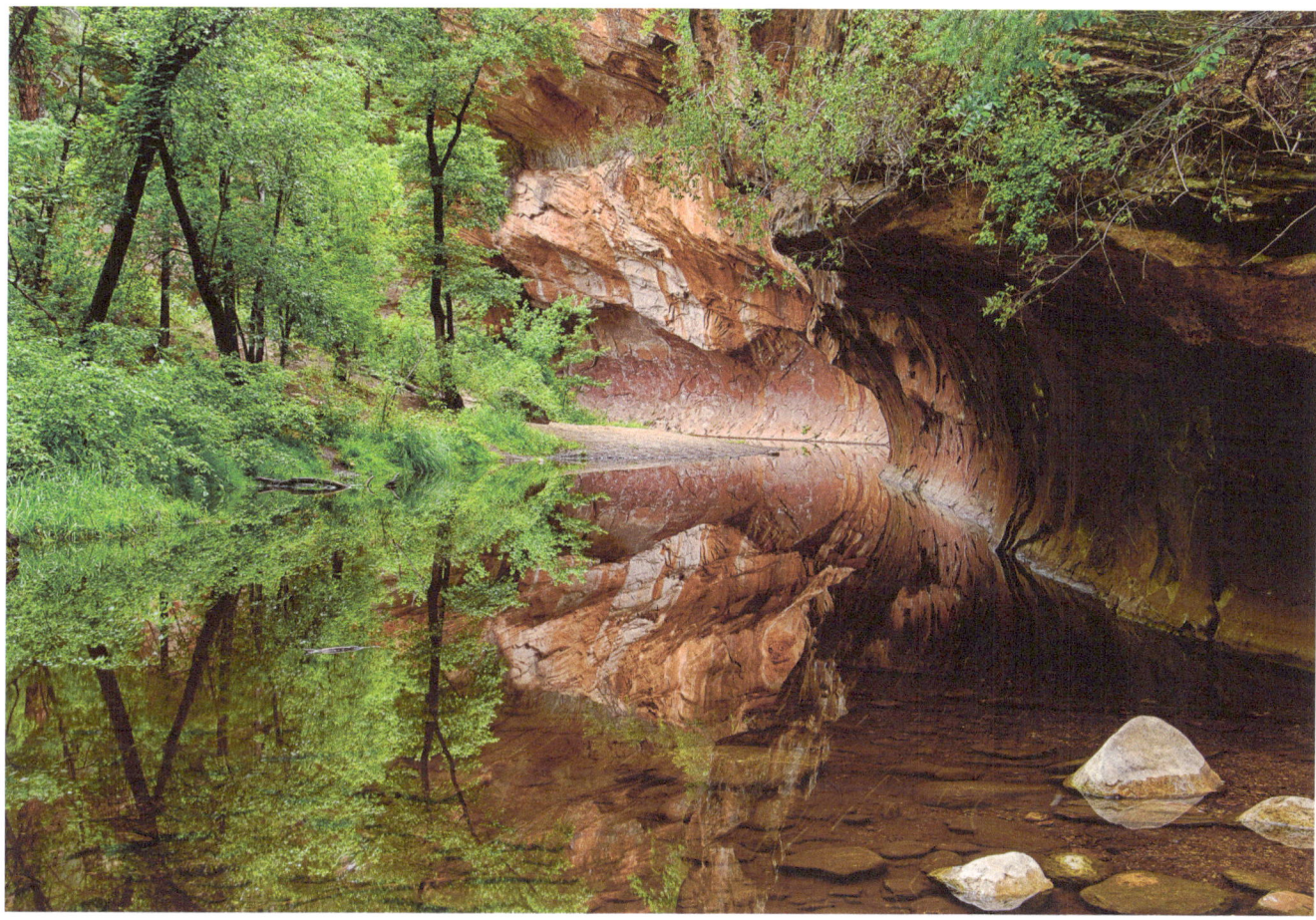

We'll end this section on water with quiet serenity. What better setting for this than Oak Creek, which we visited earlier on our journey?

Oak Creek is fantastic in the fall, yet it handles the different seasons equally well. I adore the summer months there, for everything is full, lush, and green. In the afternoon, the creek flows gently and serenely, and in many places it flows so slowly the surface becomes a perfect mirror.

Best of all, it is summer, in a warm setting, and I was completely warm and comfortable while making this photograph. What more could anyone ask?

Monumental Stories

Special places draw you back time and time again. Monument Valley, for me, is one of those places, and every time I visit it, I find a new treasure, each more incredible than the last. Our journey, for now, comes to an end with these monumental stories.

Hunt's Panorama

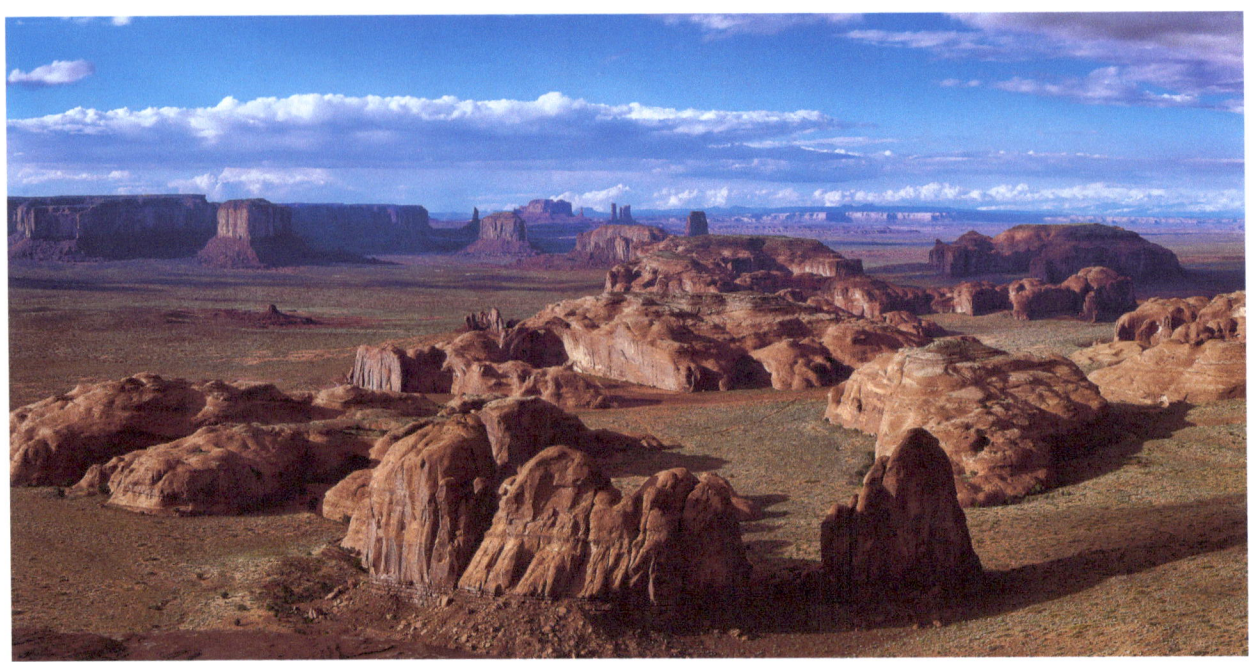

All photographers have a list of locations that they want to get to; these places haunt them, lure them, beckon them and drive them ever onward. Hunt's Mesa in Monument Valley was on my list for the longest of times. If you've talked with me, you know I would bring up Hunt's Mesa in every conversation, or at least it seemed so. It has always had an allure and appeal to me that I simply could not let go of. Finally time and circumstances came together and came together in a very big way.

Hunt's Mesa is a high mesa at one end of the valley. What makes it extraordinary is the fact that it is close to the valley, so you can see the monuments, and higher than the valley, so you are overlooking the monuments. The mesa is situated such that you can see all the monuments at once, too. In short it is the absolutely ideal location, provided that the weather is right. Complicating the planning and logistics is that fact that you must have a Navajo guide if you want to go there. Making matters even more interesting is that the way up is not easy, and only a few guides can make the long and torturous journey there. Although there is a road there, the term road is overly generous and not at all descriptive.

The day I headed up to the mesa started out with exceptionally dynamic weather, which was a very good sign. It was sunny, then raining, then sunny again, then cloudy, then sunny again, after which the cycle started all over again. The last thing I wanted when making this trip was clear sunny skies, which in the Southwest is a very real, and very frightening possibility. Today had definite potential.

As the departure time loomed, the rain came into the valley. This weather was good, because rain seldom stays long and there was an excellent chance it would clear out by the time I was up on the mesa, making conditions ideal for photography. The same rain that makes beautiful photographs, however, also makes the journey up exponentially more difficult, if not outright impossible. My success was all up to the guide, who, it turned out, didn't care a bit that it was raining, and raining hard. Off we went to the mesa. I was thrilled that I would finally be able to reach Hunt's Mesa.

I knew to expect an interesting trip on the way up there, for I knew the way was notoriously difficult. What I wasn't prepared for was the utter reality of the journey. We went down a dirt road, which had become mud, the vehicle sliding this way and that. The guide was an excellent driver, however, and he drove on like the mud wasn't even there. Had it been me, I would have stopped and turned back at that point, it being the sensible thing to do. What I didn't know was that the dangerous and slick mud was the easiest part of the adventure. Onward we went.

After a while the dirt road turned into a two-track, which is essentially just two ruts that go somewhere. They were wet and worse than the road. The guide didn't seem to realize this condition and continued forward as we slid this way and that. He expertly drove through this portion, sometimes weaving, sometime plowing through standing water. While I was gripping the seat, he was chatting as if it were a warm, spring day and he was driving on a four-lane divided highway. I pointed out that it was wet, slippery, and muddy; the comment seemed to catch him off guard. This driver was *good*.

Before I knew it, he drove right off the edge of a embankment and into a wash. Making it even more exciting was the fact the wash had flowing water, which as we've learned is best to avoid at all costs. I am not sure he noticed it had water in it at all, let alone that it was running. He continued onward faintly acknowledging that the vehicle was in a dangerous situation.

Up the other side and onward we progressed. The rest of the three-hour adventure to the mesa was even more exciting and was a meandering, hair-rising, white-knuckle, vehicle-breaking journey through more washes running with swift water, deep sand, sliprock, inclines that I would be afraid to walk up, cliffs, oil-pan-shearing boulders, blind corners, leaps of faith, and sheer insanity. It is a wonder that anyone can possibly navigate through the maze to the top, and even at that, I think the driver made it all up as he decided to see what obstacle would be the one to finally do in the vehicle he was driving. Several times he stopped, and there was no possibility whatsoever that there was a plausible way forward. He would then go straight up, sideways, or take the vehicle beyond forty-five degrees. It was an extraordinary feat of driving. When I commented on the drive, he modestly said that it was easy, and I should see it when it is hard. This driver was, indeed, *great*.

In the end we arrived on top of Hunt's Mesa, right after the storm cleared, and the late afternoon sun was once again out and shining strong. As soon as I saw that sight, I forgot about that drive, almost, and made *Hunt's Panorama*. The years and planning, plotting, and scheming were well worth the effort. But I was in for another, even more extraordinary treat.

Monumental Morning

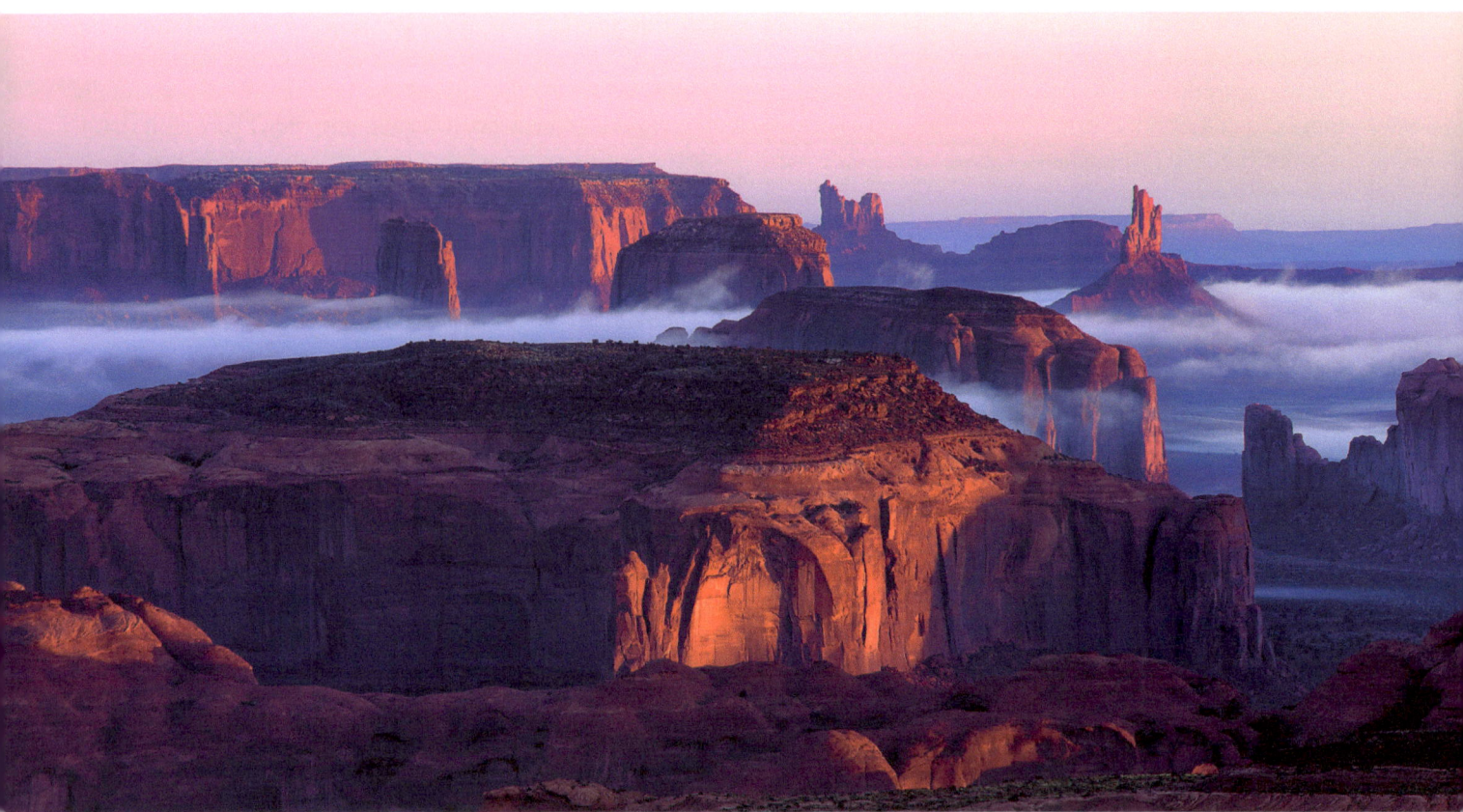

The usual Hunt's Mesa expedition is to drive up for sunset, spend the night, and photograph the subsequent sunrise. This trip was no exception. After all, since you're there, you might as well take full advantage of the situation. I was not overly optimistic about the sunrise, however, since the forecast called for clear skies. Even before I turned in for the night I could see that the skies were clear as could be, and the sunrise, while it would be gorgeous, would not be quite the photograph I was hoping for.

I arose the next morning bright and early, well before the sun. Naturally the first thing I did was look up at the sky, hoping there would be some clouds. No luck. Clear as a bell, still, and the conditions were not favorable. Still, you don't ever give up, so I packed up my gear and headed to the edge of the mesa to see what might happen. After a short hike, I reached the point I had decided was the best view and looked out over the valley.

Much to my surprise I saw a layer of fog, absolutely unprecedented and unexpected. The storms that came through the

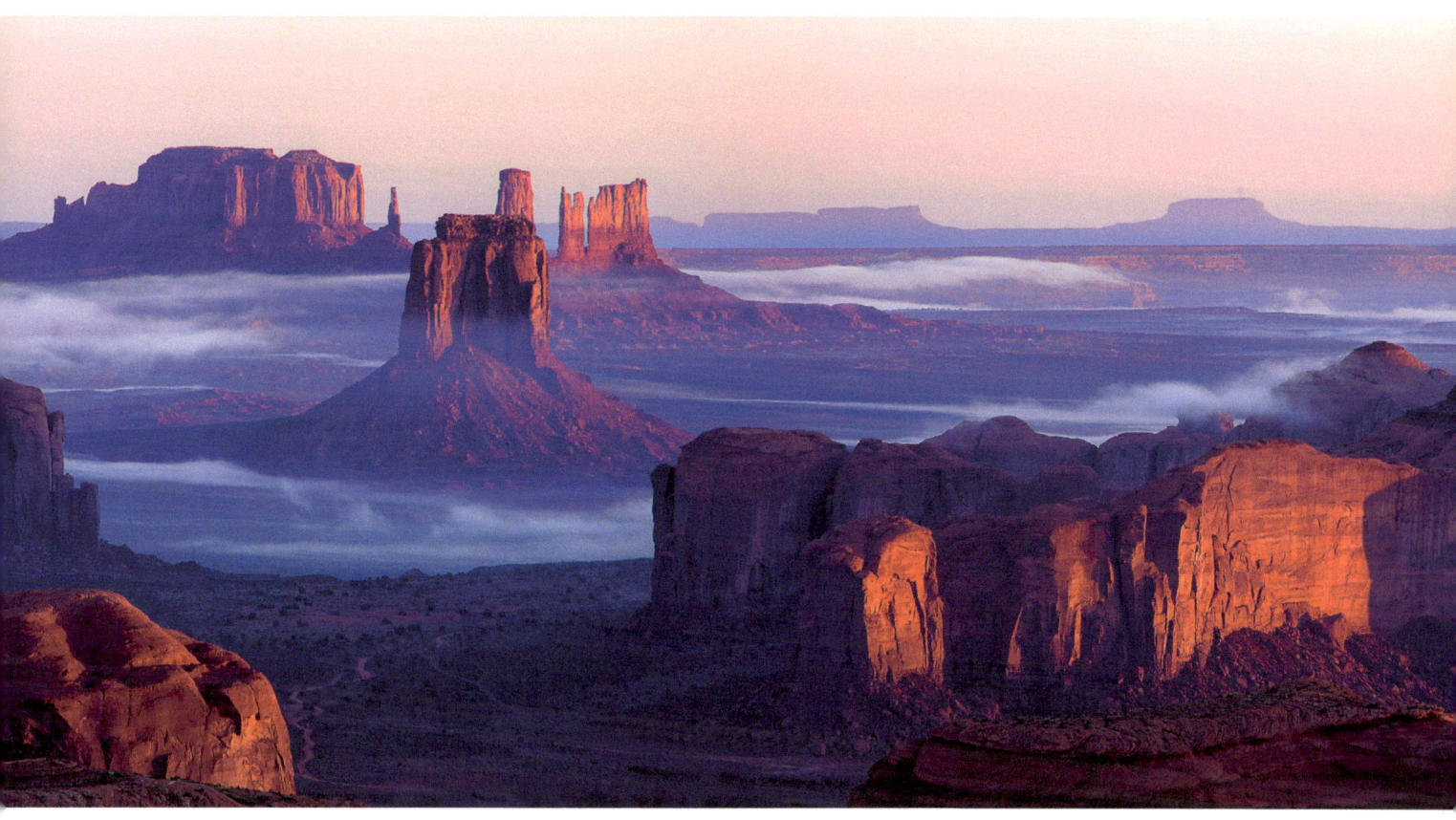

day before had dumped quite a lot of water in the valley; in addition, the humidity seemed close to 500 percent, maybe a little bit higher. If there was a surface to be found, it was soaking wet. Conditions like this do not come along every day. As sunrise approached, the fog in the valley increased and billowed out. The closer the sun came to breaking the horizon, the more outstanding the scene far below became. To add the icing on the cake, just before the sun rose, a thin band of pink appeared on the horizon, as it often does in the desert. The pink band doesn't last long, a few moments at best, but it was just enough. The pink persisted as the sun broke the horizon, perfectly lighting the buttes as they did their best to stay above the fog. The result is *Monumental Morning*. To be above the valley on one of the exceptionally rare days of heavy fog in the valley, to have the pink band, and to have all the prerequisite conditions come together is what photographers dream of and what makes all our travails worthwhile.

Valley Spirit

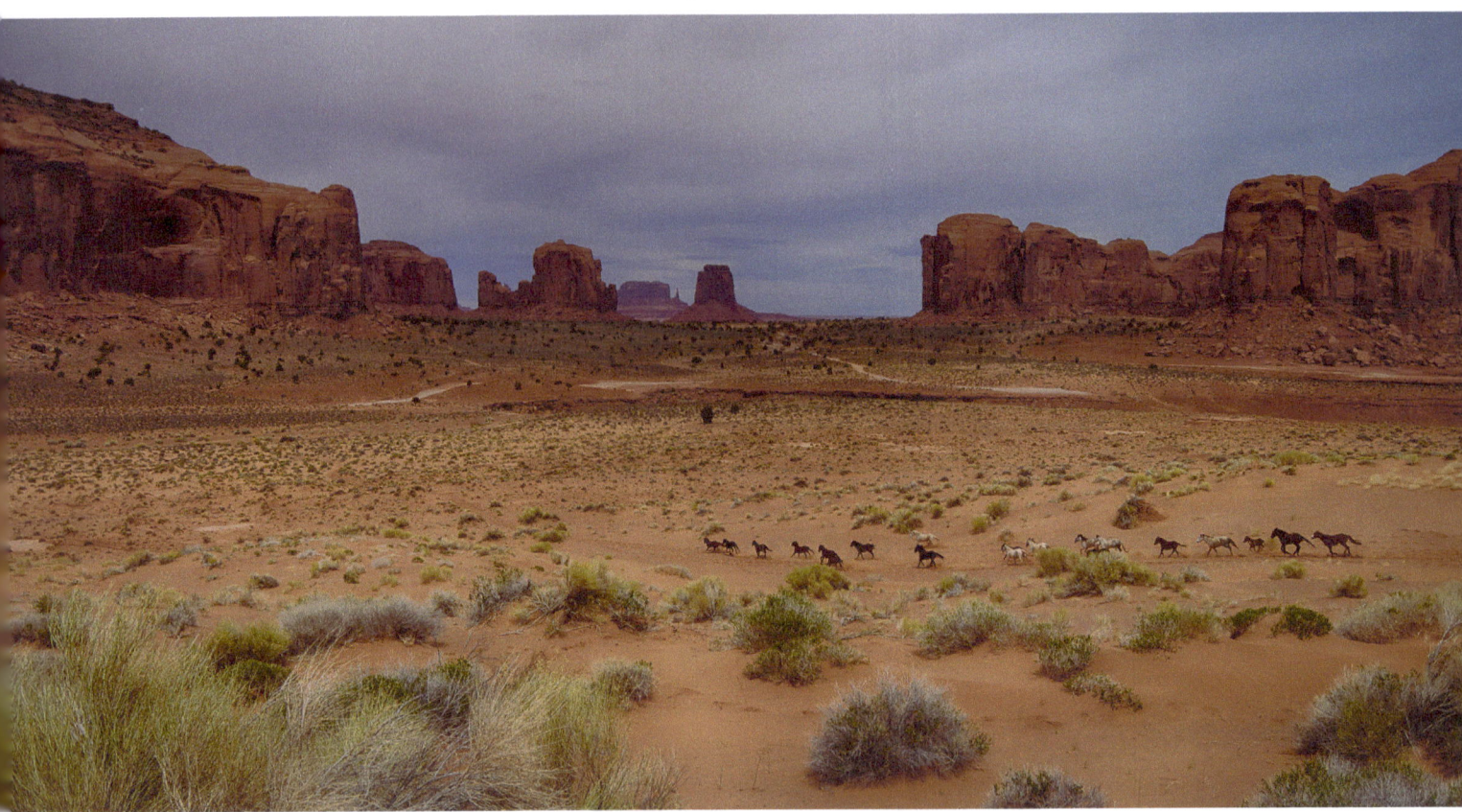

Since we're in Monument Valley for this chapter, it is only fitting that I include another one of my all-time favorites from here: *Valley Spirit*.

Again, this set conditions came together for me, a set of conditions for which I am eternally grateful. It is not every day that one has horses running through the valley against a moody backdrop of cloudy skies, and the result is, well, better than I could have ever hoped. The horses running across the open field, surrounded by tall monuments and mesas, represent the true spirit of the Wild West, and its power, beauty, and glory shines through.

Starry Mittens

Every time—and I mean every single time—I see a sunset give way to the night sky beyond, I silently give thanks for being able to witness another magnificent spectacle, for every single time it is a truly inspiring sight. Granted, some sunsets are "better" than others, but they are all wonderful in their own right. It is fitting, then, that we end with a story of the night's beginning, and for that, we'll stay where we began our day: Monument Valley.

Monument Valley has come to represent the quintessential southwestern landscape, and it has been the location for countless western movies. If you are a director and your movie or film is set in the Southwest, odds are pretty good you'll think about coming to Monument Valley. Its sunrises and sunsets are unparalleled as well, making the entire valley, any time of the day, a landscape photographer's dream.

The dream continues into the night, too. Those same towering monuments that make the perfect accompaniment to a daytime photograph also make for an compelling nighttime one as well. In nearly perfect dark skies, stars come out to play over the valley.

This photograph was made shortly after sunset; the afterglow is still in the air, and the valley itself is still settling into its nighttime role. The stars come out quickly, since there are no major cities nearby to spread light pollution here. Only the small town of Mexican Hat, in the far distance, provides any artificial light.

Starry Mittens is my tribute to that evening moment and an excellent ending to our adventure.

Photograph Locations

Cover

Yellowstone Cloudscape Yellowstone National Park, Wyoming

Introduction

Butte's Fog Monument Valley, Navajo Nation

Ready, Waiting Grand Canyon National Park, Arizona

White Tracks White Sands National Monument, New Mexico

Evening Elk Yellowstone National Park, Wyoming

Desert Southwest

Mitten's Sun Monument Valley, Navajo Nation

Mystery Saucers Mystery Valley, Navajo Nation

HooDoo Sunrise Bryce Canyon National Park, Utah

Mesa Sun Canyonlands National Park, Utah

Valley Monuments Valley of the Gods, Utah

TearDrop's Arch near Monument Valley, Navajo Nation

Antelope's Window Antelope Canyon, Navajo Nation

Alstom Panorama Grand Staircase-Escalante National Monument, Utah

Malpais Palisade El Malpais National Park, New Mexico

Tree Magic

Tree Magic near Aspen, Colorado

Ironton's Fire Ironton, Colorado

Forgotten Ironton Ironton, Colorado

Ironton's Canopy Ironton, Colorado

Reflective Kebler Gunnison National Forest, Colorado

Kebler's Leaf Gunnison National Forest, Colorado

Autumn Deer Gunnison National Forest, Colorado

Maple Guardians Manzano Mountain Wilderness Area, New Mexico

Maple's Shadow Manzano Mountain Wilderness Area, New Mexico

Tree Magic Manzano Mountain Wilderness Area, New Mexico

Sunset Maelstrom near Lewis, Colorado

Bosque's Birds

Bosque Surreal Bosque del Apache National Wildlife Refuge, New Mexico

Solo Flight Bosque del Apache National Wildlife Refuge, New Mexico

Ready Hawk Bosque del Apache National Wildlife Refuge, New Mexico

Hawk Takeoff Bosque del Apache National Wildlife Refuge, New Mexico

Egret Takeoff Bosque del Apache National Wildlife Refuge, New Mexico

Geese Drop-In Bosque del Apache National Wildlife Refuge, New Mexico

Landing Sequence Bosque del Apache National Wildlife Refuge, New Mexico

Flower Power

Bluebell Skies Yankee Boy Basin, near Ouray, Colorado
Yankee's Columbine Yankee Boy Basin, near Ouray, Colorado
Arching Color Arches National Park, Utah
Perfect Day near El Malpais National Monument, New Mexico
Calypso Orchid Rocky Mountain National Park, Colorado
Finch Attitude Amado, Arizona

Bird Prose

Finch Fellows Amado, Arizona
Pyrrhuloxia Pose Amado, Arizona
Cholla Cardinal Amado, Arizona
Cardinal Love Amado, Arizona
Bluebird Mom Tijeras, New Mexico
Bluebird Dad Tijeras, New Mexico
Bluebird Babies Tijeras, New Mexico
Roadrunner Pause Amado, Arizona

Into Autumn

Fall Bells Maroon Bells, Maroon Bell Wilderness, Colorado
Mears' Embrace Ridgway, Colorado
Divide's Autumn Ridgway, Colorado
Ashcroft's Window Ashcroft, Colorado
Gothic Fall Gothic, Colorado
Oak Variation Coconino National Forest, Arizona
Contemplative Reflection Coconino National Forest, Arizona
Bosque Afternoon Bosque del Apache National Wildlife Refuge, New Mexico
Aspen Road Gunnison National Forest, Colorado
Snowkissed Aspens Grand Mesa, Colorado
Season's End Grand Mesa, Colorado

Yesterday's Rails

Winter's Cut Rockwood, Colorado
Wintery Tefft Tefft, Colorado
C&TS #484 near Chama, New Mexico

S Curve Cumbres Pass, New Mexico
Crossing Chama Chama, Colorado

Free Spirits

Stallion's Desert Red Desert, Wyoming
Stallion Squabble Red Desert, Wyoming
Stallion Battle Red Desert, Wyoming
Mustang Moments Red Desert, Wyoming
Follow Me Red Desert, Wyoming

Yesterday's Reflections

Fiery House Cedar Mesa, Utah
Fallen Roof Cedar Mesa, Utah
Yesterday's Tower Mesa Verde National Park, Colorado
Casa Blanca Canyon de Chelly National Monument, Utah
Hovenweep's Lookout Hovenweep National Monument, Colorado
Abo Mask near Socorro, New Mexico
Abo Panel near Abo, New Mexico
Petroglyph's Alien? Petroglyph National Monument, New Mexico
Newspaper Rock Newspaper Rock State Historic Monument, Utah

Running Wild

Elk's Paradise Rocky Mountain National Park, Colorado
Rocky's Newborn Rocky Mountain National Park, Colorado
Moosen Flower Wasatch National Forest, Utah
Bighorn Flock near Ouray, Colorado
Squirrel TV Amado, Arizona

Life Unbounded

Swell Shells Satellite Beach, Florida
Point Sur near Big Sur, California
McWay's Paradise near Big Sur, California
Foggy Fishing San Simeon, California
Glade's Mill Babcock State Park, West Virginia
Yesteryear's Mill Babcock State Park, West Virginia
Mabry's Days Meadows of Dan, Virginia
Mabry's Remembered Meadows of Dan, Virginia

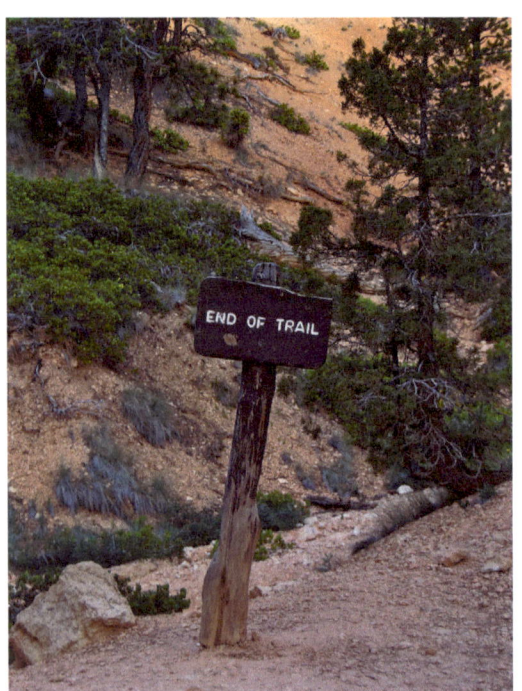

About the Author

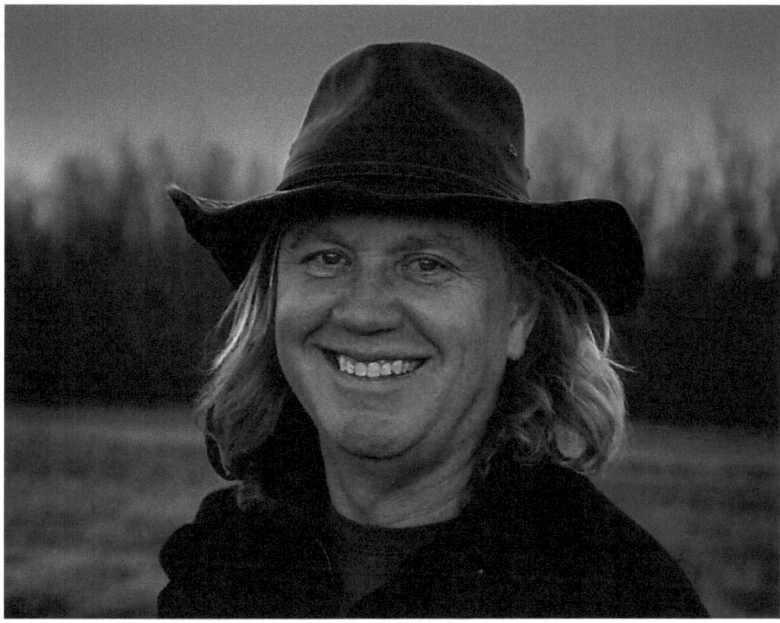

The sun sleeps on, not even thinking about rising yet. David, already standing out in a cold, wet field, waits for the sun and the wildlife to come alive. Seemingly the last place anyone else would want to be, this field springs to life with the dawn, and so does David's camera. Only the shot matters, in spite of toes threatening to move to the equator and fingers looking for a cup of coffee instead of wanting to hold the camera. He waits for exactly the right moment and then ... click. He has it.

David Schneider, a nature and wildlife photographer, focuses on bringing alive each scene and creature his camera sees. With a unique point of view and style, his prints capture the color, beauty and soul of his subjects. His affinity for nature extends into the scenic arena as well. His landscapes bring out the incredible emotion, beauty and grandeur of the Southwest and beyond; his photographs will take you from the tops of misty mountains to the shifting sands of the deep desert, letting you always be in the moment.

David lives in Tijeras, New Mexico, just outside of the Cibola National Forest. He prefers to be outside whenever possible, in his "studio"—the great outdoors. He believes in being one with nature, and not a day goes by that he doesn't find something new to be amazed and delighted by. With a lifelong interest in photography and nature, his passions combine, providing arresting photographs for everyone.

Photo by M.B. McClean

www.ingramcontent.com/pod-product-compliance
Lightning Source LLC
Chambersburg PA
CBHW041456280526
45792CB00004B/1035